中国律师实训经典

中英商务合同
精选与解读

（第二版）

林克敏 著

UNDERSTANDING
COMMERCIAL
CONTRACTS

中国人民大学出版社
·北京·

图书在版编目（CIP）数据

中英商务合同精选与解读/林克敏著．—2 版．—北京：中国人民大学出版社，2017.5
（中国律师实训经典）
ISBN 978-7-300-24558-4

Ⅰ.①中…　Ⅱ.①林…　Ⅲ.①国际贸易-贸易合同-汉、英　Ⅳ.①F740.4 ②D996.1

中国版本图书馆 CIP 数据核字（2017）第 135587 号

中国律师实训经典
中英商务合同精选与解读（第二版）
林克敏　著
Zhongying Shangwu Hetong Jingxuan yu Jiedu

出版发行	中国人民大学出版社			
社　　址	北京中关村大街 31 号		**邮政编码**	100080
电　　话	010 - 62511242（总编室）		010 - 62511770（质管部）	
	010 - 82501766（邮购部）		010 - 62514148（门市部）	
	010 - 62515195（发行公司）		010 - 62515275（盗版举报）	
网　　址	http://www.crup.com.cn			
	http://www.ttrnet.com（人大教研网）			
经　　销	新华书店			
印　　刷	北京昌联印刷有限公司		**版　　次**	2012 年 3 月第 1 版
规　　格	185 mm×260 mm　16 开本			2017 年 5 月第 2 版
印　　张	14.75 插页 2		**印　　次**	2017 年 5 月第 1 次印刷
字　　数	375 000		**定　　价**	45.00 元

谨以此书献给母校

中国人民大学，从这里，

我迈进了法律的殿堂。

序 一

　　林克敏女士是中国人民大学法律系本科 1979 年入学、1983 年毕业的校友。与她同级的人大校友或是留校任教，或是任职于政府部门或国企等单位，均已在相关岗位作出杰出成绩。林克敏女士则选择去国外留学，学成后在境内外几家知名律师事务所从事律师职业，从而积累了丰富的涉外律师工作经验。

　　本书是林克敏女士多年律师执业经验的总结，具有非常鲜明的务实特色。从书中精选的中英文合同可以看到，律师为实现委托人利益的最大化而尽职尽责的敬业精神和一丝不苟的工作作风。从这些合同范本中可以学到相关的商业模式、律师的缜密思维方式和合同的制作技巧。这些合同以英美法律和国际商业惯例为基础，同时兼顾中国法律法规的相关规定，结合具体商业交易的需要，体现出实用性很强的商业和法律智慧。

　　随着外资的大规模引入国内以及中国企业越来越多地走向海外，对于英文合同的学习和掌握变得愈加迫切，对于英文合同写作方面专门书籍的需求会与日俱增。本书作为《中国律师实训经典》系列丛书之一，对于执业律师、企业法律顾问、有志于律师职业的学子以及其他法律从业人员颇有参考价值。

中国人民大学副校长

王利明　教授

2011 年 10 月

序 二

我非常高兴地为林克敏律师的新书《中英商务合同精选与解读》作序。林克敏女士在日本名古屋大学法学研究科攻读博士课程时，我作为其指导教授，曾在合同起草以及国际商事仲裁方面对她进行过指导。作为教师的极大乐趣之一是看到所指导的学生取得杰出的学术成就，而林克敏女士的学术成就体现在这本优秀书籍中。

每位商业人士都清楚，几乎每项商业交易都需要相应的商务合同，商业交易和商务合同彼此之间是密不可分的。因此，倘若对各种商业交易缺乏广泛而深入的实际知识，则不可能胜任商务合同的起草工作。实际知识的取得需要长期实践经验的积累，不可能在短时间内完成。在这方面，林克敏女士是非常胜任的作者，她在近二十年的法律职业生涯中积累了丰富的实践经验，并将这些经验融入她的这本新书中，这正是本书最引人注目的值得推荐之处。

读者将会在本书中发现很多非常有用的商务合同范本。现在虽然从书店里也可以找到一些类似的书籍，但是本书中合同范本的质量是极为不同的，每一范本都来源于作者为其客户实际起草的商务合同，这些合同都经过相关当事方细致而全面的审核才得以完成，而不是那些经不起严格推敲的、仅为出版而虚拟的合同"样本"。对于在日常业务中需要实际使用合同范本的读者来说，这一事实是非常重要的，这正是本书最有价值的地方，而虚拟的合同"样本"是不能满足读者的实际需要的。

英文合同用语主要基于英美法律和国际习惯法，而与日常使用的英文不同。要掌握起草英文合同的专业技能，需要将学术知识和实际工作经验相结合。本书作者作为一名国际商务律师，以其丰富的专业知识和实践经验出色地完成了这一任务，这正是本书的显著特征。

"上帝是完美的，而人类则不完美。"虽然本书还存在不尽善尽美之处，仍然可能在发展中有所完善，但是，本书将在不久的将来确立其作为商务合同起草方面标准教科书的地位。

日本国立名古屋大学

荣誉教授 岩崎一生

2011 年 9 月

前　言

　　作者在从事多年的涉外业务律师职业生涯中，在多次招聘和培训年轻律师的经历中深刻体会到，高等法律院校培养出来的法律人才，即使已经通过统一司法考试并经过了律师实习期，要想成为合格的专业律师，特别是成为合格的公司涉外法务律师，其也仍然面临着漫长的路途。

　　在一项商业交易中，律师从立场定位，到起草、修改、定稿一份能够完善地保护客户合法权益的商务合同，既需要具备相应的法律知识，更需要拥有丰富经验以及准确而严谨的语言表达能力。在准备英文商务合同方面，律师还需要多年积累的涉外律师经验和法律专业英语修养。

　　在本书中，作者根据具体商业交易的性质和要求，对中英商务合同的基本结构和主要条款进行了说明，并精选一些常用的中英商务合同，以中英文本对照、辅以注解的方式进行解读，说明其内容特点、语言表达方式等。

　　为公司客户提供法律服务的年轻律师、企业法务人员、法律院校学生等，可以从本书所精选的中英合同文本中学习到起草相关商务合同的专业知识和经验，甚至可以直接以这些文本为基础或作为参考，根据实际交易的情况，起草或修改相关的商务合同（中文本和英文本）。法律院校的教师可以参考本书，在授课时讲解相关中英文合同的特点、内容等。有兴趣的一般读者，也可以从本书中了解相关合同的内容，增加法律知识。

林克敏

目　录

第1章

总 论

第1节 确立律师为客户服务的立场

　　律师为委托人（客户）服务，站在客户的立场、保护客户的合法利益原本是不言而喻的律师职责，特别是律师在为刑事案件犯罪嫌疑人的辩护中，表现得尤其明显，这一点很容易理解。但是，在商业领域，作者经常看到在已经出版的图书中或网络上流传的很多"格式合同"或"范本""样本"中，各方当事人的权利义务是很"均衡""对等"的，似乎合同的任何一方当事人都可以将这种"格式合同""范本"或"样本"下载或复制，在其中填入相应的商业交易内容后，就可以由各方当事人签字、盖章使合同生效了。这很容易使人误认为，合同的内容对当事人各方本来就应当"不偏不倚""平等均衡"，起草或修改合同的工作变得非常简单，似乎只要有这些"格式""范本""样本"就足够了，不需要专门委托律师进行商务合同的起草、审查、修改工作。

　　作者也经常看到年轻律师在起草或修改法律文书，特别是商务合同（commercial contracts）时，对于律师应当采取的立场并不是很清楚。有些律师缺乏职业训练，站在"中立""独立""不偏不倚"的第三方立场，似乎是处于法官的地位，并不代表任何一方当事人；更有些刚入职的年轻律师将合同中对自己客户有利的条款进行删除或缩减，而不能判断并修改不利于自己客户、给自己客户带来商业风险和法律风险的合同条款，因而不能有效地保护自己客户的合法合理权益、降低或规避自己客户的风险。这就使得客户失去了委托专业律师起草、审查或修改商务合同、并为此支付律师服务费的意义。

　　以上问题的发生，实在是由于这些律师对于法律专业工作的误解。"商场如战场"，在同一项商业交易中，由于律师代表着不同当事方的利益，其起草、审查或修改的法律文书之侧重点、双方当事人的权利义务内容必然不能完全是"对等"和"均衡"的。例如，在股权并购（M&A）交易中，难以想象，代表收购方的律师和代表被收购方的律师会对并购协议中双方的权利和义务持完全相同的意见，从而使得其起草的并购协议对双方完全"对等"和"均衡"。作为一名称职的律师，应当是在合法的范围内，通过自己起草或修改的合同条款最大限度地保护和体现自己客户的权利和利益，最大限度地防止和规避自己客户可能遭受的商业风险和法律风险，同时通过设定义务和责任的条款最大限度地约束对方当事人，增加其违约成本，从而尽可能促使对方当事人按合同的约定严格履行，确保自己客户实现最大限度的商业利益。

　　作者在多年的涉外律师执业生涯中深刻体会到，作为一名优秀的公司法务律师，不但要考虑客户所提出的问题和商业目的、在合同中作出相应的体现，而且要高瞻远瞩，比客户考虑得更加全面、更加深远，通过在合同中设定相应的条款，更好地保护自己客户的合法权益、规避可能的风险。当然，这需要律师勤于学习，善于分析，逐渐积累法律经验、社会经验、语言表达素养等。

在本书中，作者根据自己多年的律师执业经验，从不同当事人的立场，精选了若干商业交易的中英文合同文本，并在注解中对此进行解读，试图使读者理解各个合同文本内容的不同之处及其产生的原因，转变上述对于所谓"格式合同""范本"或"样本"的误解。

此外，在一项商业交易的协商交涉过程中，一方当事人的律师起草了商务合同草案后，对方当事人的律师往往从保护其客户的立场出发对合同草案进行修改。之后，起草方律师需要判断对方律师修改的合同草案中哪些是可以接受的，哪些是必须坚持原方案内容的，从而向自己客户提供适当的意见，进而对合同内容再次进行修改。双方律师的这种反复交涉、反复修改合同草案的过程往往会进行几个回合，在重大的商业交易中更是如此。作为一名合格的专业律师，需要丰富的经验和技巧以促使这个过程尽快顺利完成，而不是因律师未能给予自己客户适当的意见、不必要的僵硬立场、纠缠于细枝末节，从而拖延协商交涉的进程、致使当事各方迟迟不能达成一致意见。

总之，要成为一名合格的公司法务律师，需要勤于学习、善于总结、反复磨炼、常年积累，想一蹴而就是不现实的。

第 2 节　英文合同的结构和内容

英文商务合同的结构是相对固定的，在本书第 2 章中有详细说明和举例。对中国律师来说，英文合同中的一些条款似乎是"多余的、不必要的"，如"通知条款""全部协议条款"等，一些中国律师甚至认为，没有这些条款也不影响合同的完整性和法律效力。要正确理解这些条款的必要性，就需要了解英美法中的一些相关成文法和判例，特别是相关判例的影响。律师在合同中明确约定这些条款具有重要意义，对于明确当事人的权利义务、规避相关风险，都起着重要的作用。

为了使读者对商务合同有比较全面的了解，作者在本书中对中英文商务合同的基本结构和主要条款进行了说明。在此基础上，作者从商业交易的不同领域精选了一些常用的中英文商务合同文本进行解读。

第 3 节　本书的体例

为了方便读者在实践中使用本书，体现本书的实用性，本书对于精选的商务合同文本，采用中英文对照方式，并对相关合同的背景情况以及合同条款的内容、句型、应注意的方面等，以脚注的方式加以说明。合同文本中的【　】或画下横线的部分需要文本的使用者填入具体交易的相应内容。

▨ 第 4 节　如何使用本书

　　本书采用中英文对照形式，并就其内容及语言表达方面作了适当脚注，以方便读者理解和应用。如果读者在国内交易中不需要使用英文文本，可以仅参考中文文本，根据具体的交易条件和情况，将中文文本进行增加、删减、修改，以适应具体交易的需要。

第 2 章

英文商务合同的主要结构与解读

第1节　合同开始部分（签约当事人、签约日期等）

合同的开始部分首先应记载签约当事人、签约日期等。英文合同开始部分的常用表述方式如下：

【例文】

THIS AGREEMENT is made and entered into this date of 【日】 【月】 【年】 by and between：

ABC Co., Ltd.①, a company duly incorporated and existing under the laws of _____ and having its registered office at _____ (hereinafter called "**ABC**") and

XYZ Co., Ltd., a company duly incorporated and existing under the laws of _____ and having its registered office at _____ (hereinafter called "**XYZ**").

(Individually the "**Party**" and collectively the "**Parties**")

本协议由以下双方当事人于_____年_____月_____日签订：

ABC有限公司，按照_____法律正当设立并存续的一家公司，其注册地址为_____（以下简称为"**ABC**"）；以及

XYZ有限公司，按照_____法律正当设立并存续的一家公司，其注册地址为_____（以下简称为"**XYZ**"）。

（上述签约方单独称为"**一方**"，合称为"**双方**"）。

【解读】

1. 签约日期（Date of contract）

英文合同通常在一开头就列明签约日期（如同英文信函的日期记载习惯），这样做的好处是可以对签约日期一目了然。

在一般情况下，签约日期与合同生效日期一致，即"本协议自签订之日起生效"（this Agreement shall be effective as of the date of its execution）。但是，对于需要经相关政府部门审批或备案方可生效的合同，应在合同主文

---

① 本书中所选例文或合同文本中使用的公司名称均为虚拟名称。

的生效条款中作出特别约定。如果合同中没有明确约定生效日期，除非合同中有相反约定或有法律的强制性规定，一般来说签约日期即为合同生效日期。

很多中文合同将签约日期置于合同末尾，在每一方当事人签署位置的下方分别设置"　年　月　日"，由该方当事人代表签署合同时自行填入相关日期。但是，如果当事人各方不是会合在一处同时签署合同，而是通过邮寄方式在不同地点和不同时间签署合同，则可能导致各方对合同的签署日期不一致。倘若合同签署日即为合同生效日，各方会对确定合同生效日产生疑义。如像英文合同那样在合同首页写明统一的签约日期，可以避免发生这类问题。

还有些合同是各方当事人一致同意将合同生效日期回溯至签约日期之前的某个日期，只要不违反所适用法律的强制性规定，这种约定也是有效的。

2. 签约当事人的注册地（Registered address）或主要营业地（Principal office 或 Principal place of business）

在合同中写明签约当事人的注册地，其重要意义在于：

（1）有助于确定签约当事人（公司等）登记注册所依据的法律；

（2）对合同所适用的法律（准据法）的影响：通常，当事人各方会在合同中选用当事人一方注册地的法律作为合同的准据法；

（3）如果合同中没有明确约定准据法和争议解决方式，签约方的注册地对确定诉讼管辖权具有重要意义。例如，发生争议后，原告方可在被告方的注册地对被告方提起诉讼；

（4）如果合同中对法院的诉讼文书送达地址没有作出明确约定，当事人的注册地址可以成为诉讼文书的有效送达地址；

（5）对于合同项下对价的付款，在税收方面具有重要影响。例如，倘若合同中没有就对价付款的纳税负担当事方进行明确约定，收款人应当遵照其注册地的税收法律纳税。

3. 签约当事人名称（Names of parties）

当事方的法定公司全称有时很长，不便于记忆，而且会在合同中多次使用。为保持合同内容简洁、避免重复，通常在合同中第一次出现公司全称之后，紧接着在括号中定义其简称（以引号注明），以后使用其简称即可。中文"以下简称为"的英文表达方式为"hereinafter referred to as"或者"hereinafter called"；有时也可直接在括号内的引号中写上其简称，例如（"Party A"）（"甲方"）。

为了在合同中容易查找到所定义简称内容的全称，英文合同中通常会对简称使用加粗字体，例如：（"**Party A**"）（"**甲方**"）等。

4. 签约地（Place of execution）

在合同中可以写入签约地点，例如：THIS AGREEMENT is made and entered into in Beijing, the People's Republic of China as of this date of 23 July 2009 by and between：（本协议由以下双方当事人于 2009 年 7 月 23 日在中华人民共和国北京市签订：）。

在某些情况下，签约地具有一定意义，例如：倘若合同中没有明确约定准据法，日后发生争议时，签约地可以作为法院或仲裁机构确定合同准据法的一个重要因素。但在实践中，由于英文合同大多明确约定了准据法，合同签署地并不重要，很多英文合同省略了对签约地的表述。作者所接触到的大多数英文合同对签约地不作约定。

第2节　合同前言（鉴于条款）

在篇幅较长的英文商务合同中，一般有前言（序言）（Recitals）部分，以"Whereas"开头，分列数条；或者以数个"Whereas"开头的句子组合而成，因此称为 Whereas Clauses（鉴于条款）。

【例文1】

（**DISTRIBUTORSHIP AGREEMENT**）

WHEREAS：

A. The Supplier is the manufacturer of the Products（as defined in Art. 1. 1 here below）and desirous of selling the Products in the Territory（as defined in Art. 1. 3 here below）；

B. The Supplier manufactures the Products bearing the trade-marks 【　】；

C. The Distributor wishes to purchase and import the Products from the Supplier and re-sell them in the Territory through its sales network to boutiques（mono or multi-branded），department stores，specialty stores，etc.（hereinafter called the **"Customers"**）；and

D. The Parties intend to constitute their overall relationship，in order to co-operate effectively and exclusively in the marketing and distribution of the Products in the Territory through the Customers under the terms and conditions hereinafter specified.

（**经销协议**）

鉴于：

A. 供货商是指定产品（按下述第1.1条所定义）的生产厂家，希望在经销区域（按下述第1.3条所定义）销售指定产品；

B. 供货商生产的指定产品使用_____商标；

C. 经销商希望从供货商购入和进口指定产品，并在经销区域内通过其销售网络将指定产品出售给（单一品牌或多品牌的）精品店、百货商店、专卖店等（以下简称**"客户"**）；

D. 各方当事人愿意建立全面的关系，以便有效地开展排他性合作，根据本协议的下述条款和条件，在经销区域内通过客户对指定产品进行市场开发和经销。

【例文 2】

（TECHNICAL LICENSE AND ASSISTANCE AGREEMENT）

WHEREAS the Licensor has been authorized to enter into this Agreement by 【 】, which company is the ultimate proprietor of certain technology and technical know-how and expertise in relation to technology, including among others, those as set out in Schedule A attached hereto （ **"Technology"** ）; and

WHEREAS the Licensee is a sino-foreign equity joint venture company established by and between the Licensor and two other companies pursuant to a joint venture contract dated as of 【 】 （ **"JV Contract"** ）. The JV Contract provides that the Licensor shall license to the Licensee the Technology for the production of the Products and carrying on of the Business by the Licensee; and

WHEREAS the Licensee wishes to obtain a license of the Technology and the Licensor has agreed to grant such license under the terms and conditions of this Agreement;

NOW, THEREFORE, in consideration of the mutual covenants hereinafter set forth, it is mutually covenanted and agreed as follows: -

（技术许可与援助协议）

鉴于：本协议附件 A 所载明的某些技术包括其他相关技术诀窍和专有知识（以下简称 **"技术"** ）的最终所有权人【 】公司已授权许可方签订本协议；

　　鉴于：被许可方是许可方和另外两家公司根据【 】年【 】月【 】日签订的合资经营企业合同（以下简称 **"合资合同"** ）设立的中外合资经营企业。合资合同中规定许可方应将"技术"许可给被许可方使用，以便被许可方生产"产品"以及经营"业务"；

　　鉴于：被许可方希望根据本协议的条款及条件获得"技术"许可，而许可方也同意根据该等条款及条件授予该许可。

　　因此，双方考虑到本协议中所彼此约定的条款，一致同意如下：

【解读】

　　从上面的例文可以看出，前言（鉴于条款）用于记述合同双方的业务性质、签约背景情况、双方的交易意愿和缔约目的等，表明签约当事人是依据这些事实背景和目的签订本合同的。

　　关于前言（鉴于条款）的法律地位问题，即前言（鉴于条款）是否对合同当事方具有法律约束力，很多国家的法律中并无明文规定。一般认为，如果在合同后面的主文中没有对前言（鉴于条款）的法律地位作出明确约定，则其不被认为是确定法律义务的合同组成部分。

　　但是，在对合同的实质内容进行必要解释时，英美法系国家的法官通常会考虑前言（鉴于条款）的内容。因此，律师必须慎重地起草前言（鉴于条款），可以在合同中明确约定前言（鉴于条款）是合同不可分割的组成部分。

基于上述原因，前言（鉴于条款）中不宜约定合同当事方的具体权利义务（这些应当在合同主文中作出约定），以规避不必要的法律风险。

由于各类合同的签约主体及交易内容不同，其前言（鉴于条款）的内容也不尽相同，读者可以从本书后附的具体合同文本中体会。

在篇幅不长的合同中，前言（鉴于条款）可以简要叙述或者省略。

第 3 节　合同主文

在前言（鉴于条款）之后，是合同的主文部分，即合同的实质性条款，是合同各方当事人一致同意的交易事项内容以及各自的权利义务。

由于各类商务合同的性质不同，合同的实质性条款的内容和繁简程度也不尽相同，一般来说可分为以下部分：

● 合同的商务条款
● 合同的共通法律条款

作者将通过后面所精选的合同文本内容及其解读，来详细说明相关种类合同的商务条款内容及其特点。

这里仅就商务合同的共通法律条款作出简要说明。

1. 定义（Definitions）

对于篇幅较短的合同，对于在合同中第一次出现并且后面多次出现的词语，可以作出定义，并在紧接其后的括号中注明其简称（中英文简称的表达方式请参见本章第 1 节 3（签约当事人名称）中的说明）。

在较长篇幅的合同中，或者合同中需要定义的词语较多时，为了使合同语言保持简练，避免多次重复，也便于查找，通常在合同主文的最开头部分设置定义条款，对合同中出现的全部或大多数定义词语按照其首个英文字母的顺序排列（最常用方法），或按定义词语在合同中出现的先后顺序排列，或按逻辑方法排列。英文中一般将定义词语的第一个字母大写，或者将定义词语的字母全部大写，以便与普通含义的相同词语相区别。中文的定义词语则可采用黑体字或者以引号来表示，还可以添加辅助字，例如本合同（this Agreement）、该产品（the Products）、指定区域（the Territory）等。

【例文】

Article 1　Definitions

The following terms and expressions in this Agreement shall have the following meanings unless the context otherwise requires：

1.1　**"Affiliates"** shall have the same meaning as defined in the Joint Venture Agreement dated 【　】 between Licensor, ABC Co., Ltd. and XYZ Co., Ltd.

1.2　**"Business"** means the establishment and operation of the processing facilities（the **"Processing Plant"**）for the production of the Products.

1.3　**"Improvements"** means any enhancements to any item of the Technology, which advances the manufacture or processing of the Products or enhances the quality of the Products.

1.4　**"Joint Venture"** shall mean MNOP Co., Ltd.

1.5　**"Processing and Assembly Costs"** means the aggregate of the costs of JIG, tape for production and the costs of assembling components into finished Products.

1.6　**"Party"** means the Licensee or the Licensor, as the case may be, and **"Parties"** means the Licensee and the Licensor collectively.

1.7　**"Products"** means parts and components for 【　】 products using Technology or such other products as the Parties may from time to time resolve to process or produce.

1.8　**"Technology"** means and includes, among others, the items listed in Schedule A attached hereto, as well as other know-how, trade secrets and any other technical and commercial information relating to the design, manufacture, production, processing, testing, quality control, quality assurance of the Products, and/or management control, administration, supervision, reporting and/or analysis relating to or in respect of any of the foregoing in relation to the operation of the Processing Plant and/or the production of the Products, to be licensed by the Licensor to the Licensee pursuant to the terms and conditions of this Agreement or the Joint Venture Agreement. However, the Parties agree and confirm that such description is not exhaustive and shall not be deemed or be construed in any way to limit the scope of the definition set forth in this Article 1.8. The Technology shall also be deemed to include all Improvements.

1.9　**"Term"** means the term of this Agreement as set forth in Article 12 hereof.

1.10　**"Training"** means the training courses and services, details of which are set forth in Schedule B and Article 3 hereof.

第 1 条　定义

除非上下文另有规定，本协议中的下列词语应具有如下所述含义：

1.1　**"关联企业"** 具有许可方、ABC 有限公司和 XYZ 有限公司于＿＿＿＿＿＿年＿＿＿＿＿月＿＿＿＿＿签订的合资合同中所约定含义的相同含义。

1.2　**"业务"** 是指为制造"产品"而设立与经营加工设施（以下简称"**加工厂**"）。

1.3 **"改进"** 是指对 "技术" 的任何改进，并且此种改进提高了 "产品" 的制造或加工水平或提高了 "产品" 的质量。

1.4 **"合资企业"** 是指 MNOP 有限公司。

1.5 **"加工和装配成本"** 是指夹具和生产用卷带的成本以及将组件组装成成品的成本之总和。

1.6 **"一方"** 是指许可方或被许可方（视情况而定）；**"双方"** 指许可方和被许可方。

1.7 **"产品"** 是指使用 "技术" 生产的【 】产品的部件和组件或 "双方" 不时决定加工或生产的其他产品。

1.8 **"技术"** 是指包括但不限于本协议附件 A 中列明的技术项目，以及许可方根据本协议或合资合同的条款和条件，允许被许可方使用有关 "加工厂" 的经营及/或制造 "产品" 的其他专有技术、商业秘密及有关 "产品" 的设计、制造、生产、加工、测试、质量控制、质量保证及/或与任何前述方面的管理控制、管理、监督、报告及/或分析的任何其他技术资料和商业资料。不过，"双方" 同意并确认上述描述并不详尽，不应被视为或解释为以任何方式限制本协议第 1.8 条所载明的定义之范围。而 "技术" 应被视为包括所有 "改进"。

1.9 **"期限"** 是指本协议第 12 条所载明的本协议的期限。

1.10 **"培训"** 是指培训课程和服务，详见本协议附件 B 以及第 3 条。

2. 合同生效日（Effective date）

合同的生效日意味着当事人各方的权利义务开始发生，因此至关重要。通常，合同的有效期与生效日放在一起约定。下面是英文商务合同中对生效日和有效期的几种约定方式。

（1）自合同签订之日起生效

自合同签订之日起生效的约定是最常见的。

【例文】

> This Agreement shall commence upon the date of execution hereof.
>
> 本协议自签订之日起生效。

（2）自政府部门批准或备案之日起生效

如在本章第 1 节 1（签约日期）中所述，对于须经相关政府部门审批或备案方可生效的合同，应在合同中作出特别约定。

【例文】

> This Contract and its schedules require the approvals from the Ministry of Commerce of the PRC（or its authorized examination and approval authority）and shall come into force commencing from the date of approval. The same applies to amendments to this Contract and its schedules.

> 本合同及其附件须获得中华人民共和国商务部（或其授权的审批机关）的批准，自批准之日起生效。本条规定同样适用于本合同及其附件的修改。

（3）对生效日另作约定

合同各方可以对合同生效日另行作出明确约定，生效日可以与签约日不同。

【例文 1】

> This Agreement shall commence upon 【　】（the **"Effective Date"**）.
>
> 本协议自_____年_____月_____日（以下简称**"生效日"**）开始生效。

如果生效日早于签约日，下面的表述更加合适。

【例文 2】

> This Agreement shall be deemed to have commenced upon 【　】（the **"Effective Date"**）.
>
> 本协议应被视为自_____年_____月_____日（以下简称**"生效日"**）开始生效。

（4）合同中没有明确约定生效日

如在本章第 1 节 1（签约日期）中所述，如果合同中没有明确约定生效日期，除非合同中另有相反约定或有法律的强制性规定，一般来说签约日期即为合同生效日期。

（5）在满足约定的前提条件后合同生效

对有些合同（例如需要取得进出口许可证等），经各方当事人同意，合同签署后需要满足约定的条件才能生效。

【例文】

> Notwithstanding the signature of this Contract by the Purchaser and the Seller, this Contract shall become effective only when all the following conditions shall have been complied with:
>
> （i）receipt by the Seller of a letter from the Purchaser confirming that all relevant consents, import permits and licenses necessary to import and pay for the Goods in USD have been obtained; and
>
> （ii）confirmation by the Seller that it has obtained any necessary export licence for the Goods.
>
> If all the above conditions are not satisfied within forty-five（45）days of the date of the Seller's acceptance, the Seller shall have the right to amend the Contract Price and Delivery Dates by reasonable amounts or alternatively terminate the order.

尽管买卖双方签署了本合同，但只有在下述全部条件满足后，本合同方能生效：

（i）卖方收到买方的信函，确认进口该商品以及用美元支付货款所需的全部相关同意、进口许可和许可证已经取得；以及

（ii）卖方确认已经取得出口该商品所需的许可证。

如果自卖方承诺之日起四十五（45）日内上述全部条件没有被满足，卖方有权以合理数额修改本合同价格及交货日期，也可选择取消订货单。

3. 合同有效期（Term）

（1）固定期限的有效期

绝大多数合同对有效期都有明确约定。

【例文】

The term of this Agreement shall be for a period of ten （10） years from the date of signature hereof.

本协议有效期自签署之日起为十（10）年。

（2）没有具体约定有效期，一方提前发出通知可以终止合同

有些合同中没有具体约定有效期，在合同生效后，以一方向另一方提前发出通知作为合同有效期终止的条件（即使另一方没有违约行为），这通常用于双方之间长期合作的合同（如商品或服务的提供等），或者是母公司和子公司等存在高度信赖关系的当事人之间的合同。

【例文】

This Agreement shall commerce upon the date of execution hereof and shall continue in force unless and until terminated by one party giving to the other party not less than three （3） months notice to that effect.

本协议自签署之日起生效，其有效期直至一方当事人至少提前三（3）个月向另一方当事人发出通知终止本合同为止。

（3）可自动续期的合同

很多长期业务合作的合同是在约定首次固定期限的有效期后，附条件地自动续期。通常约定，除非一方在合同期满前若干天书面通知另一方不再续期，否则即自动延续合同的有效期。这种合同有效期的约定方法，可以使当事人在首个有效期中观察对方的履约情况和经济情势的发展，视具体情况决定是否将合同续期。

【例文】

> This Agreement shall come into force upon execution hereof and shall continue to be valid until _____, and shall be automatically renewed for another one year and thereafter on a year-to-year basis unless either party gives the other party a written notice to terminate this Agreement at least ninety（90）days before the expiration of the original or，as the case may be，any renewed term of this Agreement.
>
> 本协议自签署之日起生效，有效期至_____年_____月_____止；此后，倘若任何一方当事人在首个有效期或其后延续的有效期（视情况而定）届满前至少九十（90）日没有以书面形式通知另一方终止本协议，则本协议自动续期一年，其后亦以相同方式续期。

4. 合同的解除（Termination）

（1）通知解约——无需理由

在一些合同（例如房屋租赁合同、代理合同、经销合同或技术许可合同等）中，双方可以约定，合同生效一段时间之后或者在履行过程中，一方向另一方发出通知提前解除合同，无需任何理由，而仅因为业务上的需要。

【例文】

> This Agreement may be terminated by the Licensee as to the Technology on which twenty-four（24）monthly payments have been made by giving the Licensor three（3）months written notice to expire at the end of the relevant period of twenty-four（24）months or at any time thereafter.
>
> 在被许可方就使用该技术支付 24 个月的款项后，被许可方可以提前 3 个月向许可方发出书面通知，在相关 24 个月期间结束时或其后的任何时间解除本协议。

（2）通知解约——需要理由

（a）因一方违约而解除合同

在多数合同中，一方发出通知提前解除合同则需要通知方具有解约的正当理由，最常见的理由是对方违约、没有履行其合同义务。

在对方违约的情况下，通知方当事人通常给予违约方当事人纠正其违约行为的补救期，如果违约方在指定期限内没有纠正违约行为，合同即被解除。

【例文】

> If the Licensee fails to perform any of the obligations on its part hereunder and fails to remedy any such breach within thirty（30）days of

notice thereof from the Licensor, then the Licensor may serve a written notice on the Licensee declaring that this Agreement is terminated at such further date as it may designate.

如果被许可方没有履行其在本协议项下应履行的任何义务，并且在接到许可方的相关通知后 30 天内没有纠正该违约行为，许可方可以向被许可方发出书面通知，声明在其指定的日期解除本协议。

（b）因其他原因而解除合同

除了违约以外，解除合同的其他正当理由通常包括一方失去偿债能力、破产、解散等，以致其不能按合同履行义务。下面的例文，针对各方当事人的不同主体资格（公司、自然人、合伙、非公司社团等），约定在不同情况下解约的理由。

【例文】

The Contract may be terminated with immediate effect by either party giving notice of termination to the other party (the **"Defaulting Party"**)：
  (i) if the Defaulting Party shall pass a resolution for winding up or a court shall make an order to that effect, or
  (ii) if the Defaulting Party shall cease to carry on its business or subs-tantially the whole of its business, or
  (iii) if the Defaulting Party becomes or is declared insolvent, or convenes a meeting of or makes or proposes to make any arrangement or composition with its creditors, or
  (iv) if a liquidator, receiver, administrator, administrative receiver, trustee, or similar officer is appointed over any of the assets of the Defaulting Party.

有下列情形之一的，任何一方可向对方（**"违约方"**）发出解约通知，立即解除本合同：
  (i) 如果违约方通过清算决议，或者法院作出这方面的裁定；
  (ii) 如果违约方停止经营业务或者实质性地停止其全部业务；
  (iii) 如果违约方失去偿债能力，或者与其债权人召开会议或建议作出债务偿还安排或债务重整协议；
  (iv) 如果已经委任针对违约方任何资产的清算人、破产管理人、财产接收管理人、受托人或类似人员。

（3）合同解除的后果——责任的免除或保留

（a）双方均免除责任

在合同签订后，因时间流逝而解约或未能就重要条件达成一致而解约时，当事人可以不再进行交易，互相不负继续履约的责任。在此种情况下，可以使用下述例文条款：

【例文】

> Any termination under Clause 【　】 above shall discharge the parties from any liabilities for the further performance of the Agreement.
>
> 在根据上述第＿＿＿＿条解约时，双方当事人均免除继续履行本协议的责任。

（b）对于解约发生损失的赔偿

在多数情况下，在解约时，应当对继续进行过程中的工作或产品作出公平的补偿，并退还对方已支付的预付款。例如在供货合同中，供货方不仅有权对于制作过程中的未完成产品获得赔偿，而且有权对于未完成全部交易所丧失的机会成本、倘若完成全部交易应取得的利润等获得赔偿。当然，这取决于订约双方在就合同内容进行谈判时的各自实力以及交涉的结果。

【例文】

> In the case of a termination by either party pursuant to Clause 【　】, the Supplier shall be entitled to be paid a reasonable sum for any work carried out by it prior to such termination together with a reasonable profit thereon and on the uncompleted portion of the individual contract，and （subject to such payment） the Customer shall be entitled to be repaid forthwith any sums previously paid under this Agreement （whether by way of a deposit or advance payment or otherwise） provided that save as aforesaid neither party shall have any liability whatsoever to the other by reason of such termination.
>
> 倘若任何一方根据第＿＿＿＿条解约，供货方对在解约之前其已经进行的工作及其合理利润以及对个别合同的未完成部分有权获得合理数额的付款；（以该付款为条件）客户有权立即收回在本协议项下（以定金、预付款或其他方式支付）的预付款项。除上述以外，任何一方因解约对于另一方不需承担任何其他责任。

（c）解约日之前的权利义务保留

无论由于任何原因而解约，无论是否免除继续履约的责任，合同中通常会保留已经发生的权利和义务。下述几个例文条款可适用于不同情况，在例文 1 中，双方权利义务对等；而在例文 2 中，权利向一方倾斜。

【例文 1】

> The termination of this Agreement for any reason shall be without prejudice to any rights or obligations which shall have accrued or become due between the Supplier and the Customer prior to the date of termination.
>
> 无论由于任何原因而解除本协议，均不影响在解约日之前供货方和客户之间所发生或到期的任何权利或义务。

【例文 2】

The exercise by the Supplier of its right of termination under this Clause will be without prejudice to any right to damages or other remedy which the Supplier may have in respect thereof, whether under this Agreement or otherwise. The Supplier's foregoing right of termination shall not be affected by any previous waiver of its rights.

供货方按照本条行使解约的权利，不影响其在本协议项下或其他方面可享有的相关损害赔偿权利或其他补偿。供货方的上述解约权亦不因以前的权利放弃而受到影响。

（d）解约的后果——某些条款继续有效

双方可以约定，某些条款在合同解除后继续有效，这些条款通常是保密条款和争议解决条款等。

【例文】

Notwithstanding anything contained elsewhere in this Agreement, the provisions of Clause 【 】 shall survive the expiry or termination of this Agreement howsoever caused, and shall continue thereafter in full force and effect.

尽管本协议其他条款另有规定，在本协议期满终止或因任何原因而解除后，第【 】条的规定仍然继续完全有效。

5. 保密条款（Confidentiality）

商务合同是公司之间对某项具体交易中权利义务的约定，涉及保守商业秘密的问题，因此保密条款对于当事人是至关重要的。保密条款的内容通常包括商业秘密的范围、保密义务以及例外情形等。保密条款的繁简程度取决于合同的类型、商业秘密的性质、当事人对保密的要求范围和程度等。

【例文】

ARTICLE 【 】 CONFIDENTIALITY

1. No Party shall disclose to any other person any information related to the Agreement without the prior written consent of the other Party.
2. Notwithstanding the preceding paragraph of this Article, either Party may disclose information related to the Agreement to:
（1）its agents or contractors who have a need to know the same provided that such agents and contractors are first subject to the same confidentiality restrictions contained herein;

(2) any other person pursuant to a legal requirement to disclose or pursuant to any judicial authority which requires disclosure, provided that -

(a) if the Principal, its servants or agents shall become compelled by law to disclose such information, the Principal shall immediately notify the Operator of that fact so that the Operator may, if the Operator wishes, seek to prevent that disclosure;

(b) the Principal, its servants and agents will take such steps as the Operator shall require to prevent or minimize the scope of any disclosure; and

(c) in any case, if the Principal, its servant or agents are compelled to make disclosure, they will only disclose the portion of the relevant information which must be disclosed;

(3) any person whom the Operator regards has a need to know the same in respect of transactions relating to or in connection with this Agreement provided that such person is first subject to the same confidentiality restrictions as are contained herein; or

(4) any other person to the extent such disclosure shall either already be known to such person not due to a breach of this Article or shall be a matter of public knowledge.

3. Notwithstanding the complete performance of the Agreement by either or both Parties or the termination of the Agreement, the terms and conditions of this Article shall remain in full force and effect.

第【 】条　保密

1. 未经本协议另一方的事先书面同意，本协议任何一方不得将与本协议有关的任何信息披露给任何其他人。

2. 尽管有本条第 1 款的约定，本协议任何一方可以将与本协议有关的信息披露给如下人员：

(1) 该方有必要了解上述信息的代理人或承包方，但该代理人和承包方应首先遵守本协议中包含的保密条款的限制；

(2) 法律规定或司法机关要求披露给的任何其他人，但是，

(a) 如果委托人、其雇员或代理人披露上述信息是迫于法律规定，则委托人应立即将相关情况通知运营商，运营商可自行决定是否阻止该等披露；

(b) 委托人、其雇员或代理人按运营商的要求采取相应行动，以防止披露或尽量缩小披露的范围；以及

(c) 在任何情况下，如果委托人、其雇员或代理人必须进行披露时，其只能披露必须披露的相关信息。

(3) 运营商认为有必要了解涉及本协议或与本协议有关的交易之任何人士，但该人士应首先遵守本协议中包含的保密条款的限制；或者

(4) 非因违反本条款而已经知晓该信息的任何其他人，或该信息已为公众所知。

3. 即使本协议一方或双方已经履行完毕本协议，或本协议已经提前解除，本条规定仍将完全有效。

6. 陈述与保证条款（Representations and Warranties）

在大多数商务合同中均有陈述与保证条款，如当事人违反了合同中陈述与保证的内容，即构成违约，必须承担违约责任。

根据交易性质、合同内容等的不同，陈述与保证的范围有很大差异，通常包括以下几个方面：

- 当事人有权签署合同，或签署人已被当事方正当授权签署合同；
- 当事人正常存续、信誉良好（good standing）；
- 遵守法律（compliance with laws）；
- 对合同标的具有合法所有权；
- 其他陈述与保证（根据合同的具体内容，可包括对所有权、产品质量等的陈述和保证）。

【例文】

Representations and Warranties of Purchaser

1. The Purchaser represents and warrants to the Seller that：

(A) it has the requisite capacity, power and authority to enter into and perform this Agreement and to execute, deliver and perform any obligations it may have under each document to be delivered by it at the Completion；

(B) its obligations under this Agreement constitute, and its obligations under each document to be delivered by it at the Completion will, when delivered, constitute binding obligations of it in accordance with their respective terms；and

(C) the execution and delivery of, and the performance by it of its obligations under this Agreement and each document to be delivered by it at the Completion will not：

(i) result in a breach of any provision of the memorandum or articles of association of it ; or

(ii) result in a breach of, or constitute a default under, any instrument by which it is bound；or

(iii) result in a breach of any order, judgment or decree of any court or governmental agency by which it is bound.

2. The Purchaser represents and warrants to the Seller that each of the representations and warranties in this Clause is true and accurate and is not misleading as at the date of this Agreement and on the Completion Date.

3. Each of the representations and warranties in the Clause shall be construed as a separate and independent representation and warranty and （except where expressly provided to the contrary）shall not be limited or restricted by reference to or inference from the terms of any other representations and warranties in this Clause or any other term of this Agreement.

买方的陈述和保证

1. 买方向卖方陈述并保证：

（A）买方有所需的能力、权力和授权签订并履行本协议，并在交易完成时签订、交付和履行交付的文件中所记载的任何义务；

（B）买方基于本协议的义务以及在交易完成时根据交付的文件中所记载的义务，都将根据相关条款对买方构成具有约束力的义务；以及

（C）签订、交付和履行买方基于本协议的义务以及在交易完成时根据交付的文件中所记载的义务均不会：

　　（ⅰ）导致对买方公司章程的违反；或

　　（ⅱ）导致对买方应受约束的任何法律文件的违反或不履行；或

　　（ⅲ）导致对买方应受约束的任何法院或政府机构的命令、判决或法令的违反。

2. 买方向卖方陈述并保证，在本协议签订日及交易完成日，规定在本条中的陈述和保证都是真实而准确的、不会令人误解。

3. 本条中的每一项陈述和保证都是单独和独立的，除非另有相反规定，则每一项陈述和保证都不受本条中规定的其他陈述和保证以及本协议其他条款的限制和约束。

7. 补救与赔偿（Remedies and indemnities）

　　在英文合同中，对于一方当事人未按合同履行其义务和责任而给另一方当事人造成的损失和损害，通常会约定补救措施（remedies）。各类合同的标的不同，对补救措施的约定也不尽相同。例如，在买卖合同、供货合同中，对于提供的商品有瑕疵或在运输中遭到损坏或丢失的商品（除因不可抗力事件导致或应由保险公司负赔偿责任等之外），通常约定卖方或供货方应采取修理或更换的补救措施。

　　在英国法以及大多数普通法地区，赔偿（indemnities）是对于确定的损失或损害的明示赔偿义务。赔偿是补救措施（remedies）的一种，但与明示的补救措施不同；赔偿是支付金钱，而不是如上述对瑕疵商品的修理或更换等补救措施。在诉讼程序中，赔偿在法律上更易于执行。

【例文】

Each party shall indemnify and hold the other party harmless from and against any and all losses, claims, damages and liabilities (including without limitation legal fees on a solicitor-client basis and disbursements, loss of anticipated profits and special indirect or consequential damages) resulting directly or indirectly from any breach by such party of any term, condition, covenant or provision in this Agreement.

对于因一方当事人违反本协议的任何条款、条件、承诺或规定，而直接或间接地给另一方当事人造成的任何及全部损失、索赔、损害和债务（包括但不限于律师向当事人收取的律师费及垫付开支、预期利润的损失、特殊的间接或从属损害），该方当事人应对另一方作出赔偿，使另一方免受损失。

8. 免责条款（Exclusions of liability）

合同中的免除或限制责任条款是非常重要的，可以为当事人规避或减轻法律风险。但是，在英美法中存在着相关的成文法和判例，对某些种类合同中的免责条款进行限制。如果合同中的免责范围太过于宽泛，特别是在格式条款的情形下，会存在被法院认定为无效的风险；如果免责的内容含糊、不明确、可有不同的解释，则易被法院作出不利于提供该条款一方的解释。

根据合同的标的、性质、双方权利义务等的不同，必要的免责条款内容也不尽相同；这里仅举一个服务合同中免责条款的例子。

【例文】

ABC Company has no obligation，duty or liability to the Customer in contract，tort，for breach of statutory duty or otherwise beyond that of a duty to exercise reasonable skill and care.

ABC 公司对于客户不负有超越合同的、侵权的、违反法定责任或运用合理的技能及注意之外的义务、职责或责任。

9. 不可抗力（Force majeure）

从广义来看，不可抗力条款也是合同中的一种免责条款，是为与一般的免责条款相区别另设的一个单独条款。因当事方不能预见、不能避免、不能克服的不可抗力事件导致合同义务延迟履行或未能履行，该当事方可以免责。不同国家的法律对不可抗力的认定标准有不同的规定。不可抗力条款的关键是对于"不可抗力"范围的约定，一般有两种做法：概括性约定（简略）和列举性约定（详细）。下面例文是介于繁简之间的一般性约定。

【例文】

Force Majeure

1. In the event of any failure or delay by either party hereto in the performance of all or any part of this Contract due to earthquake，typhoon，flooding，fire，war，epidemics or any other force majeure beyond the control of either party，the party involved in any of these events shall inform the other party without delay by fax or by e-mail and shall within 30 days submit to the other party particulars of such event and the failure of performing of this Contract and the need of postponing the performance hereunder.

2. The parties shall，depending upon the extent of impact caused by the force majeure events，negotiate to extend the period of performance or to release the party concerned from performance of this Contract.

3. No party shall be liable for any losses and damages caused by any force majeure events.

不可抗力

1. 本合同任何一方当事人因地震、台风、水灾、火灾、战争、传染病或其他不能控制的不可抗力事件，导致没有履行或延迟履行本合同的全部或部分义务，受到影响的一方当事人应立即以传真或电子邮件方式通知对方，并在 30 天内向对方送交记载有关不可抗力事件的详情、未能履行以及需要延期履行本合同的情况。

2. 双方应根据不可抗力事件所造成影响的程度，协商决定延长相关当事方履行的期间或免除履行本合同。

3. 由于不可抗力事件造成的损失及损害，双方均不承担赔偿责任。

10.　通知条款（Notices）

在商务合同中，特别是履行期间较长、内容较详尽的合同中，通知条款是不可或缺的。合同一方有关合同的变更、解除、权利主张、要求等，均需要以适当的方式通知对方，方可生效。通知条款应规定通知的制作方式（书面方式）、送达地址、送达方法、通知被视为有效送达的时间等。英文商务合同的当事方有时还对通知的语言进行约定。

【例文】

Notices

1. All notices，requests，demands and other communications required or permitted under this Agreement shall be in writing and shall be deemed to have been duly given or made if delivered by hand，mail or sent by courier or facsimile transmission or e-mail provided that in the case of the facsimile transmission or e-mail，a confirmation copy of the notice shall be delivered by hand or sent by courier or registered prepaid mail within two（2）business days of the transmission，to the followings（until notice of a change thereof is given in writing）：

      Address：

      Facsimile no.：

      Attention：

  To：Licensee：

      Address：

      Facsimile no.：

      Attention：

2. All communications given or made in accordance with the proceeding paragraph of this Clause shall be effective, if delivered by hand, mailed or sent by courier, at the time of delivery, and if communicated by facsimile or e-mail, at the time of transmission, provided that if such delivery or transmission is made at a time which, in the destination, is later than 6 p.m. on a business day, or is on a Saturday, Sunday or public holiday, it shall be deemed effective on the next succeeding business day.

通　知

1. 按本协议所要求或允许的所有通知、请求、要求和其他通信应采用书面形式。如果通过面交、邮寄、快递、传真或电邮（在传真和电邮发出的情况下，应在发出后的两个营业日内通过面交、快递或已付邮资挂号信，发出该通知的确认副本）方式作出，发往以下地址（直至书面通知改变地址时为止），应视为正式发出或作出。

　　　　许可方：
　　　　　　地址：
　　　　　　传真：
　　　　　　收件人：
　　　　被许可方：
　　　　　　地址：
　　　　　　传真：
　　　　　　收件人：

2. 根据本条前款发出或作出的所有通信，如通过面交、邮寄或速递，则在送交时生效；如通过电邮或传真发送，则在发送时生效；倘若送交或传送的时间（按目的地时间计算）为营业日的下午六时以后或在星期六、星期日或公众假日，则应被视为于下一个营业日生效。

11. **全部协议条款**（Entire and whole agreement）

在英文合同中，通常有个"全部协议"条款，约定该合同构成各当事方之间有关该商业交易的全部和完整的协议，取代签约之前的一切相关契约性文件或口头约定等。这个条款的目的是保持合同的确定性，合同的当事方希望在一个合同或一套合同中记录该交易的全部权利义务，以排除当事方之间以前可能作出的任何其他形式的不同约定（例如初步性信件、报价、销售方面的文件等）之法律效力。同时，由于举证困难，当事方通常希望排除全部口头陈述和讨论。

【例文】

> This Agreement along with Exhibit 1 hereof constitutes the entire and whole agreement[①] among the Parties, and supersedes all previous agreements[②], whether oral or written, between them with respect to the subject matter hereof.
>
> 本协议与其附件 1 共同构成各方当事人之间的全部和完整的协议，并取代各方之间有关本协议标的之全部先前的口头或书面协议。

12. 合同变更条款（Variations）

在合同签订后，当事人有可能根据实际情况对合同内容作出修改，导致合同内容的变更。这就需要事先对合同修改的程序进行约定。通常，修改合同应采取书面方式，并由当事人各方授权代表签署。对于违反约定程序的修改，当事人可以主张无效。

【例文】

> No amendment, change, addition or deletion regarding the terms and conditions of this Contract shall be effective or binding on either of the Parties unless made in writing and executed by each of the Parties.
>
> 有关本合同条款和条件的修改、变更、增加或删除，均须采用书面方式，并由各方当事人签署，方为有效，对各方当事人产生约束力。

13. 法律的适用和争议的解决（Governing law and settlement of disputes）

除个别种类的合同以外[③]，大多数涉外合同的当事人可以选择处理合同争议所适用的法律。通常，当事人考虑到对本国法律比较熟悉、方便使用本国语言、举证和判决执行的便利、节省费用等因素，大多倾向于选择合同适用本国的法律以及接受本国法院或仲裁机构对合同争议的管辖权。

但在实践中，根据当事人各方对于合同主要义务履行地、违约方财产所在地、确保法院判决或仲裁裁决的承认和执行等因素的考虑，以及各方在合同协商交涉过程中的地位不同等因素，最终在合同中对法律适用及争议解决方式的选择会作出妥协。

---

①② 这里的"agreement"，开头字母不大写，意指当事人之间的协议内容，区别于前面的"the Agreement"（本协议）。

③ 根据《中华人民共和国合同法》（1999 年 10 月 1 日起施行）第 126 条的规定，涉外合同的当事人可以选择处理合同争议所适用的法律，但法律另有规定的除外。在中华人民共和国境内履行的中外合资经营企业合同、中外合作经营企业合同、中外合作勘探开发自然资源合同，适用中华人民共和国法律。

下面是对法律适用和争议解决约定的几种情形。

【例文 1】适用中国法律、接受中国仲裁机构的管辖

This Agreement is governed by and shall be construed in accordance with the laws of PRC. Both parties agree to resolve any dispute between them in relation to this Agreement through good faith negotiations. If the parties are unable to reach an amicable resolution，then such dispute shall be submitted to China International Economic and Trade Arbitration Commission for arbitration，which shall be conducted in accordance with the Commission's arbitration rules in effect at the time of applying for arbitration. The arbitral award shall be final and binding upon both parties.

本协议适用中国法律并按照中国法律解释。双方当事人同意通过友好协商解决有关本协议的任何争议。如果当事人通过友好协商不能解决争议，应提交中国国际经济贸易仲裁委员会，按照申请仲裁时该会实施的仲裁规则进行仲裁。仲裁裁决是终局的，对双方均有约束力。

【例文 2】适用外国法律、接受外国法院的管辖

This Agreement shall be governed by and constructed in accordance with English law and each party agrees to submit to the non-exclusive jurisdiction of the English courts as regards any claim or matter arising under this Agreement.

本协议适用英国法律并按照英国法律解释。每一方当事人同意就本协议项下发生的任何索赔或事项接受英国法院的非专属性管辖权。

【例文 3】适用被诉方国家法律、接受被诉方国家法院的管辖

Any legal proceedings instituted against the Buyer by the Seller shall be brought in the courts of the Buyer's country of domicile and any legal proceedings instituted against the Seller by the Buyer shall be brought in the courts of the Seller's country of domicile and for the purposes of such proceedings the law governing this Agreement and such proceedings shall in each case be deemed to be the law of the country in which the relevant proceedings have been instituted in accordance with this Clause.

卖方对买方提起的任何法律诉讼应由买方住所地国家的法院管辖，而买方对卖方提起的任何法律诉讼应由卖方住所地国家的法院管辖。为该等法

律诉讼的目的，按照本条约定提起相关法律诉讼的国家之法律应被视为本协议和该等法律诉讼所适用的法律。

14. **其他条款或杂项条款**（Miscellaneous clauses）

在英文合同的结尾部分，通常设置一些杂项条款，系沿用固定模式的样板条款。这些条款的目的，是对一般法律规则和本合同之间的关系作出明确区分，限定某些一般法律规则对本合同的影响范围。

（1）排除代理、合伙或合营关系（Agency partnership or joint venture excluded）

如果合同中没有相反的约定，某些种类的商务合同可能在当事人之间建立不希望发生的代理人、合伙或合营关系。作为这些关系发生的一般法律后果，可能使一方当事人的行为对另一方具有约束力或使之对第三方承担债务，发生不能预料的分担损失赔偿等。为了规避这些风险，英文商务合同中特别设定了关于排除代理人、合伙或合营关系的条款。

【例文 1】排除代理关系

Nothing contained in this Contract shall be so construed as to constitute either party to be the agent of the other.

本合同中所包含的任何内容均不应被解释为一方成为另一方的代理人。

【例文 2】排除合伙关系或合营关系

This Contract shall not operate so as to create a partnership or joint venture of any kind between the parties hereto.

本合同不应在本合同当事人之间创立任何种类的合伙关系或合营关系。

【例文 3】全面排除

Nothing in this Contract shall be construed as establishing or implying any partnership or joint venture between the parties hereto, and nothing in this Contract shall be deemed to constitute either of the parties hereto as the agent of the other party or authorize either party, (i) to incur any expenses on behalf of the other party, (ii) to enter into any engagement or make any representation or warranty on behalf of the other party, (iii) to pledge the credit of, or otherwise bind or oblige the other party, or (iv) to commit the other party in any way whatsoever, without in each case obtaining the other party's prior written consent.

本合同中的任何内容均不得被解释为设立或者默认本合同各方当事人之间存在任何合伙关系或合营关系，并且本合同中的任何内容均不得被认为当事人的任何一方成为对方的代理人或授权给任何一方当事人：（i）以对方的名义发生任何费用；（ii）以对方的名义签订任何合约或作出任何陈述或担保；（iii）用对方的信誉作担保，或者以其他方式约束或是束缚对方；或者（iv）在没有事先取得对方书面同意的情况下，以任何方式使对方承担义务。

（2）合同的转让和分包（Assignment and sub-contracting）

大多数商务合同均明确约定，合同中双方当事人的权利义务未经对方事先书面同意不得转让或分包给第三方。这是因为商务合同的当事方是特定化的，其缔约身份和履约能力对于如约履行具有非常重要的意义。

【例文 1】合同不得转让

Neither party shall assign, transfer or dispose of this Agreement in whole or in part or any right hereunder to any person or corporation without the prior written consent of the other party.

没有另一方的事先书面同意，任何一方均不得把本协议全部或部分或其任何权利转让或转移给任何个人或公司。

【例文 2】合同权利义务不可转让、分包等

Neither the rights nor the obligations of any party under this Agreement may be assigned, transferred, sub-contracted or otherwise disposed of, in whole or in part, without the prior written consent of the other party.

没有另一方的事先书面同意，任何一方均不得转让、转移、分包或以其他方式处分在本协议项下的全部或部分权利或义务。

（3）对于税款和费用的约定（Taxes and costs）

税款和费用的负担会增加当事人的交易成本，通常由费用发生方的当事人负担。在合同中没有明确约定的情况下，一般应由相关法律规定的纳税义务人负担。为了避免争议，应当在合同中对此作出明确约定。

【例文 1】

Except as specifically agreed to the contrary, any costs in relation to this Agreement and subject matter hereof which are incurred by any one of the parties hereto shall be borne by the party incurring the same.

除非另有明确的相反约定，当事人任何一方所发生的有关本协议以及本协议标的之任何费用，应由该费用发生方当事人负担。

【例文 2】

> The Vendor shall bear all legal，accountancy and other costs and expenses incurred by it in connection with this Agreement and the sale of the Property. The Purchaser shall bear all such costs and expenses incurred by it. The Purchaser shall bear all stamp duties and sales and transfer taxes including without limitation value added tax arising as a result or in consequence of this Agreement.
>
> 卖方须负担与本协议以及该财产销售有关的、由卖方发生的法律、会计和其他费用。买方须承担由其发生的全部成本和费用。买方必须负担全部印花税以及销售和转让税款，包括但不限于由于本协议所发生的增值税。

（4）签约后的违规条款和分离措施（Supervening illegality and severance）

按照当事人意愿签订合同后，有时会因合同准据法中后来颁布的法律法规或判例使得合同的部分条款变为不合法或不可履行。这些违规条款通常涉及贸易管制条款、不正当竞争条款、排除担保和责任的条款等。为了不致使合同因此而整体失效，有必要在合同中事先约定分离措施，即部分条款因违规而被分离出去，合同的其他条款仍然有效，可以执行。①

【例文】

> Should any provision in this Agreement be held to be illegal or unenforceable，in whole or in part，under any enactment or rule of law，such provision or part shall to that extent be deemed not to form part of this Agreement but the validity and enforceability of the remainder of this Agreement shall not be affected.
>
> 若本协议中的任何条款因任何法律颁布或规则而被认为全部或部分违法或不可履行，该条款或部分在该范围内应被视为并非构成本协议的一部分，而本协议的其余条款之有效性和可履行性不受影响。

（5）时间是至关重要的（Time to be of the essence）

在一些国家的法律中，除非在合同中明确约定时间对履约是至关重要的，否则，即使一方当事人没有严格按照合同约定的时间履约，并不构成对方当事人可以立即解除合同的权利；守约方必须先向违约方送达要求履行合同的合理通知（指定具体的履约期限），倘若违约方仍不履约，守约方才可以据此解除合同。因此，在某些合同中，对"时间是至关重要的"作出明确

---

① 这在英美法中被称为"蓝铅笔原则"或"红铅笔原则"（the "blue pencil" or "red pencil" rules），该原则意为：对于合同中出现部分条款不合理（不合法、不公平）、而部分条款合理的情形时，当合同中的合理条款及不合理条款可由法庭轻易予以分隔开来时，法庭只承认合理部分的条款为有效，而不合理部分的条款为无效。这就好像用一支铅笔把不合理的条款划掉（使之无效），保留合理的条款（仍然有效）。

约定，就成为"至关重要的"了。

【例文】

Time shall be of the essence of this Contract，both as regards the dates and periods mentioned and as regards any dates and periods which may be substituted for them in accordance with this Contract or by agreement in writing between the parties.

时间对本合同是至关重要的，本合同中约定的日期和期间以及按照本合同或各方当事人之间的书面协议可以取代的任何日期和期间，均是至关重要的。

（6）弃权条款（Waiver）

很多国家的法律规定，在某些情况下，由于故意或疏忽而没有行使合同项下的权利，会导致这些权利的放弃。因此，有必要在合同中对此作出明确约定。

【例文】

Any waiver of any breach of this Contract shall not be deemed to apply to any succeeding breach of the provision or of any other provision of this Contract. No failure to exercise and no delay in exercising on the part of any of the Parties hereto any right，power or privilege hereunder shall operate as a waiver thereof nor shall any single or partial exercise of any right，power or privilege preclude any other or further exercise thereof or the exercise of any other right，power or privilege. The rights and remedies provided in this Contract are cumulative and not exclusive of any rights or remedies otherwise provided by law.

对于本合同违约行为的弃权不应被视为对本合同该条款或其他条款项下将来违约行为的弃权。一方未行使或延迟行使本合同约定的任何权利、权力或优先权，不应构成放弃该项权利、权力或优先权；任何单独或部分地行使任何权利、权力或优先权，不应妨碍将来另外行使该项或其他权利、权力或优先权。本合同所约定的权利和救济是累积性的，不排除法律规定的任何其他权利或救济。

（7）合同语言（Languages）

有些合同仅需签署英文本，中文翻译件仅作为中方当事人的参考。有些合同需要中国政府部门批准方可生效，则必须签署中文本，而外方需要同时签署英文本，并通常坚持英文本与中文本具有同等法律效力。但因提交中国政府部门审批，如两种文本内容有不一致之处，应以中文本为准。

【例文】

This Contract shall be written in Chinese and English，all of which have equal legal effect. In the event of any discrepancies between the two versions，the Chinese version shall prevail.

> 本合同用中文和英文写成，两种文本均具有同等法律效力。如果两种文本有不一致之处，以中文本为准。

如果合同不需要提交中国政府审批，则根据双方协商的结果，也可以约定以英文本内容为准。

（8）签约份数（Counterparts）

为了证明签约的内容并且便于合同的履行，合同各方通常应确保各持有一份签约原件。

【例文 1】

> This Agreement has been executed in two（2）originals. Each party shall keep one original.
>
> 本协议的签约原件一式两份，双方各执一份。

有时，在签署合同时不确定需要几份签约原件，例如，需要向不同政府部门（如发改委、商务部门、工商部门、海关、外汇管理部门等）报批或备案的合同，可以对签约份数作如下约定：

【例文 2】

> （1）This Agreement may be executed in any number of counterparts, and by the Parties on separate counterparts, but shall not be effective until each Party has executed at least one counterpart.
> （2）Each counterpart shall constitute an original of this Agreement，but all the counterparts shall together constitute the same instrument.
>
> （1）本协议的签约文本份数不限，且当事人各方均分别持有签约文本，但只在每一方当事人均签署至少一份文本时，本协议方能生效。
> （2）每一文本均构成本协议的原件，但所有文本共同构成相同的协议文件。

第 4 节　合同附件、附表
（Schedules，Appendices，Annexes）

为使合同的实质性条款不因中间穿插个别事项的细节（例如，在技术许可合同中对技术内容的详细说明、在买卖合同中对一般交易条件的约定、在独家经销合同中对最低购入数量的约定等）而破坏合同内容的逻辑性，为保持合同全文的平衡，将合同中出现的个别详细部分放在合同最后的附件或附表中是一个很好的方法。

对于合同与其附件或附表之间的关系，可以在合同中作如下约定：

【例文】

> The Parties agree that the Schedules hereof shall be incorporated into and hereby made an integral part of this Agreement.
>
> 各方当事人同意，本合同的各附件应当纳入本合同中，从而构成本合同之不可分割的一部分。

第 5 节　签署部分（Signature section）

英文合同签署部分的表达方式一般为：

【例文 1】

> IN WITNESS WHEREOF，the Parties have caused this Agreement to be executed by their respective duly authorized representatives on the day and year first set forth above.
>
> For and on behalf of
> XXX CO.，LTD.　　　　　　　　　　YYY CO.，LTD.
> By ＿＿＿【签署】＿＿＿　　　　　　　By ＿＿＿【签署】＿＿＿
> Name：【签字人姓名】　　　　　　　　Name：【签字人姓名】
> Title：【签字人职务】　　　　　　　　Title：【签字人职务】
>
> 各方当事人的正式授权代表已经于本合同首页所述日期签署了本合同，特此为证。
>
> 代表：XXX 有限公司　　　　　　　　代表：YYY 有限公司
> 签署：＿＿＿＿＿＿＿＿　　　　　　　签署：＿＿＿＿＿＿＿＿
> 姓名：　　　　　　　　　　　　　　　姓名：
> 职务：　　　　　　　　　　　　　　　职务：

【例文 2】

> SIGNED by【签字人姓名】　　　　　　　　　　　　【签署】
> a duly authorized representative
> of Party A
> in the presence of：【在场见证人姓名】　　　　　　【在场见证人签署】
>
> 由【签字人姓名】　　　　　　　　　　　　　　　　【签署】
> 甲方之
> 正式授权代表
> 在场见证：【在场见证人姓名】　　　　　　　　　　【在场见证人签署】

合同签署页一般在最后页；如合同有附件或附表，则一般在合同主文和附件或附表之间。为防止一方当事人在双方签署合同后又擅自更改合同内容、对另一方不利，可以在签署时由双方代表在合同每一页的下边空白处进行简签（Initial，即签署代表的姓氏）；如合同除签字外还需盖章，也可以对合同每页均加盖骑缝章。

对于合同签署时是否需要盖章的问题，各国法律规定不同。《中华人民共和国合同法》（1999 年 10 月 1 日起施行）第 32 条规定，当事人采用合同书形式订立合同的，自双方当事人签字或者盖章时合同成立。按照中国法律，公司的法定代表人可以代表公司签署合同，无需盖章；如果不是法定代表人签字，则需要出具法定代表人对授权签字代表的委托书，也可以既签字又盖章（合同章或公司公章）。对于外国公司，要按照其管辖法律和公司章程确定签字人是否有权代表公司签署合同。例如，有些国家（地区）法律规定公司的董事有权代表公司签约；有些合同需要公司董事会决议授权的代表签约；有些特殊合同需要加盖公司印章或法团印章（Common Seal），等等。总之，要根据合同准据法和当事方所属国家的法律，确定有权代表当事方签署合同的人员以及是否需要加盖公司印章或法团印章（Common Seal）。

第 6 节　合同的编号系统（Contract numbering systems）

在英文合同中，Article 或者 Clause 均是"条"；在"条"下面的"款"及"项"通常直接用数字表示，例如"1.1"（可译作第 1 条第 1 款或第 1.1 条）、"1.1.1"（可译作第 1 条第 1 款第 1 项或第 1.1.1 条）。有些较短的合同，常不用 Article 或者 Clause，直接列出"1."、"1.1"等；在 1.1 的下面，可以用（a）（b）；再下面可以用（i）（ii）等。具体例文可以在后面精选的各类商务合同文本中看到。

需要注意的是，英文合同中条款段落的排列与中文不同，中文的表达习惯是在每条款最前面空 2 格，而英文是下一款比上一条往后缩进去排列，作者认为英文条款段落的排列更加便于区分和识别每个条款的内容，使用起来更为方便。

第

3

章

货物买卖合同精选与解读

第 1 节　进口合同精选与解读

（合同正面）

XX Co.，Ltd. XX 有限公司	Address： 地址： Tel 电话：　　　　　　　　Fax 传真：

CONTRACT OF PURCHASE[①] 进口合同

XX CO.，LTD. as Buyer hereby confirms the purchase from the undermentioned Seller of the following goods（the **"Goods"**）on the terms and conditions given below INCLUDING ALL THOSE PRINTED ON THE REVERSE SIDE HEREOF[②], which are expressly agreed to, understood and made a part of this Contract：-

买方 XX 有限公司在此确认依照本合同的条款和条件从下述卖方购买以下货物（以下简称"货物"）。**本合同的内容包括背面印制的全部条款及条件。**背面的条款及条件已获得双方明示同意及理解，并构成本合同的一部分。

SELLER'S NAME AND ADDRESS 卖方名称及地址	BUYER'S DEPT. 买方负责部门	DATE 日期
	BUYER'S CONTRACT NO. 买方合同编号	SELLER'S REFERENCE NO. 卖方参考编号

SHIPPING MARK 唛头	GOODS & QUALITY "货物"名称及质量	QUANTITY 数量	UNIT PRICE 单价	AMOUNT 金额

TERMS OF DELIVERY 交货方式	TIME OF SHIPMENT 装运时间
PORT OF SHIPMENT 装运港	
PORT OF DESTINATION 目的港	
INSPECTION 检验	PACKING 包装
INSURANCE 保险	SPECIAL TERMS & CONDITIONS（FINAL DESTINATION, ETC.） 特别条款及条件（例如最终目的地等）
PAYMENT 付款方法	

Agreed, accepted and confirmed by 双方同意、接受及确认本合同。

（SELLER 卖方）　　　　　　　　　　　（BUYER 买方）XX Co.，Ltd.
　　　　　　　　　　　　　　　　　　　　　　　　　　 XX 有限公司

BY 签署或盖章　　　　　　　　　　　　BY 签署或盖章
————————————　　　　　　　————————————
　Authorized Signature 授权代表签字　　　　　Authorized Signature 授权代表签字
DATE：日期
—————————————————————————————————————

（SEE GENERAL TERMS AND CONDITIONS ON REVERSE SIDE HEREOF 请见本页背面所列一般条款及条件）

---

①　本合同英文 Contract of Purchase，直译为"购货合同"，但实际是买方（进口方）用于进口货物的合同，译为"进口合同"对买方的合同管理更为便利。买方是贸易公司，货物进口后将销售给国内的批发商和零售商。本合同是律师受买方（进口方）委托而制作，合同内容（特别是背面的"一般条款及条件"）侧重于保护买方的权益。买方（进口方）将本合同作为标准格式的进口合同而印制使用，正面是商业条款，背面是一般条款及条件。

②　此处以及合同背面的大写字体及下划底线或粗体印刷的部分，是为符合所适用的法律中可能对于合同格式条款的要求，对于免除或减轻买方责任、加重卖方责任或限制其权利的合同内容，提请卖方的注意。请参阅《中华人民共和国合同法》（1999 年 10 月 1 日起施行）第 39、40、41 条等关于合同格式条款的规定。

Contract of Purchase（Reverse Side）进口合同（背面）
GENERAL TERMS AND CONDITIONS 一般条款及条件

1. TRADE TERMS Seller and Buyer shall be governed by the provisions of INCOTERMS 2000, as amended, with regard to the trade terms, such as FOB, FAS, C&F, CIF, used herein, unless otherwise provided for herein.

贸易术语 除本合同另有规定外，关于本合同中使用的贸易术语，例如：FOB、FAS、C&F、CIF，卖方及买方均受《2000年国际贸易术语解释通则》（INCOTERMS 2000）的规定以及其修订内容的约束。

2. SHIPMENT—运输

（1）The Goods shall be shipped and delivered strictly within the period stipulated herein. In the event of delay in shipment or delivery due to any cause not attributable to Buyer, Buyer has the option to cancel this Contract or extend the period for shipment or delivery, and if shipment or delivery is further delayed due to any cause not attributable to Buyer beyond the time so extended by Buyer, Buyer may cancel this Contract at any time thereafter, and in any such event the said extension or cancellation shall be without prejudice to any other rights and remedies available to Buyer. ①

"货物"应严格按本合同规定的期限装运及交货。如因任何不可归咎于买方的原因导致装运或交货发生延误，买方有权选择取消本合同或延长装运或交货期限。如因不可归咎于买方的原因导致装运或交货进一步迟延超过经买方按前述规定延长的时间，买方可于此后的任何时间取消本合同，并且在此种情况下，上述延期或取消不影响买方享有的其他任何权利和补救措施。

（2）When Seller shall secure the vessel or vessel's space, Seller shall, unless otherwise agreed herein, ship the Goods on a first class steamer or motor vessel classed Lloyd's △ 100A1 or equivalent, owned and/or operated by a carrier of good reputation and standing and of the type normally used for the transport of such goods. In such event, before loading of the Goods, Seller shall, at its expenses, inspect the vessel's hold for cleanliness and suitability for loading.

若由卖方洽船或订舱，除双方于本合同项下另有约定外，卖方须将"货物"以Lloyd's △ 100A1等级或相同等级的一级汽船或机动船舶运送，该船舶须由一间拥有良好信誉及名望的承运人所拥有及/或运营，而且其类别应是通常常用作运输此等货物。在此情形下，卖方须于装运"货物"之前自行承担费用检查用以装货的船舱的清洁及适合运载情况。

（3）If this Contract is on a C&F basis, Seller shall, unless otherwise agreed herein, compensate and reimburse Buyer for any additional insurance premiums incurred by Buyer as a result of charges made by Buyer's insurance company for insurance of the Goods by reason of unclassed vessel, overage vessel, broken-up vessel or any other characteristic of the vessel or vessel's space secured for the transport of the Goods. C&F (Cost and Freight) ②

如果本合同以C&F价格为基础，除本合同中另有约定外，对因使用不入级船、超龄船、解体船、或因用于运输"货物"的船舶或船舱之任何其他情况而导致买方须就"货物"投保而向其保险公司支付的额外保险费，卖方须予以补偿并偿还买方该额外保险费。

（4）In the event Buyer shall charter a vessel for ocean transportation of the Goods, all charges and expenses for loading of the Goods, including demurrage and other damages, which are to be for the account of the charterer against the shipowner or the chartered owner under the relevant charter party, shall be borne and paid by Seller.

如由买方租用船舶进行"货物"的远洋运输，卖方须承担有关租船契约中由租船人支付给船主或租船船东的全部装货费用及支出（包括滞期费及其他损失）。

（5）Immediately upon completion of the loading of the Goods, Seller shall by facsimile or any other

---

① 按合同及时交货是卖方的主要义务，延迟交货会影响买方向国内批发商和零售商及时履行交货义务，可能导致买方违约。因此本合同对卖方的按时交货义务作了较严厉的约定。

② 成本加运费价格，因保险费由买方负责，如果卖方所定船舶或船舱不适合运输"货物"而导致买方额外负担保险费，根据此款规定可归由卖方负担。

writing transmission give to Buyer a notice of shipment or delivery, showing the contract number, the name of vessel or the flight number of aircraft, the port of shipment and delivery, the description of the Goods and packing, the quantity loaded, the invoice amount and other particulars essential to this Contract.

一旦"货物"装船完毕，卖方须立即以传真或其他书面形式向买方发送装运或交货通知书。通知书中应写明合同编号、船舶名称或飞机航班号、装运及交货港口、"货物"描述及包装、装货数量、发票金额及本合同其他基本详情。

3. **PRICE**　The price described on the face hereof shall be firm and final and shall not be subject to any adjustment as a result of a price change in Seller's cost which may occur due to a change in material or labour costs or in freight rates or insurance premiums, or on account of any variation in rates of exchange or any increase in taxes or duties or imposition of any new taxes or duties.

价格　列于本合同正面的价格是确定的最终价格，且该价格不因原料价格、工资成本、运费或保险费的变更、汇率变动、增加税项或关税、征收新设税项或关税而导致卖方的成本价格变动而调整。

4. **GOVERNMENTAL APPROVAL**　Buyer shall not be responsible for failure or delay in obtaining any governmental approval necessary for the performance of this Contract or for any restriction on import or payment of taxes or charges imposed by any governmental authority after the conclusion of this Contract. ①

政府批准　对于本合同签订后未能获得或延迟获得为履行本合同所需的任何政府批准或任何政府部门实施进口限制或征收税费，买方不承担任何责任。

5. **TERMS OF LETTER OF CREDIT**　In the event the terms of the letter of credit established on account of Buyer do not conform to the terms of this Contract, Seller shall request Buyer to amend the terms of the letter of credit immediately after receipt of notice from the notifying bank, otherwise Seller shall be deemed to have waived any claim concerning such non-

conformity. ②

信用证条款　如果买方开出的信用证条款与本合同规定不相符合，卖方须在收到由通知行发出的通知后立即要求买方修改信用证的条款；否则，视为卖方放弃就该不符合的情形提出任何索赔。

6. **INSURANCE**　If this Contract is on a CIF basis, the Goods shall, unless otherwise agreed herein, be insured by Seller at a value equal to one hundred ten percent (110%) of the CIF amount.

保险　如果本合同以 CIF 价格为基础，除非双方在本合同中另有约定，卖方须为"货物"投保，保额相当于 CIF 金额的 110%。

7. **WARRANTY—保证**

（1）Seller shall convey to Buyer good and merchantable title to the Goods free of any encumbrance, lien or security interest. Seller warrants that the Goods shall fully conform to any and all specifications, descriptions, drawings and data or samples or models furnished to or by Buyer, and shall be merchantable, of good material and workmanship and free from defects, and shall be fit or suitable for the purpose(s) intended by Buyer and/or Buyer's customer(s). ③

卖方须向买方转让良好及适销的"货物"之所有权，且不附加任何障碍、留置权或担保权益。卖方保证"货物"完全符合向买方提供或由买方提供的任何及一切规格、描述、图样、数据、样本或模型，并保证该"货物"必须是适销的、以优质原料及工艺水准制造，没有瑕疵，且适合买方及/或买方客户的预定用途。

（2）Buyer shall make all claims, except for latent defects, regarding the Goods against Seller in writing within forty-five (45) days after the arrival of the Goods at the port of destination. Seller shall not be responsible for latent defects regarding the Goods unless claims for such defects are made in writing within eight (8) months after the arrival of the Goods at the

---

①　此处约定排除了买方因政府部门的批准或税收等影响合同履行的违约责任，实际上将之归为不可抗力之类（本进口合同中并无不可抗力条款，请对照出口合同中详细的不可抗力条款约定）。

②　本条要求卖方及时通知买方信用证条款与进口合同不相符合的情况，排除了卖方因未及时通知而对所遭受的损失向买方索赔，对买方有利。

③　本款对货物的质量要求作了全面的严格限定，对保护买方的权益非常有利。

port of destination. ①

买方须于"货物"运抵目的港后的四十五天内，以书面形式向卖方提出有关"货物"的所有索赔，但潜在瑕疵除外。除非于"货物"运抵目的港后的八个月内买方以书面形式提出有关"货物"潜在瑕疵的索赔，否则卖方不对潜在瑕疵承担责任。

（3） Even after the expiration of either of the above-mentioned periods, Seller shall indemnify and hold Buyer harmless from any losses and damages suffered by Buyer's customer and/or any other third party due to any defect, unfitness or unsuitability of the Goods sold hereunder. ②

即使上述两个期限均已届满，对因本合同项下售卖的"货物"的任何瑕疵、不合格或不适合情形导致买方客户及/或其他任何第三方遭受任何损失及损害，卖方须就此予以赔偿且使买方免予遭受任何损失及损害。

8. BREACH OF CONTRACT—违约③

（1） If Seller commits a breach of any of the terms, conditions or warranties in this Contract, Buyer shall have the following remedies and may recover all losses and damages caused by Seller's breach, including, but not limited to, loss of profit which would have been obtained by Buyer but for Seller's breach and all losses and damages caused by Buyer's non-fulfillment of its obligations to Buyer's customer（s） due to Seller's breach：

(i) To suspend its performance of this Contract；

(ii) To reject the shipment or delivery of the Goods；

(iii) To dispose of the Goods, if delivered, for the account of Seller in such manner as Buyer deems reasonable and to allocate the proceeds thereof towards the satisfaction of any or all of the losses and damages；

(iv) To cancel this Contract or any part thereof.

如果卖方违反本合同中的任何条款、条件或保证，买方享有以下救济，并可获赔因卖方违约而造成的所有损失和损害，其中包括但不限于，因卖方违约使买方失去的可得利润以及因卖方违约导致买方未能对其客户履行义

务而引起的全部损失及损害：

(i) 暂停履行本合同；

(ii) 拒绝"货物"的装运或交货；

(iii) 如已交货，以买方认为合理的方法代卖方处置"货物"，并分配所获收益以清偿任何或所有的损失和损害；

(iv) 取消本合同或其中任何部分。

（2） If Buyer reasonably anticipates that Seller will not or cannot perform this Contract, Buyer may demand adequate assurance, satisfactory to Buyer, of the due performance of this Contract by Seller and Buyer may suspend its performance of this Contract until such assurance is given by Seller and accepted by Buyer.

如果买方合理地预期卖方将不会或不能履行本合同，买方可要求卖方提供使买方满意的充足担保以确保其可妥善地履行本合同，并且买方可暂停履行本合同直至卖方提供该担保且买方接受该担保时为止。

（3） If Seller fails to give the abovementioned assurance to Buyer within a reasonable time or if proceedings in bankruptcy or insolvency or similar proceedings are instituted by or against Seller or a trustee or receiver for Seller is appointed, or if Seller goes into dissolution or liquidation or assigns a substantial part of its assets for the benefit of creditors, Buyer may treat such event as breach of this Contract by Seller and shall be entitled to the remedies stipulated in the first paragraph of this Clause 8.

如果卖方未在合理时间内向买方提供上述担保，或卖方申请或被申请破产或进入清算或类似程序，或已对卖方委派托管人或接管人，或卖方进入解散或清算程序，或为债权人的利益转让其重大部分的资产，买方可将此等事件视为卖方违约并有权采取本合同第 8 条第（1）款规定的救济措施。

（4） The exercise by Buyer of any of the remedies under this Clause 8 shall not be deemed a waiver of any other rights or remedies to which Buyer is or may be entitled.

买方采取上述第 8 条的任何救济措施，不得被视

---

① 本款对买方就货物的潜在瑕疵提出索赔规定了充足的时间。

② 本款是对超过上述两款索赔期限时提出索赔的兜底规定。通过第 7 条 3 个款项的约定，对买方就货物提出索赔的权利提供了全面的保护。

③ 本条从不同方面就卖方违约时买方可享有的权利以及可采取的措施作了约定，较全面地保护了买方的权益。

为买方放弃其享有或可能享有的其他权利或救济。

9. **PATENT, TRADEMARK, ETC.** Seller shall hold Buyer harmless from any claim or dispute which may arise from or in connection with infringement of any patent, utility model, design, trademark or any other industrial property rights or copyrights in connection with the Goods. Seller shall indemnify, reimburse and compensate Buyer for all losses and damages including costs, expenses and charges for defensive actions by Buyer, if Buyer should incur them as a result of such claim or dispute.

专利、商标等　因"货物"发生有关侵犯任何专利、实用新型、外观设计、商标或其他工业产权或著作权的任何索赔或争议，卖方须确保买方不受任何损害。卖方须赔偿、偿还及补偿买方因上述索赔或争议所遭受的所有损失及损害，包括买方采取抗辩行动的费用、支出及应付款项。

10. **LAW APPLICABLE**　This Contract shall be governed by and construed in all respects in accordance with the laws of the People's Republic of China.

法律适用　本合同受中华人民共和国法律管辖，并按照中华人民共和国法律解释。

11. **NON-ASSIGNMENT**　Seller shall not assign or delegate any of its rights or obligations under this Contract without prior written consent of Buyer.

不可转让　如未获得买方的事先书面同意，卖方不得转让或转移其在本合同中的任何权利或义务。

12. **CONFLICTING TERMS**　Unless otherwise specifically agreed, the provisions contained in the front page shall govern and supersede any conflicting printed terms and conditions appeared on this reverse side. ①

冲突性条文　除非双方另有明确约定，当本合同背面印刷的条款和条件与正面所载条文的内容发生冲突时，则以正面所载条文为准。

13. **LANGUAGE**　This Contract is made in Chinese and English, and both versions shall have the same effect.

签字文本　本合同用中英文两种文字作成，两种文本具有同等效力。

14. **SETTLEMENT OF DISPUTE**　Any dispute between Buyer and Seller arising from or in connection with this Contract of Purchase shall be submitted to South China International Economic and Trade Arbitration Commission in Shenzhen for arbitration which shall be conducted in accordance with the Commission's arbitration rules in effect at the time of applying for arbitration. The arbitral award is final and binding upon both parties. ②

争议解决　买方及卖方之间凡因本合同引起的或与本合同有关的任何争议，均应在深圳提交华南国际经济贸易仲裁委员会，按照申请仲裁时该会现行有效的仲裁规则进行仲裁。仲裁裁决是终局性的，对双方均有约束力。

15. **WAIVER**　No claim or right of Buyer under this Contract shall be deemed to be waived or renounced in whole or in part unless the waiver or renunciation of such claim or right is acknowledged and confirmed in writing by Buyer.

放弃权利　除非买方以书面形式承认及确认免除或放弃本合同中全部或部分的索赔或权利，否则不得视为买方已免除或放弃该索赔或权利。

16. **ENTIRE AGREEMENT**　This Contract is based on the terms and conditions expressly set forth herein and no other terms and conditions are binding on Buyer without its agreement in writing to such other terms and conditions.

完整协议　本合同是依据其列明的条款及条件而成立。除非经买方书面同意，否则买方不受其他条款和条件的约束。

17. **HEADINGS**　The headings are for convenience only and shall not affect the construction of this Contract.

标题　标题仅为方便而设，不影响本合同的解释。

---

①　本格式合同的正面是关于具体交易的商业条款，根据每项进口货物交易的具体情况由双方填写、签署，其效力优先于本合同背面适用于各项交易的一般条款和条件。

②　因卖方是境外公司，通过华南国际经济贸易仲裁委员会的仲裁解决争议，仲裁裁决可以在卖方所在国（《承认和执行外国仲裁裁决公约》的缔约国）法院申请强制执行。而买方的主要营业地在深圳，仲裁地点选择在深圳，对买方来说更为便利。

第2节 出口合同精选与解读

（合同正面）

XX Co., Ltd. XX 有限公司	Address： 地址： Tel 电话： Fax 传真：

CONTRACT OF SALE① 出口合同

XX CO., LTD. as Seller hereby confirms the sale to the undermentioned Buyer of the following goods（the **"Goods"**）on the terms and conditions given below INCLUDING ALL THOSE PRINTED ON THE REVERSE SIDE HEREOF②, which are expressly agreed to, understood and made a part of this Contract：-

卖方 XX 有限公司在此确认依照本合同的条款和条件出售下述货物（以下简称"货物"）给下述买方。**本合同的内容包括背面印制的全部条款及条件**。背面的条款及条件已获得双方明示同意及理解，并构成本合同的一部分。

BUYER'S NAME AND ADDRESS 买方名称及地址	SELLER'S DEPT. 卖方负责部门		DATE 日期	
	SELLER'S CONTRACT NO. 卖方合同编号		BUYER'S REFERENCE NO. 买方参考编号	
SHIPPING MARK 唛头	GOODS & QUALITY "货物"名称及质量	QUANTITY 数量	UNIT PRICE 单价	AMOUNT 金额

TERMS OF DELIVERY 交货方式	PORT OF DESTINATION 目的港
TIME OF SHIPMENT 装运时间	
PORT OF SHIPMENT 装运港	
INSPECTION 检验	PACKING 包装
INSURANCE 保险	SPECIAL TERMS & CONDITIONS（FINAL DESTINATION，ETC.） 特别条款及条件（例如最终目的地等）
PAYMENT 付款方法	

Agreed, accepted and confirmed by 双方同意、接受及确认本合同。

(BUYER 买方)　　　　　　　　　　　　　(SELLER 卖方) XX Co., Ltd..
　　　　　　　　　　　　　　　　　　　　　　　　XX 有限公司

BY 签署或盖章　　　　　　　　　　　　　BY 签署或盖章

　　Authorized Signature 授权代表签字　　　　　　Authorized Signature 授权代表签字

DATE：日期

(SEE GENERAL TERMS AND CONDITIONS ON REVERSE SIDE HEREOF 请见本页背面所列一般条款及条件)

---

① 本合同英文 Contract of Sale，直译为"售货合同"，但实际是卖方（出口方）用于出口货物的合同，译为"出口合同"对于卖方的合同管理更为便利。本合同是律师受卖方（出口方）的委托而制作，合同内容（特别是背面的"一般条款和条件"）侧重于保护卖方（出口方）的权益。卖方（出口方）将本合同作为标准格式的出口合同而印制使用，正面是商业条款，背面是一般条款及条件。

② 此处以及合同背面的大写字体及下划底线或粗体的部分，是为符合所适用的法律中可能对于合同格式条款的要求，对于本合同中免除或减轻卖方责任、加重买方责任或限制其权利的合同内容，提请买方注意。请参阅《中华人民共和国合同法》（1999 年 10 月 1 日起施行）第 39、40、41 条等关于合同格式条款的规定。

Contract of Sale（Reverse Side）出口合同（背面）

GENERAL TERMS AND CONDITIONS[①] 一般条款及条件

1. TRADE TERMS Seller and Buyer shall be governed by the provisions of INCOTERMS 2000，as amended，with regard to the trade terms，such as FOB，FAS，C&F，CIF，used herein，unless otherwise provided for herein.

贸易术语 除本合同另有规定外，关于本合同中使用的贸易术语，例如：FOB、FAS、C&F、CIF，卖方及买方均受《2000 年国际贸易术语解释通则》（INCOTERMS 2000）的规定以及其修订内容的约束。

2. SHIPMENT—运输[②]

(1) Partial shipment or delivery and/or transshipment shall be permitted.

可分批装运或交货及/或转运。

(2) Date of bill of lading or air waybill shall be accepted as conclusive evidence of the date of shipment or delivery.

海运提单或空运提单上的日期应作为证明装运或交货日期的结论性证据。

(3) If the vessel is not provided or nominated by Buyer in time for the shipment or delivery of the Goods under the terms of FAS or FOB or within any extension of time for such shipment or delivery granted by Seller，Seller may，at its option，extend the time of shipment or delivery of the Goods，or cancel this Contract or change any part hereof，without prejudice to any other rights and remedies Seller may have.

如果买方没有按照 FAS 或 FOB 价格或在卖方同意延长的期限内买方没有及时提供或安排船舶装运或交付"货物"，卖方可选择延长装运或交付"货物"的期限或者取消本合同或变更其中部分条款，卖方的上述选择并不影响卖方可享有的其他权利和救济措施。

(4) In case the Goods shall be carried on air transportation，risk of loss of the Goods shall pass from Seller to Buyer upon delivery of the Goods to the carrier or its agent for transportation.

倘若"货物"须经空运，"货物"损失的风险在"货物"送达到承运人或其运输代理人时由卖方转移至买方。

(5) In case Seller is required to stow，trim or level the Goods on board at the port of shipment under the

specific terms of this Contract，risk of loss of the Goods shall pass from Seller to Buyer，regardless of such requirement to Seller，in accordance with the provisions of INCOTERMS 2000，as amended，with respect to the relevant trade terms.

即使本合同列有特殊条款要求卖方在装运港口将"货物"在船上堆装、调整或平装，"货物"损失的风险仍按照《2000 年国际贸易术语解释通则》（INCOTERMS 2000）及其修订内容对有关贸易术语的规定，由卖方转移至买方。

(6) In the event Seller shall charter a vessel for ocean transportation of the Goods，all charges and expenses for discharge of the Goods，including demurrage and other damages，which are to be for the account of the charterer against the shipowner or the chartered owner under the relevant charter party，shall be borne and paid by Buyer.

如果卖方须租用船舶进行"货物"的远洋运输，买方须承担有关租船契约中规定应由租船人支付给船主或租船船东的所有卸货的费用及支出（包括滞期费及其他损失）。

3. PAYMENT—付款

(1) In case payment for the Goods shall be made by a letter of credit under this Contract，Buyer shall，unless otherwise provided for herein，establish in favor of Seller an irrevocable and confirmed letter of credit negotiable on sight draft through a prime bank of good international reputation and satisfactory to Seller immediately after the conclusion of this Contract with validity of at least twenty（20）days after the last day of the period of the relative shipment or delivery. Such letter of credit shall be in a form and upon terms satisfactory to Seller and shall authorize reimbursement to Seller for such sums，if any，as may be advanced by Seller for consular invoices，inspection fees and other expenditures for the account of Buyer. Should payment under such letter of credit not be duly effected，Buyer shall，upon notice thereof from

---

① 本合同的一般条款和条件侧重于保护卖方（出口方）的权益，如果与前面"进口合同"的一般条款和条件互相比较参照，更能体会到卖方律师的立场及合同制作技巧。

② 本条中的各款规定从不同方面明确了出口货物运输中卖方的权利，对其责任作了限定，尽可能规避卖方的风险。

Seller, immediately make payment in cash to Seller directly and unconditionally. ①

如果本合同以信用证作为"货物"付款方式，除非本合同中另有规定，买方须于本合同订立后立即开出以卖方为受益人、不可撤销、保兑及可转让的即期付款信用证。该信用证须由卖方接受的有良好国际信誉的第一流的银行开出。该信用证的有效期从装运或交货期的最后一天起计不得少于 20 天。该信用证的形式及条款必须符合卖方要求，并应规定偿还卖方代买方垫付的领事发票及检查的费用以及其他支出（如有的话）。如该信用证未能有效承兑，买方在收到卖方的通知后，必须立刻无条件地以现金直接付款给卖方。

（2）If delivery of the Goods is to be made by partial shipment or delivery, Buyer shall, without set-off or counterclaim of any kind including counterclaims against Seller arising under this Contract, make payment for each lot of partial shipment or delivery as herein provided, and the payment by Buyer of each shipment or delivery when due shall be a condition precedent to the obligation of Seller to deliver the next succeeding shipment or delivery under this Contract. ②

如分批装运或交付货物，买方须就每次分批装运或交货付款，不得以任何理由作冲抵或进行反索赔，包括基于本合同对卖方提出的反索赔。买方按本合同依时支付每一批装运和交付的"货物"的款项，构成卖方依照本合同继续履行下一批装运或交货义务之先决条件。

（3）If payment for the Goods is not effected fully by Buyer when due under terms of payment of this Contract, or, in case of payment to be made by a letter of credit, such letter of credit is not established in accordance with the terms of this Contract, such failure shall constitute a breach of this Contract substantially impairing the value of the whole Contract entitling Seller to terminate all or any part of this Contract at any time without prejudice to the rights of Seller to

recover any damages incurred thereby and/or to enforce any other rights or remedies under applicable laws, and all accounts payable by Buyer to Seller for the Goods delivered under this Contract shall, upon Seller's notice, become immediately due and payable in cash in full. Time shall be of the essence for all payments to be made hereunder. ③

如果买方未能依照本合同的付款条件于到期付款日支付所有"货物"的款项，或如以信用证付款时，该信用证没有按照本合同条款开出，此等行为均构成违约，严重损害了本合同的整体价值；卖方有权随时解除本合同或其中任何部分，但并不影响卖方追讨因上述情形所招致的任何损失及/或依照适用的法律行使其他权利或救济措施。同时，一经卖方发出通知，根据本合同买方应支付给卖方有关已交货"货物"的所有账款立即到期应付，并须以现金全部付清。对于本合同中的一切付款事宜，按时支付是极为重要的。

（4）If Buyer's failure to make payment or otherwise perform its obligations hereunder is reasonably anticipated, Seller may demand adequate assurance, satisfactory to Seller, of the due performance of this Contract by Buyer and withhold shipment or delivery of the undelivered Goods. Unless Buyer gives Seller such assurance within a reasonable time, Seller may, without prejudice to any other remedies it may have, cancel the portion of this Contract which relates to the undelivered Goods, and all accounts payable by Buyer to Seller for the Goods delivered under this Contract shall, upon Seller's notice, become immediately due and payable in cash in full. ④

如果卖方有合理的理由预料买方不支付款项或不履行其在本合同项下的其他义务，卖方可要求买方提供使卖方满意的充分担保以确保买方可妥善地履行本合同，卖方并可将未交付的"货物"暂不予装运或交货。除非买方在合理时间内将上述担保提供给卖方，否则卖方可取消本合同有关未交付的"货物"部分，且该取消不影响卖方可享

---

① 这是在信用证付款方式下有利于卖方的典型合同条款。

② 此处规定有助于避免发生买方就每批已交付货物不及时付款的问题。

③ 按合同规定付款是买方的主要义务，此处规定赋予了卖方对于买方不按合同及时付款的违约行为作出严厉处理的权利。

④ 此处规定为卖方及时收回货款提供了某种程度的保障。特别是在信用证以外的付款方式中，有助于减少卖方的损失。

有的其他救济措施；同时，经卖方发出通知后，买方根据本合同应支付给卖方的有关已交付"货物"之全部账款立即到期应付，并须以现金全额付清。

（5）All bank charges outside the People's Republic of China, including collection charges and stamp duties, if any, shall be for the account of Buyer, provided that confirming commissions shall be for the account of Buyer, regardless of being charged within or outside the People's Republic of China. ①

买方须缴付中华人民共和国以外的全部银行手续费，包括托收费用及印花税（若需缴纳）；且银行保兑手续费不论在中华人民共和国境内或境外收取，均须由买方支付。

4. **INSURANCE** If this Contract is on a CIF basis, 110% of the invoice amount shall be insured by Seller, unless otherwise agreed herein.

保险 如果本合同基于 CIF 价格，除非双方在本合同中另有约定，卖方须购买保险金额为发票金额 110% 的保险。

5. **INCREASED COSTS** Any new, additional or increased freight rates, surcharges (bunker, currency, congestion or other surcharges), taxes, customs duties, export or import surcharges or other governmental charges, or insurance premiums, including those for war and S. R. C. C. risks, which may be incurred by Seller with respect to the Goods after the conclusion of this Contract, shall be for the account of Buyer and shall be reimbursed to Seller by Buyer. ②

费用增加 在本合同订立后，卖方就"货物"而可能发生的新增或额外的运费、附加费（关于燃料、货币、港口拥塞或其他附加费）、税款、关税、出口或进口附加费、其他政府收费或保险费（包括战争及罢工、暴动和内乱险的保险费），均由买方承担，由买方偿还卖方代为垫付的上述费用。

6. **WARRANTY UNLESS OTHERWISE EXPRESSLY STIPULATED ON THE FACE OF THIS CONTRACT, SELLER MAKES NO WARRANTY OF FITNESS OR SUITABILITY OF THE GOODS FOR ANY PARTICULAR PURPOSE OR SPECIAL CIRCUMSTANCE.** ③

保证 除非在本合同正面另有明文规定，卖方并不保证"货物"适合或符合任何特定用途或特殊情形。

7. **CLAIM—索赔④**

（1）No claim may be raised by Buyer against Seller with regard to the Goods unless Buyer notifies Seller of its claim by registered airmail, containing full particulars of the claim and accompanied by evidence thereof certified by an authorized surveyor within thirty (30) days after the arrival of the Goods at the port of destination, or within six (6) months after the arrival of the Goods at the port of destination in the event of a latent defect.

除非在"货物"运抵目的港后三十天之内，或如发现"货物"有潜在瑕疵时于运抵目的港后六个月之内，买方以挂号空邮信件通知卖方进行索赔，并附上索赔详情以及经授权的检验人核证的证据，否则买方不得向卖方提出关于"货物"的索赔。

（2）Seller shall not be responsible to Buyer for any incidental, consequential or special damages. Seller's total liability on any or all claims from Buyer shall in no event exceed the price of the Goods with respect to which such claim or claims are made.

卖方没有责任就任何附带的、间接的或特殊的损害向买方作出赔偿。在任何情况下，卖方就买方提出的任一或全部的索赔须承担的全部责任不超过与该等索赔有关的"货物"之价款。

8. **PATENT, TRADEMARK, ETC.—专利、商标等⑤**

（1）Seller shall not be responsible to Buyer, and Buyer waives any claim against Seller, for any alleged infringement of patent, utility model, design, trademark or any other industrial property right or copyright, in connection with the Goods.

在"货物"被声称侵犯专利、实用新型、外观设计、商标、其他工业产权或著作权的情形下，卖方无须向买方承担责任，而买方亦放弃就该等侵权向卖方索赔。

---

① 有些国家的银行手续费是相当高的，有必要在合同中对此作出明确约定。

② 本条款将合同签订后新增费用的风险转移到买方，使卖方得以规避额外的费用负担。

③ 本条用大写字体，目的为特别提示卖方并未就货物的适用性提供特别的保证，有效地排除了卖方对货物质量的额外保证风险。

④ 本条款对买方就货物提出索赔的期限、证明方式、责任范围和赔偿限度作出了有利于卖方的约定。

⑤ 本条款对有关知识产权的侵权和损害赔偿作了有利于卖方的约定，对买方的权利作了限制。

（2）Buyer shall hold Seller harmless from any such alleged infringement on said rights arising from or in connection with any instruction given by Buyer to Seller regarding patent, utility model, design, trademark, copyright, pattern and specification.

如因买方向卖方发出关于专利、实用新型、外观设计、商标、著作权、样式及规格的指示，导致卖方被指控侵犯上述权利，买方应赔偿卖方所遭受的任何损害和损失。

9. FORCE MAJEURE—不可抗力

（1）In the event the performance by Seller of its obligations hereunder is prevented by force majeure, directly or indirectly affecting the activities of Seller or any other person, firm or corporation connected with the sale, manufacture, supply, shipment or delivery of the Goods, including, but not limited to, act of God, flood, typhoon, earthquake, tidal wave, landslide, fire, plague, epidemic, quarantine restriction, perils of the sea；war or serious threat of the same, civil commotion, blockade, arrest or restraint of government, rulers or people, requisition of vessel or aircraft；strike, lockout, sabotage, other labor dispute；explosion, accident or breakdown in whole or in part of machinery, plant, transportation or loading facility；governmental request, guidance, order or regulation；unavailability of transportation or loading facility；curtailment, shortage or failure in the supply of fuel, water, electric current, other public utility, or raw material including crude oil, petroleum or petroleum products；bankruptcy or insolvency of the manufacturer or supplier of the Goods；boycotting of Chinese goods；substantial change of the present international monetary system；or any other causes or circumstances whatsoever beyond the reasonable control of·Seller, then, Seller shall not be liable for loss or damage, or failure or delay in performing its obligations under this Contract and may, at its option, extend the time of shipment or delivery of the Goods or cancel unconditionally and without liability the unfulfilled portion of this Contract to the extent so affected. ①

因不可抗力事件直接或间接地影响卖方或者售卖、制造、供应、装运或交付"货物"的其他任何人士、商行或公司的活动，包括但不限于天灾、水灾、台风、地震、海啸、山崩、火灾、瘟疫、流行病、检疫隔离限制、海上风险、战争或类似战争的严重威胁、内乱、封锁、政府、统治者或民众的拘禁或限制，船舶或飞机被征用、罢工、封锁、破坏活动、其他劳资纠纷，部分或全部机器、设备、运输工具或装货设备发生爆炸、事故或故障，政府的要求、指引、命令或规定，缺乏运输或装货设备，燃料、水、电源、其他公用设施或原料包括原油、石油或石油产品的供给减少、短缺或缺乏，"货物"的制造商或供货商破产或资不抵债，中国的货物遭到联合抵制，现有国际金融体系发生重大改变，或者卖方不能合理控制的其他任何原因或情形，致使卖方在履行本合同义务时受到妨碍，则卖方对此不承担赔偿损失或损害的责任，亦不承担未能履行或延迟履行本合同义务的责任；卖方可以选择推迟装运或交付"货物"的时间或取消本合同受到影响而无法履行的部分，而不受任何条件的限制，亦无须为此负任何责任。

（2）Any monetary obligation hereunder shall not be excused or mitigated by reason of any force majeure event. Any obligation of Buyer hereunder shall not be excused or mitigated by reason of nonperformance of any obligation by Buyer's customer or any other third party, regardless of whether the nonperformance is due to a force majeure event or any other reason. ②

本合同项下的任何金钱债务不得以不可抗力事件为由而免除或减少。本合同项下买方的任何义务不得以买方的客户或其他第三方的任何义务的不履行为由而免除或减少，不论该不履行是因为不可抗力事件还是其他任何原因造成的。

10. CONFLICTING TERMS

Unless otherwise specifically agreed, the provisions contained in the front page shall govern and supersede any conflicting printed terms and

---

① 对照前述进口合同中没有约定单独的不可抗力条款，而本出口合同中约定了非常详细、范围广泛的不可抗力条款，体现出卖方律师对出口方（卖方）可能因遭遇不可抗力而影响其履行合同义务的防范风险约定。

② 买方在买卖合同项下的主要义务是按合同规定向卖方支付货款。这里第 9 条（2）款的约定排除了买方以不可抗力作为理由要求免除或减少应付的货款，也排除了买方以其客户或第三方的原因为理由要求免除或减少应付的货款。

conditions appeared on this reverse side. ①

冲突性条文　除非双方另有明确约定，当本合同背面印刷的条款和条件与正面所载条文的内容发生冲突时，则以正面所载条文为准。

11. **LANGUAGE**　This Contract is made in Chinese and English，and both versions shall have the same effect.

签字文本　本合同用中英文两种文字作成，两种文本具有同等效力。

12. **SETTLEMENT OF DISPUTE**　Any dispute between Seller and Buyer arising from or in connection with this Contract of Sale shall be submitted to South China International Economic and Trade Arbitration Commission in Shenzhen for arbitration which shall be conducted in accordance with the Commission's arbitration rules in effect at the time of applying for arbitration. The arbitral award is final and binding upon both parties. ②

争议解决　卖方及买方之间凡因本合同引起的或与本合同有关的任何争议，均应在深圳提交华南国际经济贸易仲裁委员会，按照申请仲裁时该会现行有效的仲裁规则进行仲裁。仲裁裁决是终局性的，对双方均有约束力。

13. **LAW APPLICABLE**　This Contract shall be governed by and construed in all respects in accordance with the laws of the People's Republic of China.

适用法律　本合同适用中华人民共和国法律，并按照中华人民共和国法律解释。

14. **WAIVER**　No claim or right of Seller under this Contract shall be deemed to be waived or renounced in whole or in part unless the waiver or renunciation of such claim or right is acknowledged and confirmed in writing by Seller.

放弃权利　除非卖方以书面形式承认及确认免除或放弃本合同中全部或部分的索赔或权利，否则不得视为卖方已免除或放弃该索赔或权利。

15. **ENTIRE AGREEMENT**　This Contract is based on the terms and conditions expressly set forth herein and no other terms and conditions are binding on Seller without its agreement in writing to such other terms and conditions.

完整协议　本合同条款及条件均已在此明示。除经卖方书面同意外，卖方不受其他条款及条件的约束。

16. **HEADINGS**　The headings are for convenience only and shall not affect the construction of this Contract.

标题　标题仅为方便而设，不影响本合同的解释。

第 3 节　出口代理合同精选与解读

出口代理合同
Export Agency Contract③

委托方：

住所地：

Principal：

Address：

---

①　本格式合同的正面是关于具体交易的商业条款，根据每项出口货物交易的具体情况由双方填写、签署，其效力优先于本合同背面适用于各项交易的一般条款和条件。

②　因买方是境外公司，通过华南国际经济贸易仲裁委员会的仲裁解决争议，仲裁裁决可以在买方所在国（《承认和执行外国仲裁裁决公约》的缔约国）法院申请强制执行。而卖方的主要营业地在深圳，仲裁地点选择在深圳，对卖方来说更为便利。

③　在外贸实务中，外贸公司（代理方）接受国内生产企业或其他经济实体（委托方或被代理方）的委托，以代理方的名义与国外买家签订出口合同，为此，代理方与委托方需要首先签订出口代理合同，代理方再据此与国外买家签订出口合同。本合同是国内委托方委托代理方将委托方的货物出口销售给国外买方，而由代理方的律师所制作的，侧重于保护代理方的利益，用作代理方的格式合同文本。

代理方：**XX** 有限公司

住所地：

Agent：XX Co．，Ltd．

Address：

委托方和代理方（以下简称"**双方**"）根据《中华人民共和国合同法》及其他相关法律法规，就委托方作为本合同项下出口货物（以下简称"**货物**"）的卖方，委托代理方出口货物的有关事项，签订本合同，具体条款如下：

This Contract is executed by and between the Principal and the Agent（the "**Parties**"）in accordance with the Contract Law of the People's Republic of China and other related laws and regulations，with respect to delegation by the Principal，acting as the seller of the exported goods（the "**Goods**"）under this Contract，to the Agent for exportation of the Goods. The Parties hereby agree as follows：

第1条 出口货物

Article 1 Exported Goods

1. 品 名：

   Name：

2. 规 格：

   Specifications：

3. 数 量：

   Quantity：

4. 包 装：

   Packing：

5. 单 价：

   Unit Price：

6. 总 值：

   Total Amount：

第2条 指定出口合同的买方

Article 2 Designated Buyer of Export Contract[①]

1. 委托方应按下述第【 】种方式指定买方（以下简称"**买方**"）：

   The Principal shall designate the buyer（s）（the "**Buyer**"）in accordance with the following method【 】：

   （1）由委托方指定买方。买方信息作为本合同附件1，构成本合同不可分割的一部分（如指定多家买方，在本合同第1条第3款限定的数量内向各买方出口的货物数量，应同时予以说明）；

   The Buyer shall be designated by the Principal. The information of the Buyer shall be attached hereto as Exhibit I and constitute an inseparable

---

① 出口合同中的买方，可以由委托方指定（委托方在国外已找到买家），也可以由代理方指定（委托方尚无确定的国外买家，委托代理方代为选定国外买家）。

part hereof（in case plural Buyers are designated，the quantities of the Goods to be exported to the respective Buyers within the limited quantity under Paragraph 3 of the Article 1 hereof shall be specified at the same time)^①；

（2）由代理方指定买方。委托方对代理方指定的买方不得提出任何异议。

The Buyer shall be designated by the Agent. The Principal shall not make any objection to the Buyer designated by the Agent.

第 3 条　交货
Article 3　Delivery

1. 委托方向买方交货的期限为：＿＿＿＿＿。

The Goods shall be delivered from the Principal to the Buyer by ＿＿＿＿＿．^②

2. 委托方应按照本合同及出口合同（以下简称"出口合同"）的规定，在装运港将货物直接交付给以下第【　】种承运人：

（1）委托方指定的承运人；

（2）代理方指定的承运人。

The Principal shall deliver the Goods directly to the carrier as indicated in the following item【　】at the port of shipment in accordance with this Contract and the export contract（s）(the **"Export Contract"**)：

（1）Carrier designated by the Principal；

（2）Carrier designated by the Agent.

3. 双方在此确认并同意，<u>代理方仅负责将本条第 1 款约定的交货期限规定于代理方与买方之间的出口合同中</u>。对于因任何原因导致货物没有在交货期限内交货的情形，代理方不向委托方、买方或任何第三方承担任何责任；在此种情形下，委托方应赔偿代理方因此遭受的全部损失或损害。

The Parties hereby confirm and agree that，**the Agent is only responsible for stipulating in the Export Contract between the Agent and the Buyer the time limit of delivery set out in Paragraph 1 of this Article 3.** The Agent shall not be liable to the Principal，the Buyer or any third parties for failure of delivery of the Goods within the time limit of delivery hereunder for any reasons. In such a case，the Principle shall indemnify the Agent for all losses or damages incurred by the Agent. ^③

---

① 由于国外买方是委托方所指定的，其相关信息以及向各买方出口的货物数量需要由委托方在本合同中明确约定，代理人据此执行，可避免发生争议。

② 依据本合同，代理方接受委托方的委托，以代理方本身名义与国外买方签订出口合同并办理货物出口手续（根据合同内容，还可能代委托方选定国外买方），而货物则是由委托方直接向国外买方发运的。

③ 在买卖合同中，卖方的主要义务是按照合同向买方交付货物。依据本合同，委托方（卖方）直接向国外买方交付货物，代理人对于委托方能否准时交货是无法控制的，本条款限定了代理人的责任范围，可使代理方有效避风险。本条款以及本合同其他条款中加下划线或粗体印刷的部分，是为符合中国法律中有关合同格式条款的要求，对于免除或限制代理方责任、加重委托方责任或限制其权利的内容，提请委托方注意。

第 4 条　运输方式与目的港
Article 4　Transportation and Port of Destination①

1. 货物采取_____运输方式，目的港为_____。

The Goods shall be transported by the means of _____ to _____ as the port of destination.

2. 双方在此确认并同意，代理方仅负责将本条第 1 款规定的运输方式与目的港规定于代理方与买方之间的出口合同中，除此之外代理方不承担有关本条款的任何其他责任。

The Parties hereby confirm and agree that, **the Agent is only responsible for stipulating in the Export Contract between the Agent and the Buyer the means of transportation and the port of destination set out in Paragraph 1 of this Article 4**, other than which the Agent shall have no responsibility related to this Article.

第 5 条　贸易术语
Article 5　Trade Term

出口合同项下的贸易术语为：_____。

The trade term under the Export Contract shall be _____ .

第 6 条　佣金、成本和费用
Article 6　Commission, Costs and Expenses②

1. 佣金

（1）本合同项下的佣金（以下简称"**佣金**"）为本合同第 1 条第 6 款规定的货物总值的【　】%。

（2）委托方应在本合同签订后 3 个工作日内，按照代理方同意的方式向代理方全额支付佣金。

Commission

（1）The amount of the commission hereunder (the "**Commission**") shall be 【　】% of the Total Amount stipulated in Paragraph 6 of Article 1 hereof.

（2）The Principal shall pay the Agent the Commission in full in the way agreed by the Agent within three (3) working days after execution of this Contract.

2. 成本和费用

（1）与出口货物有关的运输费用、商检费、港口运杂费、仓储费、报关费、保险费、税收、银行手续费以及任何其他成本和费用，全部由委托方负担；代理方对该等成本和费用并无垫付义务。代理方也可指示委托方直接向该等款项的收款方支付该等成本和费用，或者指

---

① 本条款对于代理方的重要意义，请参见前述对第 3 条的解读。

② 在出口代理合同中，双方的法律关系适用民法上的间接代理制度。虽然代理方以其本身名义与国外买方签订出口合同，但代理方为了委托方的利益办理出口业务所需的成本和费用，应当由委托方负担，本条款对此作了详细约定；而代理方则依据本合同从委托方收取报酬（佣金）。

示委托方向代理方支付该等费用，代理方在收到委托方支付的该等款项后向该等款项的收款方支付该等成本和费用；委托方应按代理方指示的时间及方式立即支付该等成本和费用，代理方对由于委托方未按代理方指示付款导致的后果不承担任何责任。

（2）除上述成本和费用以外，因代理出口货物而发生的任何其他成本和费用，亦全部由委托方承担。双方在此确认，该等其他成本和费用并未包含于本条第 1 款规定的佣金中。委托方除向代理方支付佣金外，在收到代理方发出的付款通知书后【　】个工作日内，还应向代理方足额支付本条规定的该等其他成本和费用。

Costs and Expenses

（1）All the costs and expenses such as transportation fees, inspection fees, port freight expenses, storage fees, customs declaration fees, insurance premiums, taxes and bank charges and any other costs and expenses in connection with export of the Goods shall be borne by the Principal, and the Agent is not responsible for payment of such costs and expenses on behalf of the Principal. The Agent may instruct the Principal to pay such costs and expense either directly to the payees or to the Agent who shall then pay such costs and expenses to the respective payees. The Principal shall, without delay, pay such costs and expenses at the time and in the way designated by the Agent. The Agent shall not be liable for any consequences caused by the Principal for the reasons of failure to pay such costs and expenses as instructed by the Agent.

（2）Any costs and expenses other than the above-mentioned incurred as a result of the export agency of the Goods shall be borne by the Principal. The Parties hereby confirm that such other costs and expenses shall not be included in the Commission stipulated in Paragraph 1 of Article 6 hereof. In addition to the Commission, the Principle shall pay the Agent such other costs and expenses in full under this Article within 【　】 working days after receiving the notice（s）of payment sent by the Agent.

第 7 条　签订出口合同

Article 7　Execution of Export Contract[①]

1. 委托方在此表示接受代理方现有的出口合同标准文本（以下简称"**标准合同文本**"）的既定条款和条件（该出口合同标准文本作为本合同附件 2，构成本合同不可分割的一部分），并充分注意到其中各方的权利义务、各方免除及减轻各自责任的条款。

The Principal hereby accepts the given terms and conditions of the existing

---

①　在本合同中，代理方接受国内委托方的委托，以代理方自己的名义作为卖方（Seller）与国外买方签订出口合同，出口合同的内容必须由国内委托方、代理方和国外买方三方协商一致方可签署。本条款对于三方之间在出口合同内容的协商和签订过程中可能发生的各种情况作了具体约定，有助于代理方规避可能的风险。

standard Contract of Sale used by the Agent (the "**Standard Contract**") (which shall be attached hereto as Exhibit Ⅱ and constitute an inseparable part hereof) and has paid enough attention to the terms in connection with the rights and obligations of each party thereto and with exemption and reduction of their respective responsibilities and liabilities.

2. 代理方在收到本合同第 6 条第 1 款约定的佣金后，应按照本合同的条款与买方签订标准合同文本的货物出口合同。委托方应努力促使买方接受标准合同文本的条款以及对货物的基本要求、交货期限、运输方式、贸易术语以及本合同项下有关货物出口的其他条件。

After receiving the Commission stipulated in Paragraph 1 of Article 6 hereof, the Agent shall execute with the Buyer the Export Contract on the Goods in form of the Standard Contract in accordance with terms hereof. The Principal shall try to make the Buyer accept the terms of the Standard Contract and such other conditions as the basic requirements for the Goods，term of delivery，transportation，trade term and other conditions hereunder for exportation of the Goods. ①

3. 如果买方要求对出口合同标准文本进行修改或者不同意本合同项下的货物出口条件，代理方应在确定该等合同条款前将买方的修改意见通知委托方。委托方应在收到该等意见后毫不迟延地向代理方作出书面确认，在【 】个工作日内通知代理方是否接受买方的意见。

In case the Buyer requests for modification of the Standard Contract or does not agree to the conditions for export of the Goods hereunder，the Agent, before determining such contractual terms，shall inform the Principal of the opinions of the Buyer on such modification. The Principal shall make written confirmation to the Agent without delay on whether or not to accept the Buyer's opinions after receiving such opinions，and such confirmation may not be made later than【 】working day since the Principal receives such opinions.

4. 如果因委托方迟延确认等可归咎于委托方的任何原因导致迟延签订出口合同，则由委托方自行承担相关责任，并须赔偿代理方因此遭受的全部损失。如果因可归咎于委托方的任何原因导致代理方未能签订出口合同，则本合同就拟向相关买方出口的货物数量予以取消，委托方须自行承担因此而发生的全部责任，并赔偿代理方因此遭受的全部损失。此外，委托方无权要求退还已经支付给代理方的佣金。

In case the execution of the Export Contract is delayed due to any reasons attributed to the Principal such as delay in confirmation by the Principal，the Principal shall bear on its own the related liabilities and compensate all losses suffered by the Agent as a result of such reasons. In case the Agent is unable to execute the Export Contract due to any reasons attributed to the Principle,

---

① 在本合同中，虽然代理方以自己名义作为卖方（Seller）同国外买方签订出口合同，但在实践中，三方就出口合同的具体条款和条件进行协商并最后确定时，国内委托方往往会直接或间接地参与其中，并起着重要作用。

this Contract is terminated in respect of the quantity of the Goods purported to be exported to the related Buyer，and the Principal shall bear all liabilities as a result of the said reasons and compensate the Agent for all losses suffered by the Agent. In addition，the Principal is not entitled to the Commission already paid to the Agent.

5. 如果由于买方不同意签署出口合同标准文本或本合同项下的货物出口条件或者由于委托方不同意买方的修改意见，而导致代理方未能签订出口合同，则本合同就拟向相关买方出口的货物数量予以取消。在此情形下，委托方须自行承担因此而发生的全部责任，并赔偿代理方因此遭受的全部损失。此外，委托方无权要求退还已经支付给代理方的佣金。

   In case the Agent is unable to execute the Export Contract due to the Buyer's disagreement to sign the Export Contract in the form of the Standard Contract or based on the export conditions of the Goods hereunder，or due to disagreement of the Principal to the modification opinions of the Buyer，this Contract is terminated in respect of the quantity of the Goods purported to be exported to the related Buyer. In this case，the Principal shall bear all liabilities on its own and compensate the Agent for all losses suffered as a result. In addition，the Principal is not entitled to the Commission already paid to the Agent.

第 8 条　支付货款
Article 8　Payment for Goods

1. 代理方在收到买方根据出口合同支付的货款后【　】个工作日内，应将该货款折算成人民币汇往委托方指定的银行账户，因该汇款而发生的所有成本费用由委托方承担。外币与人民币之间的汇率按照代理方汇款当日中国银行公布的外汇买入价计算。

   Within 【　】 working days after receiving the payment for the Goods made by the Buyer in accordance with the Export Contract，the Agent shall remit such payment calculated in Renminbi（**"RMB"**）currency to the bank account designated by the Principal. All the costs arising from such remittance shall be borne by the Principle. The exchange rate between the foreign exchange and RMB shall be based on the buying rate between such foreign exchange and RMB quoted by the Bank of China on the day when the Agent remits such payment. [①]

2. 如果委托方在本合同项下有欠付代理方的任何款项，代理方有权从货款中扣除该欠付款项，然后将余款支付给委托方。

   In case the Principal owes any amount of money to the Agent under this Contract，the Agent is entitled to deduct such amount of money from the payment for the Goods and then pay the rest of the payment to the Principal.

---

① 因涉及代理方从国外买方收取外汇货款以及在国内以人民币向委托方付款，对于外币与人民币之间的汇率作出明确约定，有助于避免潜在的争议。

第 9 条　货物验收

Article 9　Acceptance of Goods①．

1. 货物验收应在代理方在场的情况下，由承运人或其他收货人进行。

   The acceptance of the Goods shall be effected by the carrier or other consignees in the presence of the Agent.

2. 委托方应承担与承运人或其他收货人出具的书面验货意见相关的全部责任，代理方概不承担任何责任，委托方还应赔偿代理方因这些责任而遭受的全部损失。

   The Principal shall bear all responsibilities and liabilities related to the written opinions on acceptance issued by the carrier or other consignees. The Agent shall not bear any such responsibilities and liabilities. The Principal shall compensate the Agent for all losses suffered in connection with such responsibilities or liabilities.

第 10 条　委托方和代理方的责任

Article 10　Responsibilities of Principal and Agent②

1. 委托方的责任包括但不限于以下各项：

   （1）确切、及时地提供与订立出口合同有关的主要事实和信息；

   （2）充分理解本合同条款以及代理方根据本合同与买方签订的出口合同条款，对各方的权利义务、各方免除或者减轻各自责任的条款予以足够注意；

   （3）接受代理方现有的货物出口合同标准文本的既定条款，努力促使买方接受该等条款；

   （4）按照出口合同中对"卖方"责任和义务的约定，履行应由"卖方"履行的相关责任和义务（例如交货、选定承运人、投保等）；

   （5）确保其提供的货物符合本合同以及出口合同规定的货物数量、质量和规格，并按照本合同和出口合同规定的方式包装；

   （6）提供货物的说明书、质量证明、原产地证明等全部相关文件；

   （7）按照本合同以及出口合同的约定交付货物；

   （8）与代理方共同办理货物出口的商检、报关手续及其他相关手续，向代理方提供代理方及相关政府部门要求的全部书面资料；

   （9）按照本合同以及出口合同的约定，支付与货物出口有关的运输费、商检费、港口运杂费、仓储费、报关费、保险费、税款、银行手续费及其他成本和费用；

   （10）承担出口合同项下与货物有关的全部风险或损失；

   （11）如果代理方因代理货物出口而遭受买方或任何第三方的索赔，委托

---

①　代理方为了委托方的利益、代表委托方参与出口合同项下承运人或其他收货人的验货手续，倘若因货物存在问题而导致承运人或其他收货人拒绝收货或出具不清洁提单（Unclean（foul）B/L）等后果，理应由委托方承担相关责任。

②　本条款是基于委托方和代理方之间的间接代理法律关系，详细约定双方各自应履行的责任义务，便于在实践中执行，避免因权责约定不清而发生争议。

方须承担全部责任，并赔偿代理方由此遭受的全部损失。

The responsibilities of the Principal include but not limited to the following：

（1）to provide exactly and promptly the material facts and information related to formation of the Export Contract；

（2）to fully understand the terms of this Contract and the Export Contract signed in accordance with this Contract by and between the Agent and the Buyer，and to give full attention to the terms related to the rights and obligations of each party hereto and to exemption and reduction of their respective responsibilities and liabilities；

（3）to accept the given terms of the Standard Contract currently used by the Agent and try to make the Buyer accept such terms；

（4）to perform the relevant responsibilities and obligations that shall be performed by the "Seller"（such as delivery of the Goods，designating carrier（s）and effecting insurance）in accordance with the responsibilities and obligations of the "Seller" stipulated in the Export Contract；

（5）to ensure that the Goods provided by the Principal shall conform to this Contract and the Export Contract in terms of quantity，quality and specifications of the Goods，and be packed in accordance with this Contract and the Export Contract；

（6）to provide all the related documents such as directions，certificate of quality and certificate of origin for the Goods；

（7）to deliver the Goods in accordance with this Contract and the Export Contract；

（8）to go through the formalities together with the Agent for Goods inspection，customs declaration of the Goods and other related formalities，and to provide the Agent with all written materials required by the Agent and the related government authorities；

（9）to pay the fees for transportation，inspection，port freight，storage，customs declaration，insurance，taxes and bank service，and other costs and expenses in connection with the exportation of the Goods in accordance with this Contract and the Export Contract；

（10）to bear all risks or losses in connection with the Goods under the Export Contract；

（11）to bear all the liabilities for claims made by the Buyer or any third party against the Agent as a result of export agency of the Goods and to compensate the Agent for all the losses suffered by the Agent therefrom.

2. 代理方的责任包括以下各项：

（1）提供确切的与订立出口合同有关的主要事实和信息；

（2）在签订出口合同后，及时将出口合同副本送交委托方；

（3）尽最大努力与买方签订出口合同，并催促买方按照出口合同开立信用证或其他贸易条件下的付款委托书；

    （4）办理出口货物所需的商检、报关、对外运输及议付；但所有相关费用和开支均由委托方承担，并须提前【　】个工作日支付。代理方为了委托方的利益办理上述事项，对于该等事项的办理以及因此而发生的任何责任均由委托方自行承担，代理方概不承担任何责任；

    （5）因归咎于买方的任何原因导致出口合同的延迟履行、不完全履行或未能履行时，代理方概不承担任何责任。代理方对于因买方原因而遭受的全部损失有权获得赔偿。

The responsibilities of the Agent include the following：

（1）to provide exactly the material facts and information related to formation of the Export Contract；

（2）to deliver in time the duplicates of the Export Contract to the Principal after execution of the Export Contract；

（3）to try its best to sign the Export Contract with the Buyer and to urge the Buyer to open the L/C or other payment orders under other trade terms in accordance with the Export Contract；

（4）to handle the inspection, customs declaration, transportation to other countries and negotiation necessary for exportation of the Goods, but all the related fees and expenses shall be borne by the Principal and be paid 【　】 working days in advance. The Agent handles the said issues only on behalf of the Principal, and any liabilities related to the said issues shall be borne by the Principal on its own, and the Agent shall bear no liabilities.

（5）to bear no liabilities for delay performance, partial performance or failure of performance of the Export Contract due to any reasons attributed to the Buyer. The Agent shall be entitled to compensation for all the losses it has suffered as a result of the Buyer's reasons.

第 11 条　索赔
Article 11　Claims[①]

1. 如果买方违反出口合同项下的义务，委托方应自行决定是否就出口合同向买方或其他责任方提出索赔。如果委托方决定索赔，委托方应就索赔事宜向代理方提供索赔委托书。倘若委托方未向代理方提供该委托书，则代理方没有义务为了委托方的利益提出该索赔。

If the Buyer breaches any of its obligations under the Export Contract, the Principal shall decide on its own whether or not to make a claim against the Buyer or other related parties with respect to the Export Contract. In the event that the Principal decides to make such claim, the Principal shall provide the Agent with the power of attorney for such claims. In case the

---

[①]　虽然代理方是出口合同项下名义上的卖方，但委托方是货物的最终卖方，是否索赔应由委托方决定；在具体办理索赔过程中，名义上由代理方出面，委托方须提供必要的协助。本条款对于向国外买方的索赔作了详细约定，明确了代理方和委托方之间的分工和各自的权利义务。

Principal fails to provide such power of attorney, the Agent is not obliged to make such claim on behalf of the Principal.

2. 委托方应在出口合同规定的索赔期限前【 】个工作日向代理方提供索赔所必要的文件和资料；否则，代理方有权不予办理该索赔事项。

The Principal shall provide the Agent with the necessary documents and materials for the claims【 】working days before the time limit of claim stipulated under the Export Contract. Otherwise, the Agent has the right not to handle such claims.

3. 代理方在收到委托方出具的索赔委托书后，应负责向有关责任方提出索赔要求；委托方应协助代理方办理该索赔。

After receiving the power of attorney for claims issued by the Principal, the Agent is responsible for presenting the requests of claims to the liable parties. The Principal shall assist the Agent in such claims.

4. 代理方为委托方的利益办理索赔而遭受的损失应由委托方承担，取得的索赔收益（在扣除代理方与该索赔相关的全部费用、成本和开支后）归属于委托方。

All the losses suffered by the Agent in connection with making claims on behalf of the Principal shall be borne by the Principal, and the gains on such claims, after deduction of all the fees, costs and expenses of the Agent in connection with such claims, shall be owned by the Principal.

5. 代理方仅负责就索赔事宜向有关责任方提出索赔要求以及相关文件。代理方对于具体的索赔要求以及相关文件的准备等事项不承担任何责任，该等事项应由委托方自行办理，代理方按照本合同的约定给予必要的协助。

The Agent shall be only responsible for presenting the requests of claims and delivery related documents to the liable parties. The Agent shall not be responsible for such issues as the specific requirements for claims and preparation for related documents, which shall be handled by the Principal on its own, and the Agent shall provide necessary assistance in accordance with this Contract.

6. 对于代理方为了委托方的利益办理索赔所花费的人工费及其他相关开支，代理方有权向委托方收取代理费。

The Agent shall be entitled to charge the Principal the agent fee for handling the claims on behalf of the Principal based on the labor costs and other related expenses spent by the Agent.

第12条 违约责任
Article 12 Liabilities for Breach of Contract[①]

1. 如果委托方迟延支付本合同项下的任何款项，委托方应按每日万分之

---

① 由于代理方以其本身名义为了委托方的利益向政府部门办理报关、结汇、退税等手续，倘若委托方违约不予配合，可能会给代理方造成行政处罚等严重后果。本条款对委托方的可能违约及其救济作了明确约定，对于维护代理方的合法权益是十分重要的。

五的利率向代理方支付应付款项迟延期间的逾期付款违约金。如果委托方迟延付款超过【 】个工作日，代理方有权书面通知委托方解除本合同，并且委托方应赔偿代理方因此遭受的全部损失。本合同解除后，本款关于违约金的规定仍然有效。

In case of any delayed payment hereunder by the Principal，the Principal shall pay the liquidated damages for the payable amount at the rate of 0.05％ per day for the delayed period. In case the Principal delays in any payment for【 】working days from the due date，the Agent shall be entitled to terminate this Contract by sending the Principal a written notice，and the Principal shall compensate the Agent for all the losses suffered by the Agent. After termination of this Contract，this paragraph in terms of liquidated damages shall remain valid.

2. 如果由于委托方的原因导致未能在政府部门规定的期限内办理报关、纳税、商检、装运等有关手续，均由委托方自行承担全部责任。如因委托方违反本合同给代理方造成损失的（包括但不限于政府部门的行政处分、代理方发生的任何成本及费用等），委托方应按本合同第 1 条第 6 款规定的货物总值的【 】％向代理方支付违约金。若该违约金不足以补偿代理方的该等损失，委托方应就代理方遭受的损失作出进一步赔偿。

In case of failure of handling the formalities such as customs declaration，taxes payment，inspection or shipment within the time limits designated by the government authorities due to any reasons attributed to the Principal，the Principal shall bear all the liabilities by itself. In case the Agent suffers any losses （including but not limited to administrative punishment made by the government authorities，any costs and expenses incurred by the Agent） as a result of breach of this Contract on the part of the Principal，the Principal shall pay the Agent the liquidated damages calculated at the rate of【 】％ of the total amount of the Goods stipulated under Paragraph 6 of Article 1 hereof. In the event that such liquidated damages are insufficient to compensate the Agent for such losses，the Principal shall further compensate the Agent for such losses.

3. 如果委托方违反本合同或出口合同的任何条款，并在收到代理方的书面通知后 30 日内仍未纠正该违约行为，代理方有权以书面方式通知委托方立即解除本合同，并保留向委托方要求赔偿损失的权利。

In case the Principal breaches any terms hereof or of the Export Contract and fails to correct such breach within thirty （30） days upon receiving the written notice from the Agent，the Agent shall be entitled to terminate this Contract with immediate effect by sending the

Principal a written notice of termination，and reserve the rights for claim against the Principal for compensation of the losses.

第 13 条　合同的变更和解除
Article 13　Modification and Termination of Contract

1. 对于本合同的任何变更或修改，须经双方协商一致并签署书面文件方产生法律效力。

   Any modification or amendments hereto shall become effective only after negotiation and agreement in writing by the Parties.

2. 除本合同另有规定外，未经对方事先书面同意，任何一方不得解除本合同。

   Unless otherwise provided hereunder，neither Party may terminate this Contract without prior written consent of the other Party hereto.

第 14 条　合同效力
Article 14　Validity of Contract

1. 本合同自双方正式授权代表签字盖章之日起生效，至本合同项下的货物出口事宜办理完毕时终止。

   This Contract shall come into force after signed by the duly authorized representatives of the Parties and sealed with the corporate stamps of the Parties，and shall be valid until completion of the export agency of the Goods hereunder.

2. 本合同因任何原因而终止后，本合同终止前所发生的委托方对代理方的义务不得被免除或减轻。

   After this Contract is terminated due to any reason，the obligations of the Principal to the Agent occurred before such termination shall not be exempted or mitigated.

第 15 条　不可抗力
Article 15　Force Majeure

1. 由于不可抗力事件（包括但不限于自然灾害、罢工、战争、暴动、法律变更等），导致代理方无法履行或迟延履行本合同或出口合同项下义务而造成委托方的损失（无论该损失是直接的或是间接的），代理方均不承担任何责任。

   The Agent shall not be liable for non-performance or delayed performance of its obligations hereunder or under the Export Contract which causes losses（whether direct or indirect）to the Principal in the event of force majeure（including but not limited to natural disasters，strikes，wars，riots，changes of laws，etc.）.

2. 在发生不可抗力事件时，代理方有权要求对本合同或出口合同的全部或部分作出变更。如果委托方不同意变更本合同或出口合同，或者代理方在提出变更本合同或出口合同的要求后 7 日内未收到委托方的任何答复，则代理方可发出书面通知解除本合同，且无需为此承担任何责任。

In case of force majeure, the Agent shall be entitled to request for modification in whole or in part of this Contract or the Export Contract. In the event that the Principal does not agree to such modification，or the Agent does not receive any reply from the Principal seven （7） days after sending such request，the Agent shall be entitled to termination of this Contract by sending a written notice without any liabilities for such termination. ①

第 16 条　争议解决
Article 16　Settlement of Dispute

凡因本合同引起的或与本合同有关的任何争议，应采用以下第【　】种方式解决（本合同当事人没有选择的另一种方式不具有法律效力）：

Any dispute arising from or in connection with this Contract shall be settled in accordance with the following Item 【　】 (the other item which has not been chosen by the Parties shall be null and void)：

1. 将争议提交北京仲裁委员会，按照申请仲裁时该会现行有效的仲裁规则进行仲裁。仲裁裁决是终局性的，对双方均有约束力；或

Any dispute shall be submitted to Beijing Arbitration Commission for arbitration which shall be conducted in accordance with the Commission's arbitration rules in effect at the time of applying for arbitration. The arbitration award shall be final and binding on the Parties；or

2. 就争议向代理方住所地有管辖权的法院起诉。

Any dispute shall be brought in the courts having competent jurisdiction of the Agent's domicile.

第 17 条　其他条款
Article 17　Miscellaneous

1. 双方在此确认，委托方作为出口合同的实际当事人，享有出口合同项下的权利并承担出口合同项下的义务。代理方仅作为出口合同的名义当事人，不享有出口合同项下的权利，也不承担出口合同项下的义务。

The Parties hereby clarify that the Principal shall be an actual party to the Export Contract，having the rights and the obligations under the Export Contract. The Agent shall only be a nominal party to the Export

---

① 依据本款的规定，在发生不可抗力事件时，代理方可以通过向委托方发出通知的方式来变更或解除本合同。

Contract, having no rights and the obligations under the Export Contract. ①

2. 本合同中的标题仅为便于参考，不影响其所涉任何条款的理解或解释。

The headings in this Contract are for ease of reference only and shall not affect the interpretation or construction of any provisions to which they refer.

3. 本合同未尽事宜，由双方友好协商决定。

Any issues not covered hereunder shall be decided by the Parties through friendly negotiation.

本合同一式二份，自双方正式授权代表签字盖章之日起生效。

This Contract shall be executed in duplicate, and come into force after signed by the duly authorized representatives of the Parties and sealed with the corporate stamps of the Parties.

委托方：　　　　　　　　　　　代理方：XX 有限公司

Principal：　　　　　　　　　　Agent：XX Co. , Ltd.

_____　　_____

（授权代表/Authorized Representative）　（授权代表/Authorized Representative）

签约日期：

Date：

附件 1

Exhibit I

买方信息

Information of Buyer

（参见本合同第 2 条第 1 款）

(See Paragraph 1 of Article 2 of this Contract)

---

① 本条款进一步明确了委托方和代理方在出口合同中的实际地位，明确了双方之间的间接代理关系。

附件 2

Exhibit II

出口合同标准文本

Standard Contract on Goods Export

（参见本合同第 7 条第 1 款）

(See Paragraph 1 of Article 7 of this Contract)

■ 第 4 节　国内售货合同精选与解读＿＿＿＿＿＿＿＿＿＿

售 货 合 同	卖方合同编号：　　日期：　　年　月　日
CONTRACT OF SALE①	SELLER'S CONTRACT NO： DATE：
卖方：XX（北京）有限公司 地址： Seller：　XX（Beijing）Co.，Ltd. Address：	买方： 地址： Buyer： Address：
买卖双方特此同意，以下述条款和条件以及后附一般条款和条件签订本售货合同。<u>买方在此确认，卖方就一般条款和条件中的免除或减轻卖方责任的约定（加下划线或粗体印刷的部分）已充分提请了买方注意。买方就该等约定以及可能对买方不利的其他条款已被充分告知并予以理解，故决定签订本售货合同。买方对作为贸易公司的卖方为取得转卖利益而签订本售货合同予以充分理解。</u>	
The Seller and the Buyer hereby agree to enter into this Contract of Sale on the terms and conditions set forth below and on the General Terms and Conditions attached hereto. **The Buyer hereby acknowledges that the Seller has sufficiently called the Buyer's attention to the underlined or boldfaced provisions of the General Terms and Conditions which release or mitigate the Seller's liability and responsibility. It is therefore that the Buyer has been fully informed of, and understood, such provisions and other provisions which may be disadvantageous to the Buyer and that the Buyer has determined to enter into this Contract of Sale. The Buyer fully understands that the Seller, being a trading company, shall enter into this Contract of Sale in order to make a resale profit.** ②	

---

　　①　本合同由卖方的律师制作，用于卖方在中国国内销售货物，其内容（特别是背面的"一般条款及条件"）侧重于保护卖方权益。卖方将本合同印制为格式合同使用，合同正面是商业条款，背面是一般条款及条件。

　　②　此处以及其他处加下划线或粗体印刷的部分，是为符合中国法律中有关合同格式条款的要求，对于免除或减轻卖方责任、加重买方责任或限制其权利的内容，提请买方注意。请参阅《中华人民共和国合同法》（1999 年 10 月 1 日起施行）第 39、40、41 条等关于合同格式条款的规定。

唛　头 SHIPPING MARK	货物名称 COMMODITY	数　量 QUANTITY	单　价 UNIT PRICE	总　价 AMOUNT

合同总价 　　TOTAL：	

交货期限 TIME OF DELIVERY：	交货地 PLACE OF DELIVERY：
交货条件 DELIVERY TERMS：	目的地 PLACE OF DESTINATION：
保险 INSURANCE：	包装 PACKING：
验收方法 INSPECTION：	生产厂家 MANUFACTURER：
付款条件 PAYMENT：	特殊条款及条件 SPECIAL TERMS & CONDITIONS：

买方基于其理解能力及/或卖方的说明，已充分理解本售货合同（包括所附一般条款和条件）项下可能免除或减轻卖方责任的全部条款，且不存在任何其他不明确的条款，故签订本售货合同。

Now that the Buyer, with its ability to understand and/or the Seller's explanation, has fully understood the provisions of this Contract of Sale （including the attached General Terms and Conditions） which may release or mitigate the Seller's liability and responsibility, and that there is no any other provision which is unclear to the Buyer, the Buyer has therefore executed this Contract of Sale.

买 方：	卖 方：XX（北京）有限公司
Buyer：	Seller：XX（Beijing）Co.，Ltd.
签字盖章 BY：	签字盖章 BY：

　　（SEE GENERAL TERMS AND CONDITIONS ON REVERSE SIDE HEREOF 请见本页背面所列一般条款和条件）

Contract of Sale（Reverse Side）国内售货合同（背面）
一般条款和条件（GENERAL TERMS AND CONDITIONS）

1. 所有权的转移

"货物"的所有权自"货物"交付或根据本合同应付的所有款项支付完毕二者中较迟的时间起，从卖方转移到买方。

1. TITLE TRANSFER

Title of the Goods shall transfer from the Seller to the Buyer at the time of delivery thereof or payment of all amounts due hereunder，whichever occurs later. ①

2. 验收及索赔

买方应在"货物"交付后立即进行验收。在验收中如发现"货物"全部或部分不符合本合同规定时，买方应在自"货物"交付后 7 日以内或在买卖双方或许可本合同正面所规定的期限内以书面方式向卖方提出索赔。"货物"存在潜在瑕疵时，买方应在"货物"交付后 30 日以内以书面方式向卖方提出索赔。**如买方未在上述期限内以书面方式提出索赔，则视为所交付的"货物"符合本合同的规定。**

2. INSPECTION AND CLAIM

The Buyer shall inspect the Goods immediately after delivery. In the event that the Buyer shall discover in the course of any such inspection that all or any portion of the Goods is not in conformity with this Contract，the Buyer shall make a claim in writing against the Seller within 7 days after the delivery thereof or within the period of time which the Buyer and the Seller may have stipulated on the face of this Contract. The Buyer shall assert all claims in writing against the Seller in connection with any latent defect of the Goods within 30 days after delivery thereof. **In the event that the Buyer does not assert any claim in writing during the above-mentioned period of time，the delivered Goods shall be deemed to be in conformity with this Contract.** ②

3. 不可抗力

(1) 倘若由于卖方、"货物"的生产厂家或供货商发生了自然灾害、罢工、战争、暴动、法律的变更或者其他不可预见或不能避免的不可抗力事件，导致卖方无法履行或无法按期履行本合同项下的义务时，卖方对因其不履行或不按期完全履行本合同项下义务而造成的买方之任何损失或损害（无论是直接的或间接的）均不承担任何赔偿责任。

(2) 在发生不可抗力事件时，卖方有权要求对本合同进行全部或部分变更。如买方不同意该变更或卖方在提出变更本合同的要求后 7 日内未得到买方的任何答复，则卖方可以向买方发出书面通知解除本合同。

(3) 本合同项下的任何金钱债务不得以不可抗力事件为由免除或减轻。本合同项下买方的任何义务不得以买方的客户或任何其他第三方不履行其任何义务为理由而被免除或减少，不论该不履行是由于不可抗力事件还是其他任何原因所造成的。

3. FORCE MAJEURE

(1) **In the event that the Seller fails to perform or，fails to perform in a timely manner this Contract due to a force majeure event having occurred to any of the Seller，the manufacturer or the supplier of the Goods，such as an act of God，**

---

① 本条款也可称为所有权保留条款（retention of title clause），通常用于买卖合同中，以保护卖方的利益。卖方在交货后为了确保从买方收到货款，可以在合同中约定，在卖方向买方交货后、在收到买方的货款之前，卖方保留货物的所有权；卖方从买方收到货款后，货物的所有权才转移到买方。根据这类条款，假如买方在收货后破产，卖方根据所有权保留条款可从买方处取回货物（因卖方对货物仍然拥有所有权，可以此对抗买方的其他债权人），而无需在破产程序中与其他普通债权人按比例分配买方的剩余资产。需要注意的是，所有权保留条款中的货物多为特定物（例如机器设备等，可以其编号与其他同类机器设备相区分）；而对于种类物，因其难以与其他同种类货物相区别，在实践中则较难实现所有权的保留。

② 本条款对买方提出索赔的期限作了较短的限定，有利于卖方。需要注意的是，在实践中还要根据货物的具体情况，按照所适用的法律或行业规则，适当变更索赔期限。

strike, war, civil disturbance, change in law or any other event the occurrence of which is unforeseeable or unpreventable, the Seller shall not have any liability for any loss or damage, direct or indirect, incurred by the Buyer as a result of any such failure by the Seller to fully perform in a timely manner any of its obligations. ①

（2）The Seller has the right to offer to modify this Contact in whole or in part when a force majeure event occurs. If the Buyer objects to such offer or if the Seller does not receive any response from the Buyer within seven（7）days after the Seller submits such offer, the Seller may terminate this Contract by written notice to the Buyer. ②

（3）Any monetary obligation hereunder shall not be excused or mitigated by reason of any force majeure event. Any obligation of the Buyer hereunder shall not be excused or mitigated by reason of nonperformance of any obligation by the Buyer's customer or any other third party, regardless of whether the nonperformance is due to a force majeure event or any other reason. ③

4. 新增的费用

倘若在本合同签订后征收任何新增的、额外的或提高的税款，或者因本合同第 3 条规定的不可抗力事件而导致费用增加，所有这些税款及费用均由买方负担。如果卖方已垫付这些税款或费用，买方须将垫付的金额偿付给卖方。

4. INCREASED COSTS

If any new, additional or increased taxes are imposed after the execution hereof or any increased costs are imposed due to a force majeure event as described in Article 3 hereof, all such taxes and costs shall be borne by the Buyer. If the Seller pays such taxes or costs, the Buyer shall reimburse the Seller for the amount so paid. ④

5. 付款条件的变更

在发生以下任何一种情形时，尽管本合同中有任何相反的规定，买方仍须按卖方的要求向卖方一次性付清与本合同有关的所有应付款项：

①买方开始任何破产、清算程序或其他诉讼，或者针对买方的这些程序或其他诉讼将要开始；

②买方的营业执照被吊销或以其他形式终止，或者因任何原因不能更新；

③买方的财产被查封、没收、冻结或者被采取其他财产保全措施或执行措施；

④卖方有合理理由认为买方的财务状况已经恶化，导致买方对其债权人的一般义务或在本合同项下对卖方的义务之履约能力发生不利影响；

⑤法律、税收制度、政府政策、外汇或其他市场情况等总体商业环境发生变化，使得卖方认为履行本合同项下的任何义务在商业上成为不现实；

⑥买方未履行本合同或双方之间的任何其他合同项下的全部或部分义务，或违反本合同或双方之间的任何其他合同条款或约定的全部或一部分。

5. CHANGE OF PAYMENT CONDITION⑤

If any of the following events occurs, then, notwithstanding any provision to the contrary contained in this Contract, the Buyer shall pay, in a lump sum, to the Seller all amounts owed by the Buyer in relation hereto upon the Seller's demand：

①The Buyer commences any bankruptcy or insolvency proceeding or other action or any such proceeding or other action

---

①　本款对于不可抗力范围的宽泛约定，对卖方是非常有利的。

②　依据本款的规定，在发生不可抗力事件时，卖方可以通过向买方发出通知的方式来变更或解除本合同。

③　本款的约定，将买方以"三角债"为由拒付卖方货款的抗辩加以明确排除。

④　在合同签订后，有时，由于政府新增的税种或提高税负，以及由于不可抗力事件引起履行合同的费用增加，这些新增的税收或费用究竟由哪一方负担，会成为发生争议的原因。在合同中就此作出明确约定，有助于避免纠纷。在本合同中约定这些均由买方负担，保护了卖方的利益。

⑤　本条款所列的各种情形，都会实际影响买方如约支付货款的能力；合同约定卖方可以变更付款条件、立即收回货款，对保护卖方的利益非常重要。

shall be commenced against the Buyer;

②The Buyer's business license shall be cancelled or otherwise terminated, or it shall not be renewed for any reason;

③The Buyer's assets have been sealed up, confiscated, frozen or taken over under any other property preservation measure or execution measure;

④The Seller shall reasonably determine that an adverse change in the financial situation of the Buyer has occurred and that such change will adversely affect the Buyer's ability to fulfill its obligations to its creditors generally or its obligations to the Seller under this Contract;

⑤There shall have occurred any change in the general business conditions such as any law, tax system, government policy, or foreign exchange or other market conditions, which, the Seller considers, shall render the performance of any obligation under this Contract commercially impracticable; or

⑥The Buyer shall fail to perform in whole or in part any of its obligations under, or breach in whole or in part any term or agreement contained in, this Contract or any other contracts between the parties hereto.

6. 合同的解除

在发生本合同第 5 条规定的任何一种情形时，卖方可以独自酌情决定延长"货物"的交货期限或立即（即无须发出要求补救的催告）全部或部分解除本合同，且不影响卖方要求买方对违约行为进行损害赔偿的权利或采取其他补救措施的权利。如果卖方解除本合同，买方应按每天【　】元人民币的比率向卖方支付自"货物"交付之日至"货物"返还之日期间的租赁费用。

6. TERMINATION①

In the event that any of the events described in Article 5 hereof occurs, the Seller may, at its sole discretion, either extend the time of delivery of the Goods or immediately (i. e., without any need to send a request for remedy) terminate this Contract in whole or in part, without prejudice to its right to claim damages for breach against the Buyer or to take any other remedy. If the Seller terminates this Contract, the Buyer shall pay to the Seller the amount calculated at the rate of RMB 【　】 per day accruing from the date of delivery of the Goods through the date of returning the Goods as a rental fee.

7. 损害赔偿

(1) 如果买方违反本合同项下的全部或部分义务（包括但不限于不接收本合同项下已交付的"货物"），买方应对卖方予以赔偿，使卖方免于承担因买方违约所遭受的一切损失、费用及损害（包括但不限于卖方发生的全部保管及仓储的费用及支出）。在买方违反本合同时，应首先向卖方支付相当于本合同总价 15% 的违约金。如果该违约金不足以赔偿卖方的全部损失、费用及损害额，买方应立即补偿该不足部分。**如该违约金高于卖方的全部损失、费用及损害额，卖方对该超过部分不负返还义务。**

(2) 如果买方未如期足额付款给卖方，买方应按每天 0.05% 的利率向卖方支付逾期付款利息。

7. INDEMNITY

(1) If the Buyer breaches any of its obligations hereunder, wholly or partly, including, without limitation, failing to accept the Goods delivered hereunder, the Buyer shall indemnify and shall hold the Seller harmless from any and all losses, costs and damages incurred by the Seller on account of such breach, including, without limitation, all deposit and storage charges and costs incurred by the Seller. If the Buyer breaches this Contract, it shall first pay the Seller liquidated damages the amount of which represents 15% of the total amount hereunder. If such amount is less than the Seller's total losses, costs and damages, the Buyer shall immediately indemnify the difference. **If such amount is more than the Seller's total losses, costs and damages, the Seller shall have no obligation to return the difference. ②**

---

① 本条是在第 5 条情形发生后的补充性约定，旨在减少或避免卖方的损失。

② 需要注意的是，尽管本款对违约金作了约定，但买方有可能依据中国合同法的相关规定，请求法院或仲裁机构适当减少所约定的违约金。

（2）If the Buyer fails to pay in a timely manner any amount payable to the Seller, the Buyer shall pay the Seller a default interest calculated at 0.05% per day.

8. 争议的解决

买卖双方之间凡因本合同引起的或与本合同有关的任何争议，应采用以下第【　】种方式解决（本合同当事人没有选择的另一种方式不具有法律效力）：

① 将争议提交北京仲裁委员会，按照申请仲裁时该会现行有效的仲裁规则进行仲裁。仲裁裁决是终局性的，对双方均有约束力；或

② 就争议向卖方住所地有管辖权的法院起诉。

8. SETTLEMENT OF DISPUTE

Any dispute between the Seller and the Buyer arising from or in connection with this Contract shall be settled in accordance with the following Item【　】(the other Item which has not been chosen by the parties hereto shall be null and void)：

① Any dispute shall be submitted to Beijing Arbitration Commission for arbitration which shall be conducted in accordance with the Commission's arbitration rules in effect at the time of applying for arbitration. The arbitral award is final and binding upon both parties①; or

② Any dispute shall be brought in the courts having competent jurisdiction of the Seller's domicile. ②

9. 转让

未经卖方事先书面同意，买方不得将其在本合同项下的权利或义务转让给任何第三方。

9. ASSIGNMENT

The Buyer shall not assign or transfer its rights or obligations hereunder to any third party without the prior written consent of the Seller.

10. 签字文本

本合同用中英文两种文字作成，两种文本具有同等效力。

10. LANGUAGE

This Contract is made in Chinese and English, and both versions shall have the same effect.

11. 通知

向对方当事人发送的全部通知或其他联络，应以专人递送、传真或通过邮局以邮资已付信函的方式，按照对方为此目的随时书面指定的地址发送给对方当事人。本合同各方首次指定的地址已记载于本合同正面各自的名称项下。任何专人递送的通知在交付时被视为送达；任何以传真发送的通知在其发出时被视为送达；任何以邮资已付信函发送的通知，在信函留置于有关地址时被视为送达，或者（视情况而定）如为预付快递费用的邮件，信封上的地址书写正确的，在寄出后 3 天被视为送达。

11. NOTICE

All notices or other communications to or upon the other party shall be served by hand delivery or by facsimile or by prepaid letter sent through the post to the other party at its address which may from time to time be designated, in writing, for this purpose. The initial addresses so designated by the parties hereto are set out under their respective names on the face of this Contract. Any notice delivered by hand shall be deemed to have been served when delivered;

---

① 因卖方的主营业地在北京，选择在北京仲裁委员会以仲裁方式解决争议，对卖方来说更为便利。

② 如果以诉讼方式解决争议，选择在卖方住所地法院诉讼，对卖方较为便利。

any notice sent by facsimile shall be deemed to have been served when dispatched; and any notice served by prepaid letter shall be deemed to have been served when left at the relevant address or（as the case may be）3 days after being posted, express charges prepaid, in a duly addressed envelope.

第 5 节　国内购货合同精选与解读

（合同正面）

购 货 合 同 **CONTRACT OF PURCHASE**①	买方合同编号：　　日期：　　年　　月　　日 BUYER'S CONTRACT NO： DATE：
卖方：	买方：XX（北京）有限公司
地址：	地址：
Seller：	Buyer：XX（Beijing）Co.，Ltd.
Address：	Address：

买卖双方特此同意，以下述条款和条件以及后附一般条款和条件签订本购货合同。<u>卖方在此确认，买方就一般条款和条件中的免除或减轻买方责任的约定（加下划线或粗体印刷部分）已充分提请了卖方注意。卖方就该等约定以及可能对卖方不利的其他条款已被充分告知并予以理解，故决定签订本购货合同。卖方对作为贸易公司的买方为取得转卖利益而签订本购货合同予以充分理解。</u>

The Seller and the Buyer hereby agree to enter into this Contract of Purchase on the terms and conditions set forth below and on the General Terms and Conditions attached hereto. **The Seller hereby acknowledges that the Buyer has sufficiently called the Seller's attention to the underlined or boldfaced provisions of the General Terms and Conditions which release or mitigate the Buyer's liability and responsibility. It is therefore that the Seller has been fully informed of and understood, such provisions and other provisions which may be disadvantageous to the Seller and that the Seller has determined to enter into this Contract of Purchase. The Seller fully understands that the Buyer, being a trading company, shall enter into this Contract of Purchase in order to make a resale profit.** ②

---

①　本合同由买方的律师制作，用于在中国国内购买货物，其内容（特别是背面的"一般条款及条件"）侧重于保护买方权益。买方将本合同印制为格式合同使用，合同正面是商业条款，背面是一般条款及条件。对于本合同的内容，建议读者与本书中的"售货合同"（Contract of Sale）的"一般条款和条件"互相对照，可以看出两者在相同事项上的不同约定，体会出律师为保护其客户利益的用意所在。

②　此处以及本合同其他处加下划线或粗体印刷的部分，是为符合中国法律中有关合同格式条款的要求，对于免除或减轻买方责任、加重卖方责任或限制其权利的内容，提请卖方注意。请参阅《中华人民共和国合同法》（1999年10月1日起施行）第39、40、41条等关于合同格式条款的规定。

唛　头 SHIPPING MARK	货物名称 COMMODITY	数　量 QUANTITY	单　价 UNIT PRICE	总　价 AMOUNT

合同总价 TOTAL	
交货期限 TIME OF DELIVERY：	交货地 PLACE OF DELIVERY：
交货条件 DELIVERY TERMS：	目的地 PLACE OF DESTINATION：
保险 INSURANCE：	包装 PACKING：
验收方法 INSPECTION：	生产厂家 MANUFACTURER：
付款条件 PAYMENT：	特约条款及条件 SPECIAL TERMS & CONDITIONS：

卖方基于其理解能力及/或买方的说明，已充分理解本购货合同（包括所附一般条款和条件）项下可能免除或减轻买方责任的全部条款，且不存在任何其他不明确的条款，故签订本购货合同。

Now that the Seller, with its ability to understand and/or the Buyer's explanation, has fully understood the provisions of this Contract of Purchase (including the attached General Terms and Conditions) which may release or mitigate the Buyer's liability and responsibility, and that there is no any other provision which is unclear to the Seller, the Seller has therefore executed this Contract of Purchase.

买方：XX（北京）有限公司	卖方：
Buyer：XX（Beijing）Co.，Ltd.	Seller：
签字盖章 BY：	签字盖章 BY：

　　（SEE GENERAL TERMS AND CONDITIONS ON REVERSE SIDE HEREOF 请见本页背面所列一般条款和条件）

Contract of Purchase（Reverse Side）国内购货合同（背面）

一般条款和条件（GENERAL TERMS AND CONDITIONS）

1. 所有权的转移

"货物"的所有权自"货物"交付时起，从卖方转移到买方。

1. TITLE TRANSFER

Title of the Goods shall transfer from the Seller to the Buyer at the time of delivery thereof. ①

2. 保证

卖方在此向买方保证，"货物"自交付时起【 】年内符合本合同的规定。如买方发现"货物"在数量、规格、包装、质量或其他任何方面不符合本合同的规定或存在其他瑕疵时，买方可以向卖方提出索赔，并可独自酌情决定，在不影响就卖方违约要求损害赔偿权利的前提下，以下述方式行使其他救济的权利：（i）要求卖方采取补足"货物"数量、更换、修理或减少价款等补救措施以纠正该违约行为或瑕疵；或者（ii）立即全部或部分解除本合同。在买方根据上述（i）提出要求或根据上述（ii）解除本合同时，卖方应立即按买方要求采取补救措施，或者接受本合同的解除。

2. WARRANTY②

The Seller hereby warrants to the Buyer that，within【 】years after delivery，the Goods are in conformity with the terms of this Contract. If the Buyer discovers any non-conformity or other defect with respect to quantity, specifications，packing，quality or any other aspect of the Goods，the Buyer may assert a claim against the Seller，and in its sole discretion and without prejudice to its right to claim damages for breach against the Seller or to take any other remedy，either（i）request the Seller to remedy such non-conformity or defect，by taking such act as delivering an additional quantity，replacing，repairing or reducing the price，or（ii）immediately terminate this Contract in whole or in part. As soon as any request is made by the Buyer pursuant to（i）above or this Contract is terminated pursuant to（ii）above，the Seller shall so remedy the non-conformity in accordance with the request of the Buyer or accept the termination of this Contract as the case may be.

3. 不可抗力

(1) 如果由于买方或其客户发生了自然灾害、罢工、战争、暴动、法律的变更或其他不能预见或不能避免的不可抗力事件，导致买方无法履行或无法按期履行其在本合同项下的义务或买方与其客户之间的转卖合同项下的义务时，买方对因其不履行或不按期完全履行本合同项下义务而导致卖方发生的任何损失或损害（无论该损失或损害是直接的或间接的）均不承担任何赔偿责任。

(2) 在发生任何不可抗力事件时，买方有权要求对本合同进行全部或部分变更。如卖方不同意该变更要求或者买方在提出变更本合同的要求后 7 日内未收到卖方的答复，则买方可以向卖方发出书面通知解除本合同。

3. FORCE MAJEURE③

(1) **In the event that the Buyer's obligation hereunder，or the resale contract between the Buyer and its customer（s），fails to be performed or，fails to be performed in a timely manner due to a force majeure event having occurred to any of the Buyer or the customer（s），such as an act of God，strike，war，civil disturbance，change in law or any other event the occurrence of which is unforeseeable or unpreventable，the Buyer shall not have any liability for any loss or**

---

① 本条内容与本章第 4 节国内售货合同（Contract of Sale）的"一般条款和条件"第 1 条相比较，可以看出显著区别，这里约定货物所有权自交付时起转移到买方（无论是否付清货款），明显对买方更为有利，排除了卖方对货物所有权的保留。

② 本条内容与本章第 4 节国内售货合同（Contract of Sale）的"一般条款和条件"第 2 条（验收及索赔）相对照，区别明显；此处的约定对卖方向买方提供的货物保证更为全面、详细、期限更长，赋予买方更多的救济权利。

③ 本条内容与本章第 4 节国内售货合同（Contract of Sale）的"一般条款和条件"第 3 条相比较，对于不可抗力的范围以及处理方式的约定内容，对买方明显有利。

damage, direct or indirect, incurred by the Seller as a result of any failure by the Buyer to fully perform in a timely manner any of its obligations hereunder.

（2）The Buyer has the right to offer to modify this Contract in whole or in part when a force majeure event occurs. If the Seller objects to such offer or if the Buyer does not receive a response from the Seller within 7 days after the Buyer submits such offer, the Buyer may terminate this Contract by written notice to the Seller.

4. 合同解除

如果发生下列任何情形之一的，买方有权向卖方发出书面通知立即（即无须发出要求补救的催告）全部或部分解除本合同，且并不因此影响买方要求卖方对违约作出损害赔偿的权利或采取其他补救措施的权利：

① 卖方开始任何破产、清算程序或其他诉讼，或者针对卖方的这些程序或其他诉讼将要开始；

② 卖方的营业执照被吊销或以其他形式终止，或者因任何原因不能更新；

③ 卖方的财产被查封、没收、冻结或者被采取其他财产保全措施或执行措施；

④ 买方有合理理由认为卖方的财务状况已经恶化，导致卖方对其债权人的一般义务或在本合同项下对买方的义务之履约能力发生不利影响；

⑤ 法律、税收制度、政府政策、外汇或其他市场情况等总体商业环境发生变化，使得买方认为履行本合同项下的任何义务在商业上成为不现实；

⑥ 卖方未履行本合同或双方之间的任何其他合同项下的全部或部分义务，或违反本合同或双方之间的任何其他合同条款或约定的全部或一部分。

如果买方根据本条规定解除本合同，则买方根据本合同支付款项及接收"货物"的全部义务应立即解除。在此情况下，如果买方已经向卖方支付本合同项下的任何款项，卖方应在解除本合同的相关通知之日起 7 日内将买方的全部已付款项返还给买方。如果卖方在上述期限内未返还该款项，卖方应按每天 0.05％的利率向买方支付逾期还款利息。

4. TERMINATION①

If any of the following events occurs, then, the Buyer may, immediately (i. e. , without any need to send a request for remedy) terminate this Contract in whole or in part by written notice to the Seller, without prejudice to its right to claim damages for breach against the Seller or to take any other remedy:

① The Seller commences any bankruptcy or insolvency proceeding or other action or if any such proceeding or other action shall be commenced against the Seller;

② The Seller's business license shall be cancelled or otherwise terminated and such business license shall not be renewed for any reason;

③ The Seller's assets have been sealed up, confiscated, frozen or taken over under any other property preservation measure or execution measure;

④ The Buyer shall reasonably determine that an adverse change in the financial situation of the Seller has occurred and that such change will adversely affect the Seller's ability to fulfill its obligations to its creditors generally or its obligations to the Buyer under this Contract ;

⑤ There shall have occurred any change in the general business conditions such as any law, tax system, government policy, or foreign exchange or other market conditions, which, the Buyer considers, shall render the performance of any obligation under this Contract commercially impracticable; or

⑥ The Seller shall fail to perform in whole or in part any of its obligations under or breach in whole or in part any term or agreement contained in, this Contract or any other contracts between the parties hereto.

In the event that the Buyer terminates this Contract pursuant hereto, all obligations of the Buyer to pay any amount hereunder and to accept the Goods hereunder shall immediately terminate and, to the extent that the Buyer has made any

---

① 本条的内容与本书中"国内售货合同"（Contract of Sale）的"一般条款和条件"第 5 条（付款条件的变更）的违约情形非常相似，但结果是赋予买方解除合同、收回货款等权利。

payment to the Seller hereunder，the Seller shall repay the amount so paid by the Buyer in full to the Buyer within 7 days after the date of the applicable notice of termination. If the Seller fails to repay such amount within the applicable period of time，a default interest calculated at 0.05％ per day shall also be payable by the Seller to the Buyer.

5. 损害赔偿

如果卖方违反本合同项下的全部或部分义务，卖方应对买方予以赔偿，使买方免予承担因卖方违约所遭受的一切损失、费用及损害。在卖方违反本合同时，应首先向买方支付相当于本合同总价15％的违约金。如果该违约金不足以赔偿买方的全部损失、费用及损害额，卖方应补偿该不足部分。**如果该违约金高于买方的全部损失、费用及损害额，买方对该超过部分不负返还义务。**

5. INDEMNITY①

If the Seller breaches any of its obligations hereunder，wholly or partly，the Seller shall indemnify and shall hold the Buyer harmless from any and all losses，costs and damages incurred by the Buyer on account of such breach. If the Seller breaches this Contract，it shall first pay the Buyer liquidated damages the amount of which represents 15％ of the total amount hereunder. If such amount is less than the Buyer's total losses，costs and damages，the Seller shall indemnify the difference. **If such amount is more than the Buyer's total losses，costs and damages，the Buyer shall have no obligation to return the difference.**

6. 权利

卖方应自行承担费用解决由"货物"相关的权利（包括"货物"的所有权或适用的知识产权）所引起的或与此相关的任何索赔或争议，并确保买方不会因此受到任何损害。

6. RIGHTS②

The Seller，at its own costs，shall settle and，hold the Buyer harmless from，any and all claims or disputes which may arise from or in connection with any rights to the Goods，including ownership of，or intellectual property right applicable to，the Goods.

7. 争议解决

买卖双方之间凡因本合同引起的或与本合同有关的任何争议，应采用以下第【 】种方式解决（本合同当事人没有选择的另一种方式不具有法律效力）：

①将争议提交北京仲裁委员会，按照申请仲裁时该会现行有效的仲裁规则进行仲裁。仲裁裁决是终局性的，对双方均有约束力；或

②就争议向买方住所地有管辖权的法院起诉。

7. SETTLEMENT OF DISPUTE③

Any dispute between the Seller and the Buyer arising from or in connection with this Contract shall be settled in accordance with the following Item【 】(the other Item which has not been chosen by the parties hereto shall be null and void)：

①Any dispute shall be submitted to Beijing Arbitration Commission for arbitration which shall be conducted in accordance with the Commission's arbitration rules in effect at the time of applying for arbitration. The arbitral award shall be final and binding upon both parties；or

②Any dispute shall be brought in the courts having competent jurisdiction of the Buyer's domicile.

---

① 本条的内容与本书中"国内售货合同"（Contract of Sale）的"一般条款和条件"第7条（损害赔偿）相比较，侧重于保护买方的利益。

② 本条约定是专为保护买方利益所设，在本书中"国内售货合同"（Contract of Sale）的"一般条款和条件"里是没有的。

③ 本合同第7、8条的内容，与本书中"国内售货合同"（Contract of Sale）的"一般条款和条件"第8、9条的内容相对应，但侧重保护的当事方则彼此相反。

8. 转让

未经买方事先书面同意，卖方不得转让其在本合同项下的权利或义务给任何第三方。

8. ASSIGNMENT

The Seller shall not assign or transfer its rights or obligations hereunder to any third party without the prior written consent of the Buyer.

9. 签字文本

本合同用中英文两种文字作成，两种文本具有同等效力。

9. LANGUAGE

This Contract is made in Chinese and English，and both versions shall have the same effect.

10. 通知

向对方当事人发送的全部通知或其他联络，应以专人递送、传真或通过邮局以邮资已付信函的方式，按照对方为此目的随时书面指定的地址发送给对方当事人。本合同各方首次指定的地址已记载于本合同正面各自的名称项下。任何专人递送的通知在交付时被视为送达；任何以传真发送的通知在其发出时被视为送达；任何以邮资已付信函发送的通知，在信函留置于有关地址时被视为送达，或者（视情况而定）如为预付快递费用的邮件，信封上的地址书写正确的，在寄出后 3 天被视为送达。

10. NOTICE

All notices or other communications to or upon the other party shall be served by hand delivery or by facsimile or by prepaid letter sent through the post to the other party at its address which may from time to time be designated，in writing，for this purpose. The initial addresses so designated by the parties hereto are set out under their respective names on the face of this Contract. Any notice delivered by hand shall be deemed to have been served when delivered；any notices sent by facsimile shall be deemed to have been served when dispatched；and any notice served by prepaid letter shall be deemed to have been served when left at the relevant address or（as the case may be）3 days after being posted，express charges prepaid，in a duly addressed envelope.

第 6 节　佣金协议精选与解读

COMMISSION AGREEMENT
佣 金 协 议

THIS AGREEMENT is made as of the 【日】 of 【月】【年】. ①
本协议于 【　】 年 【　】 月 【　】 日正式签署。

BETWEEN：
签约双方为：

---

① 本协议的交易内容，是由国内一家商业公司介绍货物买卖的双方给一家香港公司，香港公司在成功进行交易后，向国内商业公司支付佣金的协议。由于本协议双方是同属一个集团内的关联公司，本协议内容相对比较简要，双方权利义务也比较对等。

（1）**MNO CO. , LTD. ,** a company incorporated under the laws of the People's Republic of China（the **"PRC"**）and having its principal place of business situated at 【 】, the RPC（ **"MNO"**）；and

MNO 有限公司，一家依据中华人民共和国（下称"**中国**"）法律设立的公司，其主要营业地址在中国【地址】（下称"**MNO 公司**"）；和

（2）**MNO HONG KONG LIMITED,** a company incorporated under the laws of Hong Kong and having its registered office situated at 【 】, Hong Kong（ **"MNOHK"**）.

MNO 香港有限公司，一家依据香港法律设立的公司，其注册地址为香港【地址】（下称"**MNO 香港香港**"）。

RECITALS:
鉴于：

MNO has introduced ABC CO. , LTD. （ **"ABC"**）and XYZ COMPANY LTD. （ **"XYZ"**）to do business with MNOHK. Accordingly, MNOHK will purchase 【 】 products（the **"Products"**）from XYZ and then resell the Products to ABC（the **"Transaction"**）. For each Transaction, MNO shall receive commission（the **"Commission"**）from MNOHK. [①]

MNO 公司介绍了 ABC 有限公司（下称"**ABC 公司**"）和 XYZ 有限公司（下称"**XYZ 公司**"）与 MNO 香港进行交易。由此，MNO 香港从 XYZ 公司购买【 】产品（下称"**产品**"），然后将产品出售给 ABC 公司（下称"**交易**"）。对于每笔交易，MNO 公司将从 MNO 香港收取佣金（下称"**佣金**"）。

NOW, THEREFORE, THE PARTIES HERETO AGREE as follows:
因此，双方协商一致，现达成如下协议：

1. COMMISSION
佣 金

1.1 Upon receiving full payment of each Transaction from ABC by MNOHK, within fourteen（14）days, MNOHK shall arrange to make the payment due to XYZ and after the actual expenses and Profit（as defined in Article 1.4 below）deducted, MNOHK shall remit the Commission to MNO.

MNO 香港在从 ABC 公司收到每笔交易的全部款项后十四（14）天内，MNO 香港应将 XYZ 公司应得的货款支付给 XYZ 公司，并在扣除实际费用和利润（如下文第 1.4 条所定义）后将佣金支付给 MNO 公司。

1.2 The Commission payable to MNO shall mean the outcome of the following formula:

MNO 公司应收取的佣金之具体计算方式如下：

Commission payable to MNO ＝ amount received from ABC － purchase

---

① XYZ 公司是一家境外生产型企业，ABC 公司是一家国内生产型企业，MNO 公司将这两家公司介绍给 MNO 香港公司，MNO 香港公司与这两家公司成功进行货物买卖后，再向 MNO 公司支付每笔交易的佣金。

price paid to XYZ — all other actual expenses spent by MNOHK to complete the Transaction（e. g. bank charges, transportation costs, interest, etc., but excluding the payroll of MNOHK）—Profit

应支付给 MNO 公司的佣金＝从 ABC 公司收到的款项—向 XYZ 公司支付的购买产品的购入价—由 MNO 香港支出的所有与完成该交易相关的其他实际费用（如银行手续费、运输费用和利息等，但不包括 MNO 香港的人工费）—利润。

1.3　MNOHK shall provide MNO with the details of its actual expenses relating to the Transaction.

　　MNO 香港应向 MNO 公司提供有关交易之实际费用的明细。

1.4　The formula to calculate the Profit：US $【　】/MT x the total weight specified in the invoice issued by MNOHK to ABC of each Transaction

　　关于利润的计算方法：【　】美元/公吨 × MNO 香港就每项交易向 ABC 公司发出的商业发票中所列产品的总公吨数

2. MNO hereby agrees to undertake all risks to the Transaction for MNOHK. In case the payment received by MNOHK from ABC is not sufficient to cover （i）the purchase price paid to XYZ, （ii）the other actual expenses spent by MNOHK to complete the Transaction and （iii）the Profit of MNOHK, MNO shall immediately pay the deficiency to MNOHK upon demand. [①]

MNO 公司在此同意为 MNO 香港承担与该交易有关的全部风险。如果 MNO 香港从 ABC 公司收到的款项不足以支付（i）向 XYZ 公司支付的购买产品的购入价、（ii）由 MNO 香港支出的所有与完成该交易相关的其他实际费用以及（iii）MNO 香港的利润，则 MNO 公司应根据 MNO 香港的要求立即向其支付该不足的金额。

3. MNO hereby further agrees and undertakes to indemnify MNOHK on demand for all demands, claims, actions, proceedings, damages, payments, direct losses, costs, expenses and other liabilities incurred by MNOHK in relation to or arising out of this Agreement and/or the Transaction hereunder.

MNO 公司在此进一步同意并承诺，根据 MNO 香港的要求向其赔付与本协议以及/或者与该交易有关或引发的 MNO 香港承担的所有支付要求、索赔、法律行动及程序、损害、付款请求、直接损失、费用、支出及其他债务。

4. Any taxes, charges and levies of any kind, which may be levied in the PRC in relation to this Agreement, shall be paid by MNO.

与本协议有关的在中国境内可能征收的任何税项、收费及其他课税，应全部由 MNO 公司承担。

5. This Agreement shall be effective from the date hereof until both parties agree to terminate this Agreement. [②]

---

① 本协议项下 MNO 公司作为贸易的中介方，承担 MNO 香港公司就每一笔货物买卖交易所可能发生的商业风险（最大风险是 MNO 香港没有收到或未全额收到 ABC 的货款），这与一般的外贸中介（介绍一笔交易成功后收取一笔佣金收入）的做法有所不同；作为 MNO 公司为 MNO 香港承担风险的对价，MNO 香港就每一笔成功的交易向 MNO 公司支付佣金。

② 本协议生效后，没有规定有效期届满的日期，即双方如没有一致同意终止，本协议就一直有效。

本协议自双方签署之日起生效，直至经双方合意而终止。

6. This Agreement shall be governed by and construed in accordance with the laws of Hong Kong.

   本协议适用香港法律，按照香港法律解释。

7. In the event of any dispute arising from or in connection with this Agreement，MNOHK and MNO shall submit the dispute to South China International Economic and Trade Arbitration Commission for arbitration in accordance with the Commission's Arbitration Rules in effect at the time of applying for arbitration. The arbitration award shall be final and binding on both MNOHK and MNO.

   就本协议发生的争议，应提交华南国际经济贸易仲裁委员会，按照申请仲裁时该委员会实施的仲裁规则进行仲裁。仲裁裁决为终局性的，对双方均有约束力。

8. This Agreement is written in both English and Chinese. In the event of any inconsistency between the two versions，the English version shall prevail.

   本协议由中文和英文作成，两种版本内容出现不一致的，以英文本为准。

IN WITNESS WHEREOF，the parties hereto have caused this Agreement to be executed as of the day and year first above written.

本协议经双方在本协议首页开头所示日期正式签订并生效，以昭信守。

MNO CO.，LTD.   MNO HONG KONG LIMITED
MNO 有限公司   MNO 香港有限公司

_____   _____

Name/姓名：   Name/姓名：

   Title/职务：   Title/职务：

第 4 章

经销协议精选与解读

经销协议（Distributorship Agreement 或 Distribution Agreement），又称分销协议或销售权协议。经销或分销是国际贸易中的重要交易方式，经销协议的双方当事人为经销商与供货商，双方通过订立经销协议，经销商在约定的期限和地域内分销供货商的指定商品。

第 1 节　经销协议的分类

经销协议，从是否授予经销商独家（独占性）经销权来划分，可以分为独家经销协议（Exclusive Distributorship Agreement）或包销协议（Sole Distributorship Agreement）和非独占性经销协议（一般经销协议）。在英文合同中，通常根据协议的内容来区分；但在协议的名称上，一般统称为 Distributorship Agreement。

Sole Distributorship Agreement 或者 Exclusive Distributorship Agreement，通常译为"独家经销协议"，也称"独家分销协议"或"包销协议"，指经销商在协议规定的期限和地域内，对指定商品享有独家经销权的经销方式。一般在经销商具有强大销售网络或者限于较小的指定地域销售指定商品时使用。如果经销商不具有强大经销实力，签订独家经销协议则对供货商不利，有可能妨碍在指定地域内指定商品的市场销售。

一般经销协议，也称非独家经销协议或非独占性经销协议（Non-Exclusive Distributorship Agreement），经销商不享有独家经销权，供货商可在同一期间、同一地域内，授权若干家经销商经销同类商品。这通常在经销商不具有强大销售网络，或不愿意承担巨大购销压力，或销售区域较为广阔、不适合限定独家经销商的情况下使用。在实践中，这类非独占性经销协议的应用范围更加广泛。

第 2 节　经销协议的特点和主要内容

经销协议是经销商（Distributor）和供货商（Supplier）约定双方权利和义务、确立双方法律关系的契约。经销协议中的经销商是买方，供货商是卖方，二者是买卖关系。供货商供应指定商品，经销人以自己的名义批量买进，利用其销售网络分销，自负盈亏。经销商向其下级经销商（Sub-distributors）或零售商（Retailers）转售指定商品时，应以经销商自己的名义进行，而不得以供货商的名义进行。

供货商在多数情况下为指定商品的生产厂家，但有时是厂家的关联贸易公司；如果协议约定供货商同意经销商向下级经销商分销或对此不作明确约定，经销商本身可以与下级经销商再签订经销协议。

经销协议的主要内容一般包括：

（1）定义，对指定商品、指定地域、使用的商标等作出限定性规定；

（2）供货商将指定商品的经销权授予经销商（独家的或非独占性）；

（3）订货与交货；

（4）定价与支付方式；

（5）数量和金额（在独家经销协议中，应规定经销商对指定商品的最低购入数量或金额）；

（6）双方的具体权利义务；

（7）经销协议的有效期限和终止、解除条件；

（8）经销商的推广促销义务，如广告宣传、市场调研和维护供货商权益等；

（9）所有权转移、风险负担；

（10）知识产权的保护；

（11）一般合同条款，包括不可抗力、通知、不可转让、保密、法律适用、争议解决、合同语言、生效及有效期条款等。

经销协议的内容繁简程度视具体交易情况而定。独家经销协议与非独占性经销协议的内容上的区别，读者可以从下面精选的两种协议文本及作者的解读和评论中具体理解和体会。

第 3 节　独家经销协议（SOLE DISTRIBUTORSHIP AGREEMENT）精选与解读

SOLE DISTRIBUTORSHIP AGREEMENT[①]
独家经销协议

THIS AGREEMENT is made and entered into this date of（*年月日*）by and between：

ABC Co.，Ltd.， a company duly incorporated and existing under the laws of（*国家名*）and having its registered office at（*公司地址*）（hereinafter called the **"Supplier"**）；and

XYZ Co.，Ltd.， a company duly incorporated and existing under the laws of（*国家名*）having its registered office at（*公司地址*）（hereinafter called the **"Distributor"**）．

（Individually the **"Party"** or collectively the **"Parties"**）

本协议由以下双方当事人于（*年月日*）签订：

ABC 有限公司，按照（*国家名*）法律正当设立并存续的一家公司，其注册地址为（*公司地址*）（以下简称**"供货商"**）；以及

XYZXYZ 有限公司，按照（*国家名*）法律正当设立并存续的一家公司，其注

---

① 本协议的背景：供货商系国际知名品牌时装的生产厂家，经销商在指定地域（某大城市）拥有强大销售网络；本协议文本系供货商委托律师所起草，侧重于保护供货商的权益。

册地址为(*公司地址*)（以下简称"**经销商**"）。

（上述签约方单独称为"**一方**"，合称为"**双方**"）。

WHEREAS：

A. The Supplier is the manufacturer of the Products（as defined in Article 1. 4 here below）and desirous of selling the Products in the Territory（as defined Article 1. 5 here below）；

B. The Supplier manufactures the Products bearing the trademarks "(*某商标*)"；

C. The Distributor wishes to purchase and import the Products from the Supplier and re-sell them in the Territory through its sales network to boutiques（mono or multi-branded）, department stores, specialty stores, etc. （hereinafter called the "**Customers**"）；and

D. The Parties intend to constitute their overall relationship, in order to co-operate effectively and exclusively in the marketing and distribution of the Products in the Territory through the Customers under the terms and conditions hereinafter specified.

鉴于：

A. 供货商是指定商品（按下述第 1. 4 条所定义）的生产厂家，希望在指定地域（按下述第 1. 5 条所定义）销售指定商品；

B. 供货商生产的指定商品使用"(*某商标*)"；

C. 经销商希望从供货商购入和进口指定商品，并在指定地域内通过其销售网络将指定商品出售给（单一品牌或多品牌的）精品店、百货商店、专卖店等（以下简称"**客户**"）；

D. 双方当事人愿意建立全面的关系，以便开展有效的独家合作，根据本协议的下述条款和条件，在指定地域内通过客户对指定商品进行市场开发和经销。

NOW, THEREFORE, in consideration of the mutual covenants hereinafter set forth, it is mutually agreed as follows：

因此，双方对于本协议中互相约定的事项，一致同意如下条款：

ARTICLE 1　DEFINITIONS

第 1 条　定义

As used in this Agreement, the following words and phrases shall[①] have the following respective meanings, unless the context otherwise specifies or requires：

在本协议中使用的下列单词和短语，除非上下文另有规定或要求，则应具有下述各自含义：

---

① Shall，通常用于第一人称，表示一般将来时态，意为"将要""计划""打算"等；但在法律英文中，表示义务或约定，译为"应当"或"必须"等。

1.1　**"Business Plan"** means the business plan agreed by the Parties and defined in **Appendix A** hereof. ①

1.1　**"商业计划书"** 是指双方同意的商业计划书，在本协议附件 A 中说明。

1.2　**"Flag-ship Store"** means the flag ship store to be opened in *(城市)* under the *(品牌)* sign.

1.2　**"旗舰店"** 是指将在*(城市)* 开设、以*(品牌)* 为标志的旗舰店。

1.3　**"Flag-ship Store Owner"** means the company that opens the Flag-ship Store.

1.3　**"旗舰店所有人"** 是指开设旗舰店的公司。

1.4　**"Products"** means the clothing lines and accessories bearing the Trademarks（as defined in Article. 1.6 herebelow）as further specified in **Appendix B** hereof, specifically excluding, however, the accessories and products（including, without limitation, glasses, bags, perfumes, etc.）, whose production has been licensed by the Supplier to third parties.

1.4　**"指定商品"** 是指使用指定商标（按下述第 1.6 条所定义）的衣物系列及配饰，将在本协议附件 B 中详细列明；但不包括由供货商已经许可第三方生产的配饰和产品（包括但不限于眼镜、手袋、香水等）。②

1.5　**"Territory"** means *(具体地区/国别)* or such other areas as may be agreed upon by Parties hereto from time to time.

1.5　**"指定地域"** 是指*(具体地区/国别)*，或者本协议双方可能不时同意的其他区域。③

1.6　**"Trademarks"** means the trademarks owned by Supplier and more particularly described in Appendix B hereof.

1.6　**"指定商标"** 是指供货商所拥有的商标，详列于本协议附件 B。

ARTICLE 2　GRANT OF RIGHT
第 2 条　授权

2.1　The Supplier hereby grants to the Distributor the exclusive right to purchase, import, distribute and sell the Products in the Territory to the Customers during the term of this Agreement subject to the terms and conditions provided herein.

2.1　在本协议有效期限内，根据本协议约定的条款和条件，供货商授予经销商在指定地域内购入、进口、并向客户分销及出售指定商品的独家

---

　　① Business Plan（商业计划书），是本协议供货商同意授予经销商独家经销权的基础，经销商能否按照商业计划书实际履行，对于供货商至关重要。因此。商业计划书作为本协议的附件 A，成为本协议的组成部分；经销商没有履行商业计划书的行为则构成违约行为，对于由此产生的后果等，在本协议第 3.2 条中有具体约定。

　　② "including without limitation…"、"include without limitation…"或 "include but not limited to…"，均表示"包括但不限于……"，即后面列举的事物尚未穷尽，是法律文书中非常有用、很常见的表达方式。

　　③ 供货商应当根据经销商销售网络的广泛程度和经销实力等情况，对经销商销售指定商品的指定地域作出限定，特别是在独家经销协议的情况下，如果供货商同意过于广大的经销地域，而经销商销售指定商品的业绩不佳，但供货商又不能再指定其他经销商销售指定商品，则会对供货商在该地域的商品销售造成限制，导致损失。

经销权。①

2.2 As indicated in Appendix A hereof the Distributor is aware that the Supplier is keen on having a Flag-ship Store opened in（城市） under （品牌） sign. The Distributor undertakes to find a company that shall open a Flag-ship Store by and no later than（日期）. The Parties agree that the Flag-ship Store shall satisfy the image, location and dimension standards required by the Supplier. It is agreed that the choice of the Flag-ship Store's Owner, the minimum purchase amounts and the Flag-ship Store requirements shall be subject to the Supplier's approval. As soon as such approval is obtained, the Parties agree to amend the overall Minimum Purchase Amounts already fixed in the Business Plan with the approved Flag-ship Store purchase amounts. It is agreed that in case the Flag-ship Store is not opened by（日期）, as provided for in this Article 2.2, the Supplier may terminate this Agreement.

2.2 正如本协议附件 A 所记述，经销商理解，供货商希望在（城市）有以 （品牌）为标志的旗舰店。经销商承诺在（日期）之前找到一家开设旗舰店的公司。双方当事人同意，旗舰店应满足供货商要求的形象、地段和规模标准；旗舰店所有人的选择、最低购货金额和旗舰店的必备条件均应得到供货商的认可。在取得该认可后，双方同意立即全面修改在商业计划书中已经确定的最低购货金额，加入经认可的旗舰店购入数量。双方同意，倘若在（日期）前没有按照本合同第 2.2 条的约定开设旗舰店，供货商可以解除本协议。②

ARTICLE 3　EXCLUSIVITY
第 3 条　独家经销权

3.1 Subject to③Article 11.1 hereof, the grant of rights to the Distributor under Article 2 shall be exclusive and the Supplier agrees not to directly or indirectly sell the Products to any party other than the Distributor in the Territory.

3.1 以本协议第 11.1 条的约定为条件，根据第 2 条授予经销商的权利是独占性的，供货商同意不直接或间接地将指定商品出售给指定地域内除

---

① 由于供货商根据本协议授予经销商独家经销权后，不得在指定地域内再将指定商品销售给其他经销商，构成对供货商本身的重要限制，因此供货商应慎重使用，通常在对经销商进行全面考察，确定经销商具有在指定地域开发市场、保证最低购入数量（详见本协议第 11 条）的情况下才授予经销商独家经销权。

② 由于旗舰店直接代表指定商品的品牌形象，会极大地影响指定商品在该地域的销售情况，供货商对经销商确保旗舰店的按期开设是签订本协议的前提条件，供货商对旗舰店的地段、规模、标准、所有权、最低购货数量和必备条件等进行事先认可也是非常重要的。

③ "Subject to…"是法律英语中常用的限定性表达方式，非常有用，意为"以……为条件""根据（或依照）……""基于……""受……限制""受……约束""视……而定"等，即必须优先满足"Subject to"后面的条件，才可以行使主句中的权利或进行主句中的行为。在本条款中使用此短语，明确了供货商授予经销商独家经销权的前提条件是要满足第 11.1 条的最低购货数量要求。

经销商以外的任何其他方。

3.2　The Parties agree that the grant of exclusivity from the Supplier to the Distributor is strictly related to compliance by the Distributor with the Business Plan（Appendix A）. Therefore，the Supplier shall be entitled to sell directly or indirectly to the Customers in the Territory upon delivery of written notice in the event that the Distributor fails to comply with the Business Plan in any contract year and fails to cure such breach within thirty（30）days after written notice of such breach has been given by the Supplier and received by the Distributor.

3.2　双方同意，供货商授予经销商的独家经销权，是与经销商严格遵守商业计划书（附件 A）密切相关的。因此，倘若在任何一个合同年度中，经销商没有遵守商业计划书，在供货商向经销商发出纠正违约行为的书面通知、经销商收到该通知后三十（30）日内，经销商仍未纠正违约行为的，则供货商有权在发出书面通知后直接或间接地将指定商品销售给指定地域内的客户。

3.3　In consideration of the exclusive right granted herein in respect of the Territory，the Distributor agrees not to distribute the Products outside the Territory directly or indirectly，or sell the Products to any party which the Distributor knows or has reason to suspect who has an intention to export outside the Territory. The Distributor further agrees that it will not sell any other products of any kind other than the Products as provided in this Agreement. As for the accessories and products（including，without limitation，glasses，bags，perfumes，etc.），whose production has been licensed by the Supplier to third parties，such products shall be purchased by the Distributor directly from the Supplier's licensed third parties. ①

3.3　作为本协议中授予经销商在指定地域内独家经销权的对价，经销商同意不直接或间接地将指定商品经销到指定地域以外、或者销售给经销商知道或有理由怀疑任何有意将指定商品出口到指定地域以外的当事人。并且经销商同意不销售本协议约定的指定商品以外的任何其他种类产品。而对于供货商已许可第三方生产的配饰及产品（包括但不限于眼镜、手袋、香水等），经销商应直接从供货商许可的第三方处购买。

ARTICLE 4INDIVIDUAL CONTRACTS②
第 4 条　个别合同

Each individual contract concluded under this Agreement between the

---

①　约定本条款内容的目的，是防止经销商通过各种渠道将指定商品销往指定地域以外，从而扰乱供货商在其他区域指定的经销商分销指定商品。

②　个别合同是相对于本协议（作为交易的基本合同）而言，指经销商从供货商每次进口指定商品时双方另行签订的进口合同，内容包括进口的指定商品名称、规格、数量、价格、交货日期、交货港口等，可以采用购货订单（Purchase Order）或售货确认书（Sales Confirmation）的形式，但其内容均应与本协议内容严格保持一致；当个别合同与经销协议的内容发生抵触时，通常以经销协议的内容为准。

Supplier and the Distributor shall strictly conform to this Agreement.

供货商和经销商在本协议项下签订的任何个别合同，均应与本协议内容严格保持一致。

ARTICLE 5　ORDER AND SHIPMENT OF PRODUCTS
第 5 条　订单与货运

5.1　The Products shall be delivered to the Distributor by the Supplier or its designee（s），FCA *（指定地点）*（INCOTERMS 2000）.①

5.1　指定商品应由供货商或其指定人按照 FCA *（指定地点）*（《2000 年国际贸易术语解释通则》）交货给经销商。

5.2　Orders by the Distributor and deliveries by the Supplier shall be according to the customary seasons of the fashion industry and according to the following guideline：

　　（a）Orders for the collection of the Spring/Summer season shall be made in July-September；

　　（b）Delivery of the collection for the Spring/Summer orders timely placed shall be made in the period 10 January through 31 March；

　　（c）Orders for the collection of the Fall/Winter season shall be made in January—March；and

　　（d）Delivery of the collection for the Fall/Winter orders timely placed shall be made in the period 1 July through 30 September.

5.2　经销商的订货以及供货商的交货，应当依时装产业的惯常季节而定，并按照下述指引进行：

　　（a）春节/夏季交货的订单，应在 7 月至 9 月发出；

　　（b）春节/夏季适时发出订单的交货，应在 1 月 10 日至 3 月 31 日的期间内进行；

　　（c）秋节/冬季交货的订单，应在 1 月至 3 月发出；

　　（d）秋节/冬季适时发出订单的交货，应在 7 月 1 日至 9 月 30 日的期间内进行。

5.3　In the event that② any shipments from the Supplier to the Distributor are delayed for more than four（4）weeks from the specified and agreed delivery date（i. e.，31/03 for S/S orders and 30/09 for F/W orders），the Supplier shall grant the Distributor a ten percent（10%）discount

---

①　FCA（Free Carrier），国际贸易术语之一，《2000 年国际贸易术语解释通则》（INCOTERMS 2000）对其规定如下：FCA 是 free carrier 也就是"货交承运人（……指定地点）"，是指卖方只要将货物在指定的地点交给买方指定的承运人，并办理了出口清关手续，即完成交货。需要说明的是，交货地点的选择对于在该地点装货和卸货的义务会产生影响。若卖方在其所在地交货，则卖方应负责装货，若卖方在任何其他地点交货，卖方不负责卸货。该术语可用于各种运输方式，包括多式联运。"承运人"指任何人在运输合同中承诺通过铁路、公路、空运、海运、内河运输或上述运输的联合方式履行运输或由他人履行运输。若买方指定承运人以外的人领取货物，则当卖方将货物交给此人时，即视为已履行了交货义务。

②　"In the event that…"表示"如果""倘若""在……情况下"，"in the event that"后面跟设定情况的从句；如果后面跟短语，则为"in the event of…"。

to its prices, as better hereafter defined, with respect to such delayed goods. A fifteen percent (15%) discount to its prices, as better hereafter defined, shall be granted to the Distributor with respect to the goods in any shipment delayed for more than six (6) weeks from the specified and agreed date (i. e. , 31/03 for S/S orders and 30/09 for F/W orders). The Distributor shall be entitled to reject any delayed shipments of more than eight (8) weeks from the specified and agreed delivery date (i. e. , 31/03 for S/S orders and 30/09 for F/W orders).

5.3　如果从指定和同意的交货日期（即春季/夏季的订单为 3 月 31 日、秋季/冬季的订单为 9 月 30 日）起，供货商向经销商的货运延迟超过 4 个星期的，则供货商对于延迟货运的商品应给予经销商 10%的价格折扣（详见后述）。如果从指定和同意的日期（即春季/夏季的订单为 3 月 31 日、秋季/冬季的订单为 9 月 30 日）起，向经销商的货运延迟超过 6 个星期的，则对于延迟货运的商品应给予 15%的价格折扣（详见后述）。如果从指定及同意的交货日期（即春季/夏季的订单为 3 月 31 日、秋季/冬季的订单为 9 月 30 日）起，向经销商的货运延迟超过 8 个星期的，则经销商有权拒绝延迟的货运。①

5.4　The provisions of Article 5.3 above shall apply only to the extent that the delay has been caused by the Supplier's fault. Article 5.3 shall therefore not apply in the event that the delay is the result of the Distributor's behaviour (e. g. , without limitation, if the Distributor has failed to open or delayed the opening of a letter of credit).

5.4　上述本协议第 5.3 条的约定仅适用于因供货商过错引起的延迟货运。第 5.3 条不适用于因经销商的行为（例如，包括但不限于因经销商没有开具或延迟开具信用证的情况）造成的延迟货运。

ARTICLE 6　PRICES
第 6 条　价格

6.1　The Supplier shall sell the Products to the Distributor at such prices as set forth in the FOB Euro price list (the **"Price List"**) as determined by the Supplier from time to time, with a 15% discount.

6.1　供货商向经销商销售指定商品的价格，设定在 FOB 欧元价格表（以下简称**"价格清单"**）中，以供货商不时决定的价格为准，并优惠 15%。

6.2　Unless otherwise agreed, prices of the Products shall always be quoted in *(货币名称)* currency and referred to delivery FCA *(指定地点)* (INCOTERMS 2000).

6.2　除非另有约定，指定商品价格总是以*(货币名称)* 报价，并根据《2000 年国际贸易术语解释通则》，采用 FCA（货交承运人）交货到*(指定地点)*。

① 作为本协议标的物时装的销售具有很强的季节性，本协议中对于延迟货运的不同情况设定了不同折扣率以及拒绝收货的权利等，有助于在发生延迟货运时及时确定双方的权利和责任。

ARTICLE 7　PAYMENT
第 7 条　付款

In relation to the orders made, Distributor shall make payments for the Products by an irrevocable letter of credit payable at sixty (60) days net according to UCP 500 and issued by a first rate Hong Kong bank within thirty (30) days after the date of the order confirmation by Supplier of each individual order.

对于已发出的订单，经销商应根据 UCP500①，以 60 天付款的不可撤销信用证作为指定商品的付款方式，信用证应在香港的一流银行开立，并应在供货商确认每个订单后的 30 天内开出。

ARTICLE 8　　SALES SEASON REPORTING REQUIREMENTS AND HANDLING OF STOCK
第 8 条　销售旺季的报告要求及库存处理

The Distributor hereby agrees to submit to the Supplier a written report for each sales campaign which specifies the unit and gross sales of the Products and information relating to selling prices within thirty (30) days after the end of each sales campaign. Furthermore, at the end of each sales season, but in any event no later than the end of August for the Spring/Summer and March for the Fall/Winter, the Distributor shall submit to the Supplier the net sales of the Products, and an accurate inventory of the stock of Products unsold. Such end-of-season report shall specify how and to whom the Distributor intends to sell the remaining unsold stock. The Distributor shall sell the unsold Products in an appropriate manner so as to protect the image of the Trademarks and in accordance with the professional business practice for products of equal standard and image.

经销商在此同意，在每个促销活动结束后 30 日内，向供货商提供一份书面报告，具体说明在销售活动中指定商品的单位销售额和销售总额以及有关销售价格的信息。此外，在每个销售旺季结束时（在春夏季不得晚于 8 月底，在秋冬季不得晚于 3 月底），经销商应向供货商提供指定商品的净销售额以及未销售指定商品的准确库存量。此类季节末报告应说明经销商计划销售库存未售商品的方法以及销售对象。经销商应采用恰当的方式销售未售商品，以保护指定商标的形象，遵守同等标准和形象产品的业界商业惯例。

ARTICLE 9　PRODUCT WARRANTY
第 9 条　产品保证

9.1　　The Supplier warrants that the Products supplied to the Distributor hereunder shall be free from defect in material or workmanship in

---

① UCP500，即《跟单信用证统一惯例》国际商会第 500 号出版物，英文全称为 Uniform Customs and Practice of Documentary Credit，ICC Publication No. 500，1993 revision. 该惯例最早是由国际商会在 1933 年颁布的，目的是制定一套能够约束信用证有关当事人并能为各方共同遵守的统一、明确的规则，同时也为从事国际结算的银行和国际贸易的相关人士提供处理实际业务和解决有关纠纷案例的重要依据。

accordance with its General Conditions of Sales attached hereto (**Appendix C**). Any product warranty claim must be communicated in writing no later than thirty（30）days after receipt of such Products. This warranty constitutes the Supplier's sole warranty in respect of the Products supplied hereunder.

9.1 供货商保证，按照本协议附件 C "一般销售条件"，向经销商供应的指定商品不存在材料或者工艺上的瑕疵。对于产品质量的任何索赔，应在收到该等产品后 30 天内以书面方式进行沟通。本保证构成供货商对于按照本协议提供指定商品的唯一保证。[①]

9.2 It is agreed that the Distributor shall only return any defective Products after the prior written authorization by the Supplier. The Parties undertake to make all necessary efforts to solve any controversy in good faith and mutual agreement.

9.2 双方同意，经销商在供货商事先书面授权的情况下，方可退还任何瑕疵产品。[②] 双方保证，本着诚意和互相同意的方式，采取一切必要的努力解决任何争议。

ARTICLE 10 USE OF TRADEMARKS
第 10 条 指定商标的使用[③]

10.1 The granting of the right to use the Trademarks to the Distributor hereunder shall，subject to Article 12 hereof，include the right to use the Trademarks in respect of the promotion and sale of Products in the Territory. The Distributor shall at all times supervise the use of the Trademarks in the Territory to ensure compliance with this Agreement and appropriate use thereof that promotes and maintains the goodwill and reputation in the Territory attaching to the Products and the Trademarks. Furthermore, the Distributor shall ensure that use of the Trademarks is consistent with the marketing，image promotion，distribution and public relations programs and plans as defined from time to time by the Supplier.

10.1 授权经销商使用指定商标，应受到本协议第 12 条的约束，包括在指定地域内推销和销售指定商品时使用指定商标的权利。经销商应始终监督在指定地域内指定商标的使用，以确保符合本协议的约定以及适当使用，在指定地域内推广和维护附属于指定商品和指定商标的商誉和名誉。此外，经销商应确保指定商标的使用符合供货商所不时指定

---

① 因本协议系供货商的律师所起草，故尽量将供货商对产品质量的保证范围进行较窄的限定；如果规定的过于宽泛，会增加供货商的责任和风险。

② 此处明确约定经销商在供货商事先书面授权的情况下方可退还瑕疵产品，是为了避免经销商单方面任意退货，增加供货商的商业风险和损失。

③ 因本协议中的指定商品系国际知名品牌时装，指定商标的正当使用及其保护对指定商品的销售具有重要意义，故此在协议中作出较详细的约定。

的市场推广、形象推广、分销和公共关系的项目和计划。

10.2 The Distributor hereby acknowledges that the title to and/or the right to use the Trademarks vests solely in the Supplier as the Trademark owner and the Distributor shall not contest the ownership or validity of the Trademarks. Upon termination or expiration of this Agreement，the right to use the Trademarks granted by the Supplier to the Distributor shall be terminated and all such rights shall revert to the Supplier unconditionally and without any consideration and the Distributor agrees thereupon to discontinue use of the Trademarks.

10.2 经销商在此承认，供货商作为指定商标的所有人，对指定商标拥有唯一的所有权以及/或使用权，经销商不得对指定商标的所有权或有效性提出异议。在本协议解除或者期满时，供货商授予经销商的指定商标使用权亦随即终止，所有该等权利将无条件地、无需任何对价地回归供货商，经销商同意不再继续使用指定商标。

ARTICLE 11 MINIMUM PURCHASE REQUIREMENTS
第 11 条 最低购货条件①

11.1 In consideration of the exclusive rights granted to the Distributor hereunder，the Distributor agrees to purchase certain minimum annual volumes of Products（**"Minimum Purchase Amounts"**）during the term，as follows：

(a) In the first five years of the Agreement，the Distributor shall purchase from the Supplier each relevant year no less than （金额）；

(b) In the 6th through 10th years of the Agreement，new Minimum Purchase Amounts shall be agreed in good faith between the Supplier and the Distributor no later than June 30，（年份）. Should the Supplier and the Distributor be unable to find an agreement，the Parties shall have the option to terminate this Agreement by providing written notice of six months. In this case，the minimum purchase guarantee provided under Clause 11.3 during such six months after the service of the notice shall apply.

11.1 作为授予经销商本协议项下独家权利的对价，经销商同意，在本协议期限内每年购买指定商品的最低金额（**"最低购货金额"**）如下：

(a) 在本协议的前五年，经销商每一年应从供货商处购买的指定商品金额不少于_____（金额）；

(b) 在本协议的第六至第十年，新的最低购货金额由供货商和经销商在_____年 6 月 30 日前诚意协商确定。如果经销商和供货商

---

① 在独占性经销协议中，由于供货商在指定地域内只能指定一家经销商销售指定商品，故通常都规定经销商对指定商品的最低购货量，以便保障供货商的最低商业利益。在作者的律师业务中，曾处理过外国供货商与香港经销商的独家经销协议中没有约定最低购货条件，而经销商因市场原因购销指定商品数量甚少，外国供货商欲向经销商索赔而无合同依据的案例。

未能达成新的协议，各方有权提前 6 个月发出书面通知解除本协议。在此种情形下，在通知送达后的该 6 个月期间内，适用第 11.3 条规定的最低购货保证。

11.2 In this Article，the "**purchase amounts**" shall be invoice amounts exclusive of any shipping costs，taxes or other such costs of acquisition.

11.2 在本条款中，"**购货金额**"是指不包括任何运输成本、税款或其他购置成本的发票金额。

11.3 In the event the Distributor fails to achieve 80％ of the Minimum Purchase Amounts for any year or 90％ for any two consecutive years，the Supplier may elect to terminate this Agreement by providing written notice of one year. During such year after notice is provided，both Parties shall continue to fulfil their obligations under this Agreement. If in such year the purchases by the Distributor in any seasonal order decreases more than 10％ compared to the same seasonal order one year earlier，the Supplier shall have the right to accelerate the termination by providing 30-days written notice. Should the Supplier elect not to terminate the Agreement pursuant to the foregoing，the Distributor shall pay to the Supplier an amount corresponding to the 30％ of the difference between the Minimum Purchase Amount and the actual amount invoiced by the Supplier to the Distributor during the relevant year within 30 days of the issuing by the Supplier of the latest invoice of such year.

11.3 如果经销商在任何年度没有达到最低购货金额的80％，或者连续两个年度没有达到最低购货金额的90％，供货商可以选择提前一年以书面通知解除本协议。在通知发出后的该一年期间内，双方均应继续履行本协议项下的各自义务。如果在该一年期间内，经销商在任何一个季节订单的购货金额和前一年度相同季节订单相比减少超过10％，则供货商有权提前 30 天书面通知解除本协议。如果供货商选择不按前述规定提前解除本协议，经销商应在该年度供货商开具最后一次发票后的 30 日内，向供货商支付相当于最低购货金额与供货商向经销商开具的实际发票金额之间差额的 30％金额。

ARTICLE 12　INTELLECTUAL PROPERTY RIGHTS
第 12 条　知识产权①

12.1 The Distributor acknowledges that any and all trademarks，trade names，designs，inventions and other intellectual property rights，including the Trademarks，used in connection with or embodied in

---

① 如前所述，因本协议中的指定商品系国际知名品牌时装，本条中对指定商品知识产权的权属、使用、保护以及侵权处理等事项，均作了较详细的规定。倘若作为合同标的物的商品并非属于知名品牌或知识产权保护在合同中不占重要地位，律师可以在合同中对知识产权条款作比较简要的约定。

the Products are and shall remain the sole property of the Supplier, and the Supplier shall not in any way be challenged or disputed by the Distributor. In the event that the Distributor becomes aware that such intellectual property rights of the Supplier are claimed or infringed upon by a third party, the Distributor shall promptly inform the Supplier thereof and, in the event that the Supplier decides to take any action in respect thereof, shall render reasonable assistance to the Supplier to enable the protection of such rights.

12.1　经销商确认，用于指定商品或指定商品所包含的任何及全部商标、商品名称、外观设计、发明和其他知识产权，包括指定商标，均属于供货商的专有财产，经销商不得以任何方式对该等知识产权提出质疑或争议。如果经销商获悉供货商的该等知识产权被第三方索赔或侵权，经销商应立即通知供货商，在此种情形下，由供货商决定为此采取何种行动，经销商应向供货商提供合理的协助以保护该等知识产权。

12.2　The Distributor may use the Trademarks only in connection with the sale and promotion of Products in the Territory but shall ensure that such Products clearly identify the Supplier as the owner of such Trademarks. In the event that the Distributor makes materials bearing the Trademarks or related trade name for the purpose of advertising or promotion of the Products or otherwise, the Distributor shall submit to the Supplier copies thereof and obtain advance approval in respect of the same. The Distributor shall not use any other trademark or trade name in connection with the marketing, promotion or sale of the Products.

12.2　经销商仅在指定地域内销售和推广指定商品时方可使用指定商标，同时须确保指定商品本身清晰地表明供货商为指定商标的所有者。如果经销商在为指定商品做广告、促销或在其他方面需要使材料带有指定商标或者相关的商品名，经销商应向供货商提交该等材料的复印件并为此事先取得供货商的批准。经销商不得将任何其他商标或商品名用于指定商品的市场推广、促销或销售。

12.3　It is agreed that, upon termination of this Agreement, the right of the Distributor to use the Trademarks and any other of the abovementioned intellectual property rights shall be terminated and all such rights shall thereupon revert to the Supplier unconditionally and without consideration and the Distributor shall discontinue the use thereof.

12.3　双方同意，在本协议解除时，经销商使用指定商标和上述其他知识产权的权利也随之终止，所有这些权利应无条件地无偿返还给供货商，经销商不得继续使用上述知识产权。

12.4　The Supplier shall bear no liability whatsoever for any alleged infringement or suit with regard to intellectual property rights of a third party which may arise in connection with the sale of the Products by the

Distributor conducted in compliance with this Agreement. In the event that such a claim or suit is made against the Distributor，the Supplier shall be promptly notified thereof，and the Supplier shall furnish the Distributor with such evidence and information available to the Supplier as reasonably requested by the Distributor to assist the Distributor in defending such claim. The Distributor shall bear the legal cost involved in defending the claim.

12.4　对于经销商按照本协议规定销售指定商品所发生的第三方声称的知识产权侵权或者诉讼，供货商不承担任何责任。如果此种索赔或者诉讼是针对经销商而提起，经销商应立即通知供货商；在经销商提出合理要求时，供货商应尽可能向经销商提供相关证据和信息，以协助经销商对该索赔进行抗辩。经销商应承担对该索赔进行抗辩所发生的相关法律费用。

ARTICLE 13　CONFIDENTIALITY
第 13 条　保密

All confidential information of the Parties furnished to each other in connection with this Agreement shall be kept in strictest confidence，shall not be disclosed to any third party and shall be used only for the purpose for which it was originally received. In the event of necessity to disclose such confidential information to its employees, the Parties shall take every procedure reasonably required to cause such employees to keep the information in confidence.

双方均应对与本协议有关而提交给对方的保密信息严格保密，不得向任何第三方披露，而仅用于其接受保密信息的本来目的。如果有必要向其雇员披露保密信息，双方应采取全部必要的合理措施，使接受该等信息的雇员对此保密。

ARTICLE 14　PROMOTION AND ADVERTISING
第 14 条　促销和广告推广①

14.1　For the purpose of general advertising and sale promotion activities，the Parties agree as follows：

(a) The Distributor shall spend HK＄3 million per annum for the first three years of validity of the present Agreement. Starting from the 4th year and for the subsequent years of validity of the present Agreement, the Distributor shall spend, each commercial season, 6% of the seasonal sell-in regularly

---

①　在独家经销合同中，通常就经销商对于促销推广指定商品的义务作出约定，这对于在指定地域内迅速开拓并占领相关市场具有极为重要的意义。而且在多数情况下，由经销商全部负担宣传推广的费用，这也是供货商授予经销商独家经销权的条件之一。在本协议中，指定商品系新打入指定地域的商品，供货商为了使指定产品迅速占领当地市场，同意与经销商分担宣传推广费用。

confirmed and delivered by the Supplier.

(b) The Supplier shall contribute by reimbursing to the Distributor, pursuant to the terms set forth in Article 14.3, in the amount of 50% of the overall amount spent by the Distributor. More precisely, the Supplier's contribution shall be as follows:

(i) HK $ 1.5 million per annum, during the first three years of validity of the present Agreement;

(ii) starting from the 4th year and for the subsequent years of validity of the present Agreement, 50% of the amount spent by the Distributor up to a maximum of 3% of the seasonal sell-in regularly confirmed and delivered to the Distributor.

14.1 为了进行一般广告推广和促销活动，双方同意如下：

(a) 在本协议现行有效期的头三年，经销商应每年花费 300 万元港币用于广告和促销活动。在本协议现行有效期的第四年和随后的年度，经销商应将每个商业季节由供货商定期确认的季节批发和交货的 6% 用于广告和促销活动。

(b) 供货商根据第 14.3 条约定的条件向经销商偿付其总花费数额的 50%，更确切地说，供货商的偿付具体如下：

(i) 在本协议现行有效期内的头三年，每年 150 万元港币；

(ii) 在本协议现行有效期内的第四年和随后年度，经销商花费的 50%，最多达到定期确认的季节批发以及向经销商交货的 3%。

14.2 For the purpose of organizing promotional and exceptional events, such as fashion shows, opening events, celebrations, the Parties agree as follows:

(a) The Distributor shall spend HK $ 2 million per annum for the first five years of validity of the present Agreement;

(b) The Supplier shall contribute by reimbursing to the Distributor, pursuant to the terms set forth in Article 14.3, the amount of HK $ 2 million per annum for the first five years of validity of the present Agreement.

14.2 对于有组织的推广和特别活动，例如时装表演、开幕仪式、庆祝活动等，双方同意如下：

(a) 在本协议现行有效期的头五年，经销商每年的花费为 200 万元港币；

(b) 在本协议现行有效期的头五年，供货商根据第 14.3 条约定的条件，每年偿付给经销商 200 万元港币。

14.3 It is understood that in the event that the Parties mutually agree to reduce the advertising expenditures for any year during the term of this Agreement, each Party's contribution shall be reduced proportionally.

14.3 各方知悉，在本协议有效期内，如果双方均同意减少任一年度的广告开支，每一方的开支按比例减少。

14.4 With regard to the obligations set forth in Articles 14.1 and 14.2 above, the Parties agree that:

(a) the Supplier shall organize institutional advertising (i.e. CD-ROM, catalogues, posters, etc.) and bear the entire costs;

(b) the Distributor shall organize local advertising. In this regard, the Distributor shall submit to the approval of the Supplier a seasonal plan for all the advertising initiatives to be made in each commercial season, i.e.:

(i) on or before November 30th for any and all initiatives relating to the subsequent Spring/Summer seasons;

(ii) on or before May 31st for any and all initiatives relating to the subsequent Autumn/Winter seasons.

(c) the Supplier shall approve in writing the above initiatives in full or partially on or before December 31 for the Spring/Summer seasons and June 30 for the Autumn/Winter seasons.

(d) the Distributor shall issue and send to the Supplier the invoice/s for the sum of money approved by the Supplier and which is payable by the Supplier to the Distributor according to the allocation of expenses set forth in Article 14.2 hereof provided that the Distributor has supplied the Supplier evidence of the aforementioned advertising activity and pertaining expenditure, such as relevant invoices, on or before:

(i) May 15 for the Spring/Summer commercial season in course;

(ii) November 15 for the Autumn/Winter commercial season in course.

(e) No promotional activities relating to the Products, the Trademark or the boutique (s) shall be implemented by the Distributor until and unless written approval has been obtained from the Supplier.

14.4 关于上述第 14.1 条和第 14.2 条约定的义务，双方同意：

(a) 供货商应组织建立永久声誉的广告（如光盘、目录、海报等），并承担全部费用。

(b) 经销商负责组织当地广告。在此方面，经销商应就每个商业季节全部广告活动的季节计划取得供货商的同意，具体如下：

(i) 在 11 月 30 日或之前，制订出下一个春夏季节的全部计划；

(ii) 在 5 月 31 日或之前，制订出下一个秋冬季节的全部计划。

(c) 供货商应在 12 月 31 日或之前以书面方式全部或者部分批准上述春夏季节计划，在 6 月 30 日之前全部或者部分批准秋冬季节计划。

(d) 在经销商已经于下述日期或之前向供货商提供上述广告活动以及相关开支的凭证（例如发票）之条件下，经销商应向供货商开具并发送经供货商认可款项的发票，供货商应根据本协议第 14.2

条约定的分摊方式向经销商支付相应费用：

(i) 春夏商业季节：5 月 15 日；

(ii) 秋冬商业季节：11 月 15 日。

(e) 除非已经取得供货商的书面认可，经销商不得进行有关指定商品、指定商标或者精品店的促销活动。

14.5 In addition, the Distributor shall be at its discretion to provide rental support to the boutiques by means of a subsidy to the maximum amount of US \$ 1.00 per square meter per shop per day, provided that such support is granted to a maximum of five (5) premium location shops.

14.5 此外，经销商可以自主决定向精品店提供租金支持，支持方式采用每家店铺每天每平方米最多补助 1 美元的方式，但这种补助最多只能给予 5 家优质地段店铺。

14.6 The Supplier shall have the exclusive control of the overall image of the Products and the Trademarks as marketed, offered and presented in the Territory. In particular, any activities of the Distributor which could reflect directly or indirectly on the image and public perception of the Products and the Trademarks shall be submitted for the prior approval of the Supplier. The foregoing shall apply, without limitation, to the following: image of points-of-sale, "corners", "shops-in-shops" (location and the Trademarks display); furnishing and decoration of points-of-sale, "corners", "shops-in-shops"; visual merchandising; institutional pictures; press releases and promotional news reports.

14.6 供货商有权独自控制在指定地域内所销售、提供与展示的指定商品和指定商标的整体形象。特别是经销商可能直接或者间接地影响指定商品和指定商标的形象和公众观感的任何活动，均应取得供货商的事先批准。上述活动包括但不限于：销售点、"售货角"或"店中店"（位置和指定商标所展示）的形象、装修和装饰；视觉营销、企业形象图片、新闻发布以及促销新闻报道。

ARTICLE 15   RETAIL PRICES

第 15 条   零售价格

The Distributor shall suggest the correct retail price of the Products to its Customers in the Territory. The Distributor shall communicate to the Supplier the retail price list no later than three (3) days prior to the beginning of the relevant season's sales campaign. The Distributor undertakes to monitor compliance with the retail price by its Customers.

经销商应在指定地域内向其顾客提示指定商品的正确零售价格。经销商应在不迟于开始相关季节的销售活动 3 天前就指定商品的零售价格表与供货商进行沟通。经销商保证监督其客户实施相同的零售价格。

ARTICLE 16　TERM

第 16 条　合同期限

Unless earlier terminated in accordance with the provisions hereof，this Agreement shall be effective as of the date of its execution and shall remain in force up to *（年月日）* . This Agreement shall not be automatically renewed without the Parties' express consent. Notwithstanding the foregoing, either Party may terminate this Agreement as to any or all of the Products，by giving the other Party 6（six）months written notice to terminate with respect to such Products. During such period after notice is provided，both Parties shall continue to fulfil their obligations under this Agreement.

除非本协议按其条款提前解除，本协议自签署之日起生效，有效期至＿＿＿＿年＿＿＿＿月＿＿＿＿为止。除非经双方明示同意，本协议不得自动续期。尽管有前述规定，任何一方就指定商品的任何部分或全部，可以提前 6 个月向对方发出书面通知，就该等指定商品解除本协议。在发出通知之后的期间，双方均应继续履行其在本协议项下的各自义务。

ARTICLE 17　TERMINATION

第 17 条　协议的解除

17.1　Either Party hereto may terminate this Agreement forthwith by notice in writing upon the happening of any one or more of the following events with respect to the other Party：

（a）Insolvency，bankruptcy or going into administration or any likely insolvency proceedings；

（b）Assignment for the benefit of creditors；

（c）Attachment of assets so as to materially impair the business of the affected Party；

（d）Expropriation of business assets so as to materially impair the business of the affected Party；

（e）Dissolution or liquidation；

（f）Appointment of a trustee or receiver for all or any part of assets；

（g）The other Party commits any breach of the provisions of this Agreement and，in the case of a breach capable of remedy，fails to remedy the same within thirty（30）days after receipt of a written notice requiring it to be remedied.

17.1　任何一方如发生下列情形之一的，另一方可以书面通知立即解除本协议：

（a）资不抵债、破产、被接管或任何类似破产程序；

（b）为债权人利益的转让；

（c）资产被扣押，以致严重损害受影响一方的业务；

（d）企业资产被征收，以致严重损害受影响一方的业务；

（e）解散或清算；

（f）委任全部或部分财产的托管人或接管人；

（g）一方违反本协议的规定，在能够就违约采取补救措施的情况下，收到要求采取补救措施的书面通知后 30 天内，没有采取补救措施。

17.2 The Supplier shall be entitled to terminate this Agreement upon delivery of written notice, which shall have effect from the moment it is received by the Distributor, in the following cases:

(a) major changes in the Distributor's company structure involving new ownership or control which is not initiated by the Supplier;

(b) the Distributor or the Distributor's shareholders acquiring inte-rests or shareholdings, either directly or indirectly, in companies or entities which compete with the Supplier in respect of its products as are more particularly set out in Appendix D.

17.2 在下列情形下，供货商有权发出书面通知解除本协议，解约通知在经销商收到时立即生效①：

(a) 经销商的公司架构发生重大变更，事关供货商不予接纳的新所有权或控制权；

(b) 经销商或其股东直接或者间接收购的公司或实体的权益或股权，就本协议附件 D 所详列商品与供货商存在竞争关系。

ARTICLE 18　DISTRIBUTOR GUARANTEE
第 18 条　经销商的保证

The Distributor hereby guarantees to the Supplier the performance by the Distributor as well as by any of its sub-distributors (to the extent within its power and control) of the Products of all the duties and obligations imposed upon the Distributor by this Agreement in relation to the Products. ②

经销商在此向供货商保证，经销商以及（在其权力和控制范围内）的任何下级经销商履行本协议项下经销商对指定商品的全部责任和义务。

ARTICLE 19　MUTUAL INDEMNIFICATION
第 19 条　互相赔偿

19.1 Neither the Supplier or the Distributor is an agent of the other, and neither Party shall hold itself out or act as such nor shall the Distributor assume or create any obligations or liability expressed or implied on behalf of the Supplier, nor bind the Supplier in any manner whatsoever except as provided herein. Each Party shall indemnify and hold harmless the other Party against any liability arising from breach of any representation or warranty made in this Agreement.

---

① 通常，合同的各方当事人是基于对彼此的了解并相信对方能够完成交易才签约的，彼此了解的方面也包括对方的组织结构、股权关系或控制权等。如果在签约后这些方面发生重大变更，有可能影响到该方的履约能力，甚至与另一方形成竞争关系。因此，有必要作出类似本协议第 17.2 条的约定，赋予供货商相应的解约权。

② 在独家经销协议中，供货商通常会同意经销商授权下级经销商分销指定商品，因而需要经销商保证下级经销商遵守本协议的约定。（对比：在非独家经销协议中，供货商通常不允许经销商再授权下级经销商分销指定商品，详见本章第 4 节。）

19.1 经销商或供货商均不是对方的代理人；任何一方不得自称或代表对方；经销商也不得代表供货商承担或者设立任何明示或者默示的义务；除了本协议中另有明确规定外，不在任何方面对供货商具有约束力。倘若任何一方违反本协议中的陈述或保证，应对另一方作出赔偿或者确保其不受损害。

19.2 This Agreement shall not constitute the Supplier and the Distributor as partners, joint venturers, or principal and agent. The legal relationship of all the Parties shall be that of independent contractors. No Party shall be entitled to obligate or bind any other Party to a third party in any respect.

19.2 本协议并不在供货商和经销商之间建立合伙、合营或者代理关系。双方之间是独立的合同缔结者的法律关系。任何一方均无权在任何方面为另一方建立对于第三方的义务或者责任。

ARTICLE 20　EVENTS UPON TERMINATION
第 20 条　协议终止时的处理

Upon termination of this Agreement by either Party as provided herein, or upon expiration of the Agreement:

(a) Any indebtedness of either Party to the other Party not already due shall become immediately due and payable as of the effective date of termination or expiration of this Agreement. In no event shall any Party be liable for any debts of any other Party to its Customers or other creditors.

(b) The Supplier may, at its option, repurchase or provide for transfer of any and all of the Products at the original prices in the Price List and all marketing and point-of-sale material for the Products then owned by the Distributor. Should the Supplier not exercise the option to repurchase or provide for transfer of any and all of the Products, the Distributor may sell all remaining Products for a period of six (6) months from termination or expiration hereof.

(c) Except for termination for cause, neither Party shall have any further obligation or liability to the other, other than the obligations set forth in this Article 20.

在任何一方按照本协议约定解除本协议或本协议因期满而终止时：

(a) 在本协议解除或期满的生效日，任何一方对于另一方的未到期债务均视为到期，并应立即支付。在任何情况下，任何一方对于另一方向其客户或其他债权人的债务不负任何责任。

(b) 供货商可以选择回购或安排转让全部或部分指定商品，其价格为价格表原价加上经销商届时拥有的指定商品之全部推广和销售点材料的费用。如果供货商没有行使回购或安排转让全部或部分指定商品的选择权，经销商可以在本协议解除或者期满后 6 个月内销售剩余的指定商品。①

---

① 需要注意的是，在合同期满或提前解除时，如果供货商选择不回购或转让指定商品，给予经销商销售剩余商品的时期不宜过长，以免影响供货商在该区域内授权其他经销商或自行销售指定商品。

（c）除非有理由解除本协议，任何一方对于另一方均没有本协议第 20 条规定义务以外的任何其他义务或责任。

ARTICLE 21　·NOTICES

第 21 条　通知

21.1　All notices, requests, demands or other communications under this Agreement between the Supplier and the Distributor shall be given in writing and in the English language and shall be deemed to have been duly given or made via facsimile, when a facsimile message is sent and receipt thereof confirmed by electronic means; and, in the case of courier, when delivery thereof is confirmed in writing.

21.1　供货商和经销商之间在本协议项下的全部通知、要求、催促或其他联络均应采用书面形式，以英文进行。如果用传真方式发送，当传真信息被发送并以电子手段确认接收时，则视为已被送达；如果用快递方式发送，当以书面方式确认投递时，则视为已被适当送达。

21.2　All notices required under this Agreement and other communications affecting the interest of any Party shall be addressed as follows：

To the Supplier：

ABC CO., LTD. ,

Address：

Fax：

To the Distributor：

XYZ CO., LTD.

Address：

Fax：

21.2　本协议所要求的全部通知以及影响任何一方利益的其他联络，均应发送到下列地址：

致供货商：

ABC 有限公司

地址：

传真：

致经销商：

XYZ 有限公司

地址：

传真：

ARTICLE 22　ASSIGNMENT

第 22 条　本协议的转让

This Agreement shall not be assigned by either of the Parties to any third party without the prior written consent of the other Party hereto.

没有对方当事人的事先书面同意，任何一方均不得将本协议转让给任何第三方。

ARTICLE 23　NON-WAIVER
第 23 条　不弃权

No omission or delay on the part of any Party hereto in requiring a due and punctual fulfillment of the obligation by the other Party hereunder shall be deemed to constitute a waiver by the omitting or delaying Party of any of its rights to require such due and punctual fulfillment of the obligation and of any other obligations of the said other Party，or a waiver of any remedy it might have hereunder.

任何一方没有要求或迟延要求对方适当及按时履行其在本协议项下的义务，不能视为构成没有要求或迟延要求的一方放弃其要求对方适当及按时履行该义务以及任何其他义务的权利，也不得视为其放弃本协议项下可采取的任何补救措施的权利。

ARTICLE 24　FORCE MAJEURE
第 24 条　不可抗力

No Party shall be liable in respect of failure of performance of its obligations hereunder if occasioned by act of God，war（declared or undeclared），fire，flood，epidemics，interruption or shortage of transportation，embargo，accident，explosion，inability to produce or shortage of supply of materials，equipment，or production facilities，prohibition on import or export，government orders，regulations，rationing，or strike，lockout，or other labor troubles interfering with the transportation of the Products，or with the supply of raw materials entering into their production，or any other cause beyond the control of the Party. ①

因天灾、战争（宣战或未宣战）、火灾、洪水、瘟疫、交通中断或运输工具短缺、贸易禁运、意外事件、爆炸而引起材料、设备或生产设施的无法制造或者供应短缺、进出口禁令、政府指令、管制、定量配给，或者罢工、封锁或其他劳工纠纷妨碍指定商品的交通运输或其生产所用原材料的供给，或者一方当事人无法控制的其他事由发生时，任何一方均不承担其未履行本协议义务的违约责任。

ARTICLE 25　ARBITRATION
第 25 条　仲裁

All disputes，controversies or differences which may arise between the Parties，out of or in relation to or in connection with this Agreement，or its breach，formation，termination or nullity shall be settled through bona fide negotiations between the Parties. In the event such negotiations fail to yield any satisfactory settlement of the foregoing disputes，the Parties may require

---

① 本协议中的不可抗力范围相当广泛，这是因为供货商在交易中如因不可预料、不可避免或不可控制的不可抗力事件影响其按时生产及交货给经销商，则有可能构成违约；为防止和避免这种风险，在本协议中将不可抗力作广泛的约定，对供货商是比较有利的。

the final adjudication through binding arbitration under the UNCITRAL Rules of Arbitration and Conciliation by one or more arbitrators appointed in accordance with these rules. The arbitration proceedings shall be conducted in English and shall take place in Milano（Italy）. The award rendered by the arbitrator（s）shall be final and binding on the Parties and enforceable in any court of competent jurisdiction. ①

双方之间可能发生的因本协议引起、与本协议有关的违约、合同的成立、解除或无效有关的所有争议、争执或分歧，均应通过双方的友好协商解决。如果通过协商不能就前述争议达成满意的解决方案，双方可根据联合国国际贸易法委员会的仲裁和调解规则，通过有拘束力的仲裁裁决最终解决争议，根据该规则可以委任一名或多名仲裁员。仲裁程序采用英语进行，仲裁地点为米兰（意大利）。仲裁员作出的裁决是终局性的，对双方均有约束力，在有管辖权的任何法院可以强制执行。

ARTICLE 26   GOVERNING LAW
第 26 条   适用法律

Unless otherwise specifically provided herein, this Agreement shall be governed as to all matters, including validity, construction and performance, by and under the laws of Italy.

除非本协议中另有其他明确约定，本协议的所有事项（包括有效性、解释和履行）均适用意大利国法律。

ARTICLE 27   ENTIRE AGREEMENT
第 27 条   协议的完整性

This Agreement constitutes the entire agreement between the Parties and supersedes all previous agreements, whether oral or written, between them with respect to the subject matter hereof. No amendment, change, addition or deletion regarding the terms and conditions hereof shall be effective or binding on either of the Parties unless reduced to writing and executed by each of the Parties.

本协议构成双方之间的完整协议，取代此前双方就本协议标的所订立的全部协议（无论是口头的或者书面的协议）。除非双方签订书面协议，对本协议条款和条件的任何修改、变更、增加或删减对任何一方均不具有效力或约束力。

IN WITNESS WHEREOF the Supplier and the shareholder of the Distributor have signed this Agreement on the day and year first set forth above in two original copies, each one consisting of（页数）pages including the Appendices to be retained by each Party. This Agreement however will be

---

①   本协议的供货商公司总部设在意大利米兰，其在本交易中的地位比较强势，故双方同意仲裁地点设在意大利米兰；第 26 条约定本协议适用意大利国法律。

final and binding upon the Parties when each original copy is executed by the Distributor upon its incorporation as provided herein.

兹证明，供货商和经销商的股东已经于本协议开头所述日期签署了本协议，每份包含附件在内共有_____页，一式两份，每一方各持一份。一旦经销商按本协议约定设立后，即签署本协议的每一份原件①，本协议即对双方具有最终约束力。

ABC CO. , LTD.

XYZ HK CO. , LTD.
(AS Shareholder of XYZ CO. , LTD.)

_____

_____

By：

By：

Title：

Title：

ABC 有限公司

XYZ 香港有限公司
(作为 XYZ 有限公司的股东)

_____

_____

签署人：

签署人：

职务：

职务：

APPENDICES
附 件

Appendix A：Business Plan
附件 A：商业计划书

Appendix B：List of Products and Trademarks
附件 B：指定商品和指定商标的清单

Appendix C：General Conditions of Sale
附件 C：一般销售条件

Appendix D：Particulars of Competing Products
附件 D：竞争商品的明细

---

① 在本协议起草时，经销商公司尚未设立，系由其股东与供货方共同起草并签署本协议，因此本处作此约定。在商务实践中，有时合同一方当事人的股东与另一方之间先就合同内容达成一致后，才为履行该合同而设立合同该方当事人。

▓ 第4节 非独家经销协议（NON-EXCLUSIVE DISTRIBUTORSHIP AGREEMENT）精选与解读__

NON-EXCLUSIVE DISTRIBUTORSHIP AGREEMENT[①]
非独家经销协议

Agreement Serial No.：

协议编号：

Agreement Date：

签约日期：

Party A：

Registered Office：

Fax No.：

甲方：

注册地址：

传真号码：

Party B：

Registered Office：

Fax No.：

乙方：

注册地址：

传真号码：

On the principles of mutually beneficial arrangements, trust and for the growth and development of both Parties hereto, the Parties have engaged in friendly negotiations for Party A to appoint Party B for distributing and developing the commercial market for the products, the details of which are set forth in Schedule 1 hereof（hereinafter referred to as the **"Products"**）, and agreed as set forth below：

甲乙双方本着互利、诚信、共同发展的原则，经过友好协商，就甲方授权乙方经销及宣传推广本协议附件1详列的甲方产品（以下简称**"本产品"**）事宜，达成如下协议：

1. Appointment of Distributor

第1条　委任经销商

During the term of this Agreement, Party A hereby appoint Party B as the

---

① 本协议的背景：甲方（供货商）的母公司系外国知名电子产品生产厂商，甲方公司是其母公司在香港设立的贸易公司。本协议系非独家经销协议，甲方可以在指定地域内向乙方以外的多家经销商销售指定产品。本协议文本系甲方（供货商）委托律师所起草，侧重于保护供货商的权益。

authorized non-exclusive distributor of the Products in the designated territory（hereinafter referred to as the **"Territory"**, and more particularly defined in Clause 3 below）for the distribution of the Products in accordance with the terms and conditions of this Agreement as set forth herein. Party A may, at its absolute discretion, to appoint one or more distributor（s）within the Territory any time as it sees fit. [①]

甲方在此授权乙方作为非独家经销商在本协议有效期限内根据本协议规定的条款和条件，在指定区域内（详见本协议第 3 条，以下简称 **"指定地域"**）经销本产品。甲方有绝对的酌情权在其认为合适的任何时间授权其他经销商在指定地域内经销本产品。

2. Party B's Customers

第 2 条　乙方的客户

Party B may, within the Territory, promote and develop new customers for the Products, except the customers which are considered as the Party A's customers at any time.

除在任何时候被认为是甲方的客户以外，乙方可在指定地域内就本产品进行推广并发展新客户。

3. Designated Sales Territory

第 3 条　指定的销售地域

The designed sales Territory that Party B may promote and distribute the Products is limited to the geographical Territory falling within _____ .

乙方可以推广和经销本产品的指定销售地域限于_____地理区域内。

4. Trademark

第 4 条　商标

The trademark "*（商标名）*"（hereinafter referred to as the **"Trademark"**）used in the Products has been registered by *（甲方母公司名称）*, the parent company of Party A. The parent company of Party A shall obtain the valid registration of the Trademark and its effective renewals and provide Party B with the copies of the registration documents（including application documents）as attached in Schedule 2（copy of the Notice of Application Acceptance of the Trademark Registration）. [②]

本产品使用甲方的母公司（*甲方母公司名称*）申请注册的 "*（商标名）*" 商标（以下简称 **"该商标"**），甲方母公司应获得该商标的有效注册及其有效期续展，并向乙方提供该商标的注册证明文件（包括注册申请文件）的复印件（详见本协议附件 2：该商标注册申请受理通知书的影印件）。

---

① 由于经销商在指定地域不具有强大的销售网络，或经销商不愿意承诺最低购货数额，或销售地域较为广阔，供货商不宜授权经销商独家经销产品。在这些情况下，供货商选择与经销商签订非独家经销合同更加合适。

② 供货商的母公司对该商标拥有所有权，在本协议签订时，该商标在指定地域的注册申请已经被受理，尚未完成注册程序，故供货商仅能提供该商标注册申请受理通知书的影印件。

5. Price and Payment of the Products

第 5 条　本产品的经销价格及付款方式

5.1　The prices of the Products are set forth in Schedule 3 （The Prices of the Products） hereof. The prices of the Products may be adjusted or altered upon the mutual agreement of the Parties.

5.1　本产品的价格详见本协议附件 3（本产品价格表）。经甲乙双方协商同意，可以修改或变更本产品的价格表。

5.2　Party A and Party B agree that the prices listed in Schedule 3 shall be principally fixed. Where there is a relatively great change in the market situation and a Party requests to adjust the prices，the requesting Party shall consult the other Party and execute a written supplemental agreement for the confirmation of the changed prices of the Products. If no agreement can be reached by the Parties，the prices shall be the original prices set forth hereunder.

5.2　甲乙双方同意，附件 3 的价格表基本上不变。如果市场行情发生较大变动，一方要求变更本产品的价格时，须与另一方协商并签订书面的补充协议以确定变更后的本产品价格。如果双方未能达成一致协议，则按照本协议的原定价格表执行。

5.3　Party A and Party B agree that the payment of the Products shall be made as follows：

Party A shall issue an invoice to Party B at the beginning of each month for the Products of the preceding month. Party B shall pay to Party A the invoiced amount within the month when the relevant invoice is received. Where Party B does not agree with such invoice，the parties shall promptly verify the same together and confirm the difference with each other. Party A shall reconcile the difference in the next invoice and Party B shall confirm Party A's adjustment in writing.

5.3　甲乙双方同意，本产品的付款方式如下：

甲方应于每月初向乙方发出上个月货款的发票，乙方应在收到发票之月内支付甲方货款金额；乙方如有异议，双方应及时共同核对并确认，对货款差额，甲方须在下次发票中予以调整，乙方应对甲方的调整予以书面确认。

6. Quality Standards and Warranties

第 6 条　质量标准和保证

6.1　Party A hereby warrants that the Products comply with the quality requirements under ISO _____ in relation to the standards thereof.

6.1　甲方保证所提供的本产品质量符合 ISO _____相关标准中规定的质量要求。

6.2　The warranty period of the Products shall be one （1） year commencing from the date the Products are delivered to Party B.

6.2　本产品的质量保证期自本产品交付给乙方之日起为期壹年。

6.3　Party B agrees not to modify, or otherwise reassemble or re-package the Products in any means without first receiving written approval from Party A. ①

6.3 乙方同意，在未获得甲方事先书面同意之前，不得对本产品以任何方式进行变更或者重新装配或重新包装。

6.4 Where there is any quality problem in any of the Products that causes the return of such Product to Party B during the warranty period of such Product and after the inspect and test conducted by both Party A and Party B, it is confirmed that the problem is caused by the quality of such Product, then Party A shall change another Product of the same type and the same specifications to Party B free of charge. Subject to this Clause, Party A has no further responsibility in respect of the Products. ②

6.4 在本产品的质量保证期内，倘若因本产品的质量问题导致向乙方退货，经甲乙双方进行检测后确认为是由于本产品的质量问题所引起，甲方应予以免费更换同类品种、同种规格的本产品。除此以外，甲方不承担有关本产品的任何其他责任。

7. Purchase Orders，Confirmation of Quantity and Delivery Period

第 7 条 购货订单、数量确认、交货期

7.1 For each purchase, Party B shall send a purchase order which is duly signed and affixed with Party B's company chop to Party A by fax or by any other written forms. After receiving Party B's purchase order, Party A shall confirm the delivery date with Party B by returning a confirmed purchase order which is duly signed and affixed with Party A's company chop to Party B by fax or by any other written forms. ③

7.1 在每次购货时，乙方应通过传真或其他书面方式向甲方发送经乙方适当签字盖章的购货订单。甲方在收到乙方的购货订单后，应确认交货日期，再通过传真或其他书面方式向乙方发送经甲方适当签字盖章的确认购货订单。

7.2 Party A and Party B agree that the "Cargo Receipt" issued by Party A for each delivery of the Products and signed by Party B after the receipt of the Products shall be the final evidence of the quantity and amount of such sale and purchase of the Products. ④

7.2 甲乙双方同意，以甲方在交付每批本产品时出具的、并由乙方在收货后签署的《交货收据》作为确认每次买卖本产品的数量和货款结算的

---

① 本协议交易商品系进口电子产品，经销商承诺不随意变更或者重新装配或重新包装本产品，对确保本产品的原装质量至关重要。

② 此条款确保供货商对瑕疵产品的保证责任仅限于换货，排除了经销商对利润损失等间接损失的索赔。

③ 对于购货订单的双方书面确认是非常重要的。实践中常发生买方电话订货，或买方发出未签字盖章的订单，卖方未经书面确认回复就交付货物，而买方不付款的纠纷；在诉讼或仲裁程序中，如果买方否认曾向卖方订货，卖方需要证明买方确实曾经订货、卖方已经据此交货的充足证据。

④ 本协议下的交货方式是卖方在指定地域内直接交付本产品给买方，并非海运或空运方式交货。因此卖方随本产品交付给买方的《交货收据》（买方签收）可以作为交货证明。

最终证据。

7.3 Delivery Period: For the Products set forth hereunder, Party A shall deliver the Products within 30 to 45 days after the confirmation of the relevant purchase order.

7.3 交货时间：就本协议所约定的本产品，甲方应于确认相关购货订单后30日至45日内交付本产品。

7.4 The title to the Products shall remain with Party A prior to receipt of the full payment from Party B for a particular order of the Products. ①

7.4 在甲方就本产品的具体订单从乙方收到全额付款之前，本产品的所有权仍然属于甲方。

7.5 All risks of loss in the Products shall pass to Party B upon delivery of the Products to Party B by Party A in accordance with this Agreement. Upon delivery of the Products as agreed, Party B shall assume the all risks of loss, including but not limited to, due to any natural disaster, damage and other loss of property caused to the Products delivered, except such loss is caused by the acts or omissions of Party A. ②

7.5 在甲方按照本协议将本产品交付给乙方之后，本产品的损失风险全部转移到乙方。一旦如约定交付本产品，除因甲方的行为或疏忽造成的损失以外，乙方应承担全部损失风险，包括但不限于因自然灾害对本产品造成的损害和其他损失。

8. Responsibilities of the Parties
第 8 条　双方责任

8.1 During the term of this Agreement, Party B shall use its best effort to promote and sell the Products within the Territory.

8.1 在本协议有效期限内，乙方应尽其最大努力在指定地域内推广及销售本产品。

8.2 Party B shall undertake all advertising and promotional activities after consultation with and in accordance with Party A's instructions. Party B shall bear all costs and expenses for such advertising and promotional activities, unless otherwise expressly agreed in writing by the Parties. ③

8.2 乙方应与甲方协商并按照甲方指示开展全部广告和促销活动。除非双方以书面方式另有明确约定，这些广告和促销活动的成本和费用应全部由乙方负担。

---

①　按照本协议下的付款方式，从供货方交货到收款之间有一段时间，在供货方未收到已交付的本产品款项之前，对已交付的本产品保留供货方的所有权是十分必要的；在经销商破产等情况下，供货方有权将未付款的本产品从经销商处收回，可有效地保护供货方的合法权益。

②　在供货方向经销商交付本产品后，倘若发生不可抗力事件或归咎于经销商或第三方的其他事件，致使本产品发生损坏或灭失，根据本条款其风险已经转移到经销商处，供货方可以避免遭受损失。

③　本条款可以避免因经销商进行不必要的宣传活动，增加供货商的推广费用。

8.3　Party A may, at its own absolute discretion and at the request of Party B, provide technical assistance or after-sale services in connection with the Products to Party B's customers. ①

8.3　甲方有绝对的酌情权，根据乙方的要求，可向乙方的客户提供与本产品相关的技术支持或售后服务。

8.4　Party B agrees to inform Party A of any information or complaints in connection with the Products received from Party B's customers. Party B also agrees to cooperate with Party A in handling and resolving any issues pertaining the Products in a manner satisfactory to Party A. ②

8.4　乙方同意将收到的乙方客户对于本产品的任何信息或投诉通知甲方。乙方同意以甲方满意的方式与甲方合作，处理及解决有关本产品的任何问题。

8.5　The Parties hereto hereby undertake that their business activities carries out hereunder do not violate any applicable laws and regulations. In the event that a Party commits a breach of this Clause and causes any loss or damages to the other Party, the defaulting Party shall bear all legal liabilities and indemnify the other Party for all its losses and damages so incurred.

8.5　双方在此保证，其在本协议项下所进行的经营活动不违反所适用的法律法规。如因任何一方违反本条规定并给对方带来任何损失或损害，违约方须承担所有法律责任并赔偿给对方造成的全部损失和损害。

8.6　Party B shall be solely responsible for any disputes, claims, losses, infringements and liabilities, etc. between itself and its customers. Party A would not participate in such disputes, claims etc. between Party B and its customers and shall not be responsible for any losses of Party B's customers.

8.6　乙方应负责自行解决与其客户之间的任何争议、索赔、损失、侵权和违约责任等，甲方不介入乙方与其客户之间的这些纠纷、索赔等，也不对乙方客户的任何损失负责。

8.7　Party B shall not distribute the Products outside the Territory as provided in this Agreement.

8.7　乙方不得在本协议规定的指定地域之外分销本产品。

8.8　Party B agrees and hereby warrants that it shall not distribute any products manufactured by other manufacturers which infringe the Trademark, trade name, package design, etc. of the Products. ③

8.8　乙方同意并在此保证不经销其他生产厂家侵犯本产品的商标、商号、包装设计等所制造出的任何产品。

----

① 通常，供货商会就经销商销售的本产品提供技术支持和售后服务，本条规定的目的是将这方面的主动权掌握在供货商手中。

② 本条内容是经销合同中的常用条款，对于维护供货商以及本产品的商业信誉很重要。

③ 根据本条款，经销商销售本产品的假冒商品或侵权商品等时，供货商可追究经销商的违约责任。

8.9　Party B shall not do any acts which may damage Party A's intellectual property rights and the image of the Products and the brand names. Party B shall assist Party A in monitoring the market situation, immediately report to Party A of any infringing acts and assist Party A in taking any protective measures.

8.9　乙方不得进行有损甲方知识产权以及本产品形象和品牌的行为。乙方须协助甲方进行市场监督，对任何侵权行为须立即向甲方报告并协助甲方采取保护措施。

8.10　In the event that Party B becomes aware of any claims arising from the Products for personal injury or for monetary damages, Party B shall forthwith notify Party A of any such claims, and shall deal with such claims as Party A may see fit. Party B shall indemnify Party A against all claims for personal injury and damages alleged to have resulted from Party B's negligence or wilful conduct (including all legal fees incurred by party A in defending such claims).

8.10　如果乙方获悉因本产品而发生任何人身伤害或金钱损失的索赔，乙方应立即通知甲方，并按甲方认为适当的方式处理该索赔。对于主张是由于乙方的过失或故意行为所导致的人身伤害及损害的全部索赔，乙方应向甲方作出赔偿（包括甲方对该索赔进行抗辩而发生的全部律师费用）。

9. Cessation of Supply and Liabilities Upon Breach

第 9 条　停止供货与违约责任

9.1　Where any of the following events occurs, Party A is entitled to stop the supply of the Products to Party B and reserves its rights to claim against Party B for breach of this Agreement:

(1) Where Party B fails to pay Party A any outstanding amount of the Products, Party A is entitled to stop the supply of the Products to Party B; in addition, Party A is entitled to claim against Party B interest on such outstanding amount at the rate of 1% per month commencing from the due date until the date such outstanding amount has been fully paid by Party B. ①

(2) Where Party B is announced to be wound up or is going to be wound up, Party A is entitled to forthwith cease the supply of the Products to Party B and request immediate payment of any outstanding amount of the Products from Party B.

(3) Where Party B is in breach of provisions hereof by selling the Products to any wholesalers or knowingly sell to any third party (including wholesalers and retailers) the Products for the purpose of resale outside the Territory, Party A is entitled to stop the supply of the Products to Party B and claim against Party B for any losses and damages arising

---

① 对经销商延迟支付货款计收利息的约定，可以有效促使经销商向供货商按时支付货款。

from the breach of this Agreement by Party B. ①

9.1　倘若乙方发生以下任何情形之一的，甲方有权停止向乙方提供本产品，并有权追究乙方的违约责任：

(1) 倘若乙方未能按期向甲方支付本产品货款，甲方有权停止向乙方提供本产品；并在从乙方收回所欠付本产品货款的同时，有权要求乙方支付利息，利息按乙方应付但未付金额的月息 1‰计算，从应收账款到期日开始计算利息，直到乙方将应付货款完全结清为止。

(2) 倘若乙方被宣告破产，或乙方处于濒临破产状态，甲方有权立即停止向乙方继续提供本产品，并有权向乙方立即追讨所欠付的本产品货款。

(3) 倘若乙方违反本协议的规定，将本产品销售给指定地域外的其他批发商，或者在知情的情况下向任何第三方（包括批发商和零售商）出售本产品以便运往指定地域以外作转售之用，甲方有权停止向乙方继续提供本产品，并有权向乙方追讨因乙方违反本协议而使甲方遭受的一切损失和损害。

9.2　Where there is no breach of this Agreement by Party B, Party A shall give Party B three (3) months' prior written notice before ceasing the supply of the Products to Party B. In case that the supply has been ceased without prior notice, Party B shall be entitled to return all existing stocks.

9.2　在乙方没有违约的情况下，甲方如要停止供货必须于 3 个月前以书面通知乙方。在没有事前通知而停止供货的情况下，乙方有权将现有存货退回。

10. Intellectual Property Rights

第 10 条　知识产权

10.1　The patents, trademarks, copyrights, packing designs and all other intellectual property rights of the Products (hereinafter referred to as **"Party A's IP Rights"**) shall belong to Party A and/or the parent company of Party A. Unless otherwise authorized hereunder, Party B has no right, ownership or interest on Party A's IP Rights.

10.1　有关本产品的专利权、商标权、著作权、包装设计以及其他全部知识产权（以下简称"**甲方知识产权**"）均属于甲方及/或甲方母公司所有，除了本协议授予的权利以外，乙方对甲方知识产权没有其他权利、所有权或权益。

10.2　Party B shall not register the trademarks, the patents and other intellectual property rights in respect of the Products in any jurisdiction and in any class of products. ②

---

① 经销商通过各种手段将本产品转售到指定地域以外，会扰乱供货商的整个销售网络，破坏供货商的价格体系，使供货商遭受损失，需要在协议中明文禁止。

② 本条款可有效防止经销商在供货商尚未就本产品注册知识产权的管辖权范围内抢先注册，给供货商造成损失。

10.2 乙方不得在任何管辖权范围内和任何商品类别内注册本产品的商标权、专利权及其他知识产权。

10.3 Party B hereby warrants that it shall not do any act which may cause any damage to Party A's IP Rights or cause confusion to the public (including but not limited to any representations or acts which may lead the public to believe that Party B has the ownership of Party A's IP Rights).

10.3 乙方保证不作任何行为以致可能损害甲方知识产权或者在公众中可能引起的任何混淆（包括但不限于可能导致公众认为乙方对甲方知识产权拥有所有权的任何陈述或行为）。

10.4 Where Party A discovers that any third party who has business cooperation with Party B infringes Party A's IP Rights, Party A shall immediately inform Party B, and Party B shall stop any business cooperation with such third party forthwith. Where an infringing act has been committed, Party B shall not handle with the infringing items without the prior written consent from Party A.

10.4 如果甲方发现与乙方业务合作的任何第三方进行侵害甲方知识产权的侵权行为，甲方应立即通知乙方，乙方必须立即停止与该第三方的任何业务合作。如果侵权行为已经发生，乙方在未获得甲方的书面同意前不得擅自处理侵权物品。

10.5 If it comes to Party B's knowledge of any infringement or threat of infringement by any third party to Party A's IP Rights, Party B shall immediately notify Party A in writing. If Party A decides to take any administrative or legal proceedings to prohibit such infringing acts, Party B shall provide Party A with all necessary assistance, including but not limited to making complaints to the relevant authorities or initiating litigation in courts, etc.①

10.5 若乙方知悉任何第三方对甲方知识产权的任何侵权或侵权威胁，乙方应立即以书面方式通知甲方。如果甲方决定通过行政或诉讼程序等方法制止该侵权行为，乙方须向甲方提供一切必要的协助，其中包括但不限于向相关行政机关投诉或向法院起诉等。

11. Confidentiality

第 11 条　保密

Party A and Party B shall keep strictly confident on the contents of this Agreement or any business and technical data and information of the other Party obtained as a result of this Agreement and shall not disclose or divulge the same to any third party without the written consent of the other

---

① 对于指定地域内侵犯供货方/其母公司知识产权的行为，如果以供货方或其母公司（境外公司）名义向指定地域的有关行政机关投诉或提起诉讼等，会面临程序上的要求和过程等，可能拖延时日，难以及时阻止侵权行为；而以乙方（当地公司）名义向当地有关行政机关投诉或提起诉讼等，更为便捷，可以迅速有效地阻止侵权行为，因此本条款的约定是十分必要的。

Party. This Clause survives the termination or expiration of this Agreement.

有关本协议的内容以及甲乙双方由于本协议而获得的对方的商业及技术数据和信息，甲方及乙方应严格保密，在未得到对方的书面同意前不得向任何第三者披露或泄露。本条的规定在本协议解除或期满终止后仍然继续有效。

12. Term

第 12 条　协议有效期

12.1　This Agreement shall come into force and effect upon execution and shall continue to be valid until（*年月日*），and shall be automatically renewed for another one year and thereafter on a year-to-year basis unless either Party gives to the other Party a written notice to terminate this Agreement at least three（3）months before the expiration of the original or，as the case may be，any extended term of this Agreement.

12.1　本协议自签订之日起生效，有效期至____年____月____止；此后，如果甲方或乙方在最初有效期或任何续期后的有效期届满日前至少 3 个月没有以书面方式通知对方终止本协议，则本协议自动续期一年；其后亦以同样方式逐年续期。

12.2　This Agreement may be terminated by either Party by giving the other Party at least three（3）months' prior written notice but without prejudice to the rights and remedies of either Party against the other in respect of any antecedent claim or breach of the terms and conditions herein contained. [①]

12.2　倘若甲乙任何一方欲中途解约，应提前 3 个月书面通知另一方，方可解除本协议；本协议的解除并不影响任何一方对另一方就先前的索赔或违反本协议中所含条款和条件的权利及救济。

13. Termination

第 13 条　解约

Either Party hereto may immediately terminate this Agreement in whole or in part without notice to the other Party，if any of the following events occurs to the other Party：

（1）its business licence being cancelled by the relevant authorities or be ordered to cease business；

（2）its assets being frozen，seized，enforced or applied for auction by any third party or withheld due to delay of tax payment；

（3）being served by a third party or filed by the Party itself a petition for bankruptcy，company restructuring or winding-up；

（4）decide to amalgamate，deduce the registered capital，transfer whole or a substantial part of its business；

（5）fails to perform its obligations provided in this Agreement and does not

---

①　本条款约定的解约，是在双方均没有违约行为的前提下提前解除终止本协议，这类条款又称为"break clause"（中断条款），与下述第 13 条因一方违约而提前解除本协议的情况不同。

cure the non-performance within 30 days after a written demand from the non-defaulting Party;

(6) its financial situation become deteriorating or be considered to have the possibility that its financial situation will be deteriorating;

(7) there is a substantial change in Party B's business.

甲方或乙方发生下列情形之一的，对方当事人无需发出通知，可立即解除本协议的全部或其一部分：

(1) 被相关政府部门吊销营业执照或者被责令停止营业；

(2) 其财产被任何第三方冻结、扣押、强制执行或被申请拍卖，或因延迟缴税而被扣留；

(3) 被第三方申请或者该当事人自己申请破产、公司重组或清算；

(4) 该当事人决定合并、减少注册资本、转让其业务的全部或重要部分；

(5) 不履行其在本协议项下的义务，虽经守约方当事人以书面要求违约方予以纠正，但在该要求发出后 30 日内违约方仍然没有纠正违约行为；

(6) 其财产状况恶化，或者被认为有可能恶化；

(7) 乙方业务发生重大变更。

14. Compensation

第 14 条　损害赔偿

14.1　Where either Party fails to cure any breach hereof within thirty（30）days after a written demand from the non-defaulting Party, the non-defaulting Party has the right to terminate this Agreement immediately.

14.1　倘若甲乙任何一方违反本协议，在守约方向违约方发出纠正违约行为的书面要求后 30 日以内违约方仍没有纠正违约行为，守约方有权以书面方式通知违约方立即解除本协议。

14.2　Any Party terminating this Agreement in accordance with the preceding Clause 13 or this Clause 14.1 may claim against the other Party for all losses and damages so suffered.

14.2　倘若甲乙任何一方根据上述第 13 条或本协议第 14.1 条的约定解除本协议，对于由此蒙受的一切损害和损失，可要求对方当事人给予赔偿。

15. Force Majeure

第 15 条　不可抗力

15.1　In the event of any failure or delay by either Party hereto in the performance of all or any part of this Agreement due to earthquake, typhoon, flooding, fire, war, epidemics or any other force majeure beyond the control of either Party, the Party involved in any of these events shall inform the other Party without delay by fax or by email and shall within thirty（30）days provide the other Party with particulars in writing of such event and the failure of performing of this Agreement or the need of postponing the performance hereunder.

15.1　甲乙任何一方因地震、台风、水灾、火灾、战争、传染病或其不可控制的其他不可抗力事件，致使其不能履行或延迟履行本协议的，受到影响的一方当事人应立即以传真或电子邮件方式通知对方，并应在 30 日内向对方送交有关不可抗力事件的详细情况以及不能履行本协议或需要延期履行本协议的书面说明。

15. 2　The Parties may，depending upon the extent of impact caused to this Agreement by such force majeure event，negotiate to extend the period of performance or to release the Party concerned from performance of the Agreement.

15. 2　甲乙双方可根据不可抗力事件对本协议造成影响的程度，协商决定受影响的当事人延期履行或免除履行本协议。

15. 3　No Party shall be liable for any losses and damages caused by any force majeure events.

15. 3　对于不可抗力事件造成的损失和损害，甲乙双方均不承担赔偿责任。

16. Governing Law and Jurisdiction

第 16 条　适用法律及管辖权

16. 1　This Contract shall be governed by and construed in accordance with the laws of Hong Kong.

16. 1　本协议适用香港法律，按照香港法律解释。

16. 2　Any dispute arising from or in connection with this Agreement between the Parties shall be submitted to the non-exclusive jurisdiction of the Hong Kong courts. ①

16. 2　凡因本协议引起的或与本协议有关的任何争议，甲乙双方接受香港法院的非专属管辖权。

17. Assignment

第 17 条　转让

Party B shall not assign or transfer any of its rights or obligations under this Agreement to any third party without the prior written consent of Party A. ②

乙方在未得到甲方的书面同意前，不得将乙方在本协议项下的任何权利或义务转让给任何第三方。

18. No Waiver

第 18 条　权利的不放弃

No failure on the part of the non-defaulting Party to exercise，and no delay on its part in exercising any right hereunder shall operate as a waiver thereof，nor shall any single or partial exercise of any right under this Agreement preclude any other or further exercise of it or the exercise of any other right or prejudice or affect any right against the defaulting Party.

倘若守约方没有行使以及没有及时行使其在本协议项下的任何权利，并不构

---

① 在此条款下，原告方可以根据自己诉讼的便利以及被告可执行资产的具体情况，决定提起诉讼的地点。

② 供货方是基于对经销商履约能力（包括其资产、经营状况、销售网络、管理层情况等）的了解和信任，将本产品的经销权授予经销商的，通常不允许经销商将经销协议项下的权利业务擅自转让给第三方。

成守约方放弃其在本协议项下的任何权利；对本协议项下权利的单项行使或部分行使不妨碍守约方另外行使或进一步行使其他权利，也不损害或影响其对于违约方的任何权利。

19. Notice

第 19 条　通知

Any notice or other communication to be given, made or served under this Agreement shall be by facsimile transmission or by courier addressed to the relevant Party at its correspondence address or facsimile number as stated herein.

根据本协议而发出、作出或送达的各种通知或其他联络，应使用传真或快递方式进行，发送到本协议所记载的相关当事人的通信地址或传真号码。

20. Relationship between the Parties

第 20 条　双方的关系

No Party hereto shall declare itself as the agent of the other Party or has any authority to create or assume any obligation of any kind for or on behalf of the other Party.

本协议任何一方不得声称自己是另一方的代理人或声称其有权代表另一方设定或承担任何义务。

21. Miscellaneous

第 21 条　其他条款

21.1　This Agreement shall not be amended, supplemented or modified except by a written instrument signed by or on behalf of each Party.

21.1　对本协议的任何修改、补充或变更，应以书面方式进行，由各方当事人签署后生效。

21.2　Any provision hereof which is illegal, invalid or unenforceable shall be severable and shall not affect the remaining provisions of this Agreement.

21.2　倘若本协议的任何条款违法、无效或不可执行，则应将该条款分离出去，本协议其他条款的有效性不受影响。

21.3　This Agreement constitutes the entire agreement between the Parties hereto as to the subject matter contained herein and supersedes all previous undertakings, commitments and agreements whether oral or written relating to the subject matter hereof.

21.3　本协议构成双方当事人之间有关本协议标的之完整协议，取代此前有关本协议标的之全部口头或书面保证、承诺和协议。

21.4　This Agreement shall be executed in duplicate, each Party shall have one of them. Each counterpart shall have the same legal effect.

21.4　本协议正本一式两份，双方当事人各执壹份，具有同等法律效力。

AS WITNESS whereof this Agreement has been executed on the day and year first above written.

本协议已经于上述首页所述日期签订，特此为证。

For and on behalf of
Party A：
代表甲方：

_____

Name：
姓名：
Position：
职务：
For and on behalf of
Party B：
代表乙方：

_____

Name：
姓名：
Position：
职务：

Schedule 1
附件 1

The Specifications of the Products
本产品的规格

Schedule 2
附件 2

Copy of Notice of Application Acceptance of Trademark Registration
该商标注册申请受理通知书影印件

Schedule 3
附件 3

The Prices of the Products
本产品价格表

第5章

知识产权、专有技术类许可合同的精选与解读

第 1 节　商标及商誉使用许可协议精选与解读_____

商标及商誉使用许可协议
TRADEMARK & GOODWILL
LICENCE AGREEMENT①

本协议由下述双方当事人于【年】【月】【日】签订：

THIS AGREEMENT is executed on the【日】day of【月】【年】by and between：

EF（香港）有限公司，一家依据中华人民共和国（下称"**中国**"）香港特别行政区（下称"**香港**"）法律正当成立并存续的有限公司，其主营业所地址为【 】（下称"**许可方**"）；以及

EF（HONG KONG）CO.，LTD.，a corporation duly organized and existing under the laws of Hong Kong Special Administrative Region（hereinafter called the "**HKSAR**"）of the People's Republic of China（hereinafter called the "**PRC**"）and having its principal place of business at【 】 （hereinafter called the "**Licensor**"）；and

GH 有限公司，一家依据中国大陆法律正当成立并存续的有限公司，其注册地址为【 】（下称"**被许可方**"）。

GH CO. LTD.，a corporation duly organized and existing under the laws of the mainland China and having its registered office at【 】（hereinafter called the "**Licensee**"）.

鉴于：

WHEREAS：

A. 许可方是本协议第 1 条描述的商誉（下称"**该商誉**"）以及**本协议附件 1** 记述的"【 】"商标（下称"**该商标**"）的所有权人，该商誉和该商标用于许可方或其关联公司生产的某些【 】产品（下称"**该产品**"）之市场推广和销售；

Licensor is the proprietor of the goodwill as set out in Clause 1 hereof（hereinafter called the "**Goodwill**"）and the trademark in **Schedule 1** hereof（hereinafter called the "**Trademark**"）being used for the marketing and

---

① 本协议是一家香港公司将其在中国内地注册的商标及商誉许可一家内地公司使用的协议。许可方（香港公司）多年以来通过向内地市场进口销售其产品，积累了相当的商誉；现香港公司为了扩大其产品在内地市场的占有率，许可本协议的被许可方（内地公司）使用该等商标和商誉在内地宣传推广及销售许可方的产品。本协议虽系许可方的律师所起草，但双方权利和义务基本上是比较对等的。

selling of certain 【 】 products （hereinafter called the "**Products**"） produced by the Licensor or its related companies；

B. 被许可方希望取得在中国内地使用该商誉和该商标进行市场推广和销售该产品（下称"**该业务**"）的许可；

Licensee is desirous of acquiring a license to use the Goodwill and the Trademark in marketing and selling the Products in the mainland China （hereinafter called the "**Business**"）；

C. 许可方同意按照本协议的条款和条件授权被许可方使用该商誉和该商标。

The Licensor has agreed to provide such license for the Licensee to utilize the Goodwill and the Trademark under the terms and conditions of this Agreement.

双方当事人通过友好协商，一致同意如下：

WHEREBY IT IS AGREED through friendly negotiation as follows：

1. 许可方同意授权被许可方使用该商誉，该商誉包括下述信息、服务和专有技术，构成许可方在中国内地（下称"**该区域**"）迄今为止从事的、而将由被许可方从事的附属于该业务的全部基本商誉：

（a）客户名单、供货商和第三方承包商的名单、与该业务有关以及/或者用于从事该业务的全部联系人名单；

（b）包含用于从事该业务的知识、专业技能、专有技术或其他信息的文件、通信和其他资料；

（c）有关该业务的客户和其他人士的介绍，以及有关该等人士（视情况而定）的背景情况；

（d）被许可方将在其经营中使用的、有关该产品的市场推广、促销及包装的信息；以及

（e）在本协议有效期内，被许可方可能不时合理要求的其他信息、知识以及/或者协助。

The Licensor agrees to provide to the Licensee a right to use the Goodwill①which shall include the following information，services and know-how and constitute all of the essential Goodwill attaching to the Business hitherto carried on by the Licensor in the mainland China （hereinafter called the "**Territory**"），and to be carried on by the Licensee：-

（a）Customer lists，supplier and third party contractor lists，and lists of all contacts related to and/or useful in carrying on the Business；

（b）Documents，correspondence and other materials containing knowledge，expertise，know-how or other information which is useful in carrying on the Business；

（c）Introductions to customers and other persons relating to the Business，

---

① 商誉，是指企业所拥有和控制、能为企业未来获得超额利润的无法具体辨认的无形资产。读者可以从本条中具体列举的商誉各项内容理解本协议项下商誉的含义。许可方向被许可方提供并授权使用商誉，为被许可方成功从事该产品的推广和销售提供了重要的条件。

> together with background knowledge relating to such persons as appropriate;

（d）Information concerning marketing, promotion and packaging of the Products which will be useful to the Licensee in its operations; and

（e）Such other information, knowledge and/or assistance as the Licensee may reasonably request from time to time during the term of this Agreement.

2. 在本协议有效期内，根据本协议规定的条款和条件，许可方同意授权被许可方使用该商标，用于推广与销售该产品、提供该产品的售后服务以及有关该业务的所有其他方面。被许可的该产品仅限于在该区域内推广与销售。

The Licensor also agrees to grant to the Licensee for the term of this Agreement and on the terms and conditions set out in this Agreement a right to use the Trademark in connection with the Products marketed and sold, the provision of after-sale services in relation to the same, and all other aspects of the Business. The licensed Products shall be marketed and sold in and limited to the Territory.

3. 本协议项下的许可是非独占性的，许可方可以授权该区域内的其他方使用该商誉和该商标。在此情况下，本协议双方应就本协议条款的修订可行性进行诚意协商。本协议项下的授权包括被许可方将与该产品有关的该商标和该商誉在该区域内再授权许可使用的权利。

The license hereunder is non-exclusive in nature and the Licensor may grant others in the Territory the right to use the Goodwill and the Trademark. In such circumstances, the parties hereto shall negotiate in good faith concerning possible amendments to the terms hereof. The grant under this Agreement includes the right for the Licensee to grant sub-licenses to use the Trademark and the Goodwill in connection with the Products in the Territory. ①

4. 作为本协议项下授权许可的对价，在被许可方每一会计年度结束后的 30 天内，被许可方应按其年度审计报表中所记载的该产品年度净销售额的【　】％向许可方支付许可费。

As consideration for the grant of the license under this Agreement, the Licensee shall pay annually to the Licensor within thirty（30）days after the end of each fiscal year of the Licensee a royalty calculated at the rate of 【　】％ of the annual net sales of the Products as shown in the Licensee's annual audited accounts.

5. 倘若被许可方没有在约定的日期付款，须按年息【　】％的利率逐日计算逾期付款利息，直至许可方收到付款之日为止。

If the Licensee fails to make payment on the required date, late interest

---

① 可以看出，根据本条款的授权，在本协议有效期内，（1）许可方本身可以继续使用该商标和该商誉；（2）许可方可以在该区域内授权除被许可方以外的其他方使用该商标和该商誉；（3）被许可方可以在该区域内再授权其他方使用该商标和该商誉。

shall accrue at the rate of 【 】% per annum calculated daily until payment is received by the Licensor.

6. 根据许可方不时提出的要求，被许可方应提供其年度净销售额的证据，或者向许可方提供其报表和记录，以便许可方可以对此进行核实。①

   Licensee shall provide such evidence of its annual net sales, or access to its books and records so that Licensor may verify same, as the Licensor may request from time to time. ①

7. 在本协议有效期内，被许可方应将许可费汇入许可方指定的银行账户或者以许可方通知的其他方式付款。

   During the term of this Agreement, the royalty shall be remitted by the Licensee to the bank account designated by the Licensor or be paid by other means notified by the Licensor.

8. 本协议的有效期为自本协议签订之日起 2 年，根据双方的一致同意可以续期。

   The term of this Agreement shall be for a period of two (2) years from the execution date of this Agreement and be renewable by the mutual agreement of both parties.

9. 倘若被许可方没有履行其在本协议项下的任何实质性义务或实质性地违反本协议的规定，或者在接到许可方要求纠正该违约行为的书面通知后 30 天内仍然没有纠正相关违约行为，许可方有权向被许可方发出书面通知解除本协议，而不影响到解约日为止可能发生的任何权利或义务。

   The Licensor shall have the right to terminate this Agreement without prejudice to any rights or liabilities which may have occurred prior to the date of such termination immediately by written notice to the Licensee upon the Licensee's failure to perform any substantive obligations under this Agreement or the occurrence of a substantial breach of the provisions of this Agreement, or failure to rectify any relevant breach within thirty (30) days upon the receipt of written notice by the Licensor requesting rectification of such breach.

10. 倘若被许可方失去偿债能力或破产，或进入清算程序（无论是主动清算或以其他方式清算），或者被许可方的主要资产被任何第三方占有、没收、征用或占用，或者被许可方成为无能力或无法充分履行本协议项下的义务，本协议则自动终止。

    This Agreement will automatically cease, in the event that the Licensee becomes insolvent or bankrupt, or goes into liquidation (whether voluntarily or otherwise), or the Licensee's substantial assets have been possessed, confiscated, expropriated or occupied by any third party, or the Licensee becomes incapable or unable to fully perform its obligations under this Agreement.

11. 对于许可方和被许可方之间因本协议发生的或与本协议有任何关联的任

---

① 由于本协议的双方系多年合作伙伴，一向比较守约，故本协议中没有规定许可方有权聘请独立审计师对被许可方的财务记录进行审计的条款。在实践中经常发生被许可方少报销售额，从而少支付许可费的情况。如果双方是新的合作伙伴，许可方担心被许可方少报、少缴许可费，可以参考本书第 5 章第 2 节（技术许可与援助协议）第 4.8 条的规定，加入相应的审计和检查条款。

何争议，本协议的违反、解除或无效或者对于本协议中所包含规定的争议，双方应尽最大努力通过友好协商方式解决。

If there is any dispute between the Licensee and the Licensor arising out of, relating to, or connected in any way with this Agreement, the breach, termination or invalidity hereof, or the provisions contained herein, the parties hereto shall use their best endeavors to resolve the dispute through friendly negotiation.

12. 本协议适用香港法律，按照香港法律解释。双方接受香港法院的非专属性管辖权。

This Agreement shall be governed by and construed in accordance with the laws of HKSAR, and the parties submit to the non-exclusive jurisdiction of the courts of HKSAR.

13. 本协议是双方当事人之间的完整协议，取代双方之间以前的所有协商、谅解、承诺或其他安排。

This Agreement is the entire agreement between the parties hereto and supersedes all prior negotiations, understandings, commitments or other arrangements between the parties.

14. 在双方签订本协议后，如有必要，许可方应尽快将本协议副本以及其他有关文件提交给中国主管机关进行备案。

After the execution of this Agreement by the parties, if necessary, the Licensor shall file a duplicate copy of this Agreement together with other relevant documents with the Chinese competent authorities for record as soon as possible. [①]

15. 本协议签署一式两份，经签署并交付的每一份协议均为原件，由双方各持一份。

This Agreement shall be executed in duplicate, each of which when so executed and delivered shall be an original and be kept by each of the parties hereto.

作为签约凭证，双方当事人由其正式授权代表于本协议首页所载明的日期已经签订本协议。

IN WITNESS WHEREOF the parties have entered into this Agreement through execution by their duly authorized representatives as of the date first above written.

代表：**EF（香港）有限公司**
For and on behalf of
EF（HONG KONG）CO. , LTD.
签署（Sign）： _____
姓名（Name）：

---

① 按照中国相关法规的规定，商标使用许可合同须在商标局进行备案。

职务（Title）：

代表：**GH** 有限公司
For and on behalf of
GH CO. , LTD.
签署（Sign）：_____
姓名（Name）：
职务（Title）：

附件 1：该商标明细
Schedule 1：Details of the Trademark

1. 商标图形：
   Logo of Trademark：
2. 商标注册类别：
   Class of Trademark Registration：
3. 商标注册号：
   Trademark Registration No. ：
4. 许可使用的商品种类：
   Commodities subject to licensing：

第 2 节　技术许可与援助协议精选与解读

技术许可与援助协议
TECHNICAL LICENSE AND ASSISTANCE AGREEMENT

目　录
CONTENTS

技术许可与援助协议
TECHNICAL LICENSE AND ASSISTANCE AGREEMENT①

本协议于【 】年【 】月【 】日由以下双方签订：

THIS AGREEMENT is executed this 【日】 day of 【月】 【年】 by and between②：

ABC 有限公司，为一家根据【某外国】法律注册成立并存续的公司，其注册地址在【 】（以下简称"**许可方**"）；及

ABC CO. , LIMITED, LIMITED, a corporation incorporated and existing under the laws of 【某外国】 with its registered office at 【外国地址】 (hereinafter referred to as the "**Licensor**")；and

XYZ 有限公司，为一家根据中华人民共和国（以下简称"**中国**"）法律注册成立并存续的有限公司，其法定地址在【国内地址】（以下简称"**被许可方**"）。

XYZ CO. , LTD.，a company incorporated and existing under the laws of the People's Republic of China（hereinafter referred to as the "**PRC**"）with its legal address at 【国内地址】, the PRC（hereinafter referred to as the "**Licensee**"）.

鉴于：

WHEREAS：

（A）本协议**附件 A** 所载明的关于【 】技术的某些技术、专有技术和专门技能（以下简称"**该技术**"）的最终所有权人 MNO 有限公司已授权许可方签订本协议。

The Licensor has been authorized to enter into this Agreement by MNO Co. , Limited③, which company is the ultimate proprietor of certain technology and technical know-how and expertise in relation to 【 】 technology, including among others，those as set out in Schedule A attached hereto（hereinafter referred to as the "Technology"）.

（B）被许可方是许可方和另外两家公司根据【 】年【 】月【 】日签订的合资经营企业合同（以下简称"**合资合同**"）设立的中外合资经营企业。合资合同中规定许可方应授权被许可方使用该技术，供被许可方生产合营企业产品并经营其业务。

The Licensee is a Sino-foreign equity joint venture company established

---

① 本协议是一家中外合资经营企业（被许可方 XYZ 公司）与其股东之一（许可方 ABC 公司）之间关于技术许可与援助的协议，由于双方之间的特殊关系和共同利益所在，本协议双方的权利义务约定比较平衡。而在一般的技术许可协议中，侧重于保护许可方权利的情况比较常见。

② 本协议的许可方 ABC 公司是一家外国公司，与一家中国公司及另一外国公司共同投资设立了被许可方 XYZ 公司（中外合资经营企业）；许可方根据本协议及合资合同将该技术授权被许可方使用，加工生产营企业的产品。

③ 该外国公司（MNO 公司）是本协议许可方（ABC 公司）的母公司，是本协议项下技术的最终所有权人，授权许可方将该技术许可被许可方使用。

by and between the Licensor and two other companies pursuant to a joint venture contract dated as of 【日期】 (hereinafter referred to as the "JV Contract") . The JV Contract provides that the Licensor shall license to the Licensee the Technology for the production of the Products and the carrying on of the Business by the Licensee. ①

(C) 被许可方希望获得该技术的使用许可，而许可方同意根据本协议的条款及条件授权该许可。

The Licensee wishes to obtain a license of the Technology and the Licensor has agreed to grant such license under the terms and conditions of this Agreement.

因此，双方达成一致协议如下：

WHEREBY IT IS AGREED as follows：

第 1 条　定义

Definitions

除非上下文另有规定，下列词语具有如下含义：

The following terms and expressions shall have the following meanings unless the context otherwise requires：

1.1 **"该业务"** 是指为生产该产品而设立与经营加工设施（以下简称**"该加工厂"**）。

"Business" means the establishment and operation of the processing facilities (hereinafter referred to as the **"Processing Plant"**) for the production of the Products.

1.2 **"营业日"** 是指许可方及被许可方所在国的持牌银行（视情况而定）通常的营业日（星期六、星期日或公众假日除外）。

"Business Day" means a day (other than Saturdays, Sundays or public holidays) in which licensed banks in the countries of the Licensor and the Licensee，as the case may be，are generally open for business.

1.3 **"改进"** 是指对该技术的任何改进，此种改进提高了该产品的制造或加工水平或者提高了该产品质量。

"Improvements" means any enhancements to the Technology，which advances the manufacture or processing of the Products or enhances the quality of the Products.

1.4 **"合营企业"** "合营企业" 即被许可方，是许可方和另外两家公司共同设立的一家中外合资经营企业。

"JV Company" means the Licensee，a Sino-foreign equity joint venture company jointly established by and between the Licensor and two other companies.

1.5 **"加工装配成本"** "加工装配成本" 是指合营企业加工装配该产品的成本总和。

---

① 请参考本书第 6 章第 1 节的合资合同（该合同第 8 章 "技术援助"）。

"**Processing and Assembly Costs**" means the aggregate of the costs for processing and assembly of the Products by the JV Company.

1.6 "**一方**"是指许可方或被许可方（视情况而定）；"**双方**"指许可方和被许可方。

"**Party**" means the Licensee or the Licensor，as the case may be，and "**Parties**" means the Licensee and the Licensor collectively.

1.7 "**该产品**"是指使用该技术加工生产的【 】产品或双方不时决定加工生产的其他产品。

"**Products**" means 【 】 products processed or produced using the Technology or such other products as the Parties may from time to time resolve to process or produce.

1.8 "**该技术**"是指并尤其包括本协议附件 A 中列明的技术项目，也包括许可方根据本协议或合资合同的条款和条件，授权被许可方使用的有关该加工厂的经营以及/或者生产该产品的其他专有技术、商业秘密，以及有关该产品的设计、制造、生产、加工、测试、质量控制、质量保证以及/或者与前述内容有关的管理控制、管理、监督、报告以及/或者分析的任何其他技术资料和商业资料。但是，双方同意并确认，上述描述并不详尽，不应被视为或解释为以任何方式限制本条款所载明的定义之范围。而该技术应被视为包括其全部改进。

"**Technology**" means and includes，among others①，the items listed in Schedule A attached hereto，as well as other know-how，trade secrets and any other technical and commercial information relating to the design， manufacture， production， processing， testing， quality control， quality assurance of the Products， and/or management control， administration， supervision， reporting and/or analysis relating to or in respect of any of the foregoing in relation to the operation of the Processing Plant and/or the production of the Products，to be licensed by the Licensor to the Licensee pursuant to the terms and conditions of this Agreement or the JV Contract. However，the Parties agree and confirm that such description is not exhaustive and shall not be deemed or be construed in any way to limit the scope of the definition set forth in this Article. The Technology shall also be deemed to include all Improvements.

1.9 "**有效期**"是指本协议第 12 条所载明的本协议有效期。

"**Term**" means the term of this Agreement as set forth in Article 12 hereof.

1.10 "**该培训**"是指培训课程和服务，详见本协议**附件 B**以及第 3 条的规定。

---

① Among others 或者 among other things，是英文合同中比较常用的短语，意为"其中之一""包括""尤其""格外""除了别的以外（还）""……及其他（东西）""以及其他种种事实（问题）"等。在本条款中的用法是指附件 A 所列举的技术内容并非穷尽列举该技术的全部内容，除此之外，还包括其他相关技术内容。

"**Training**" means the training courses and services，details of which are set forth in **Schedule B** and Article 3 hereof.

第 2 条　授权

Grants

2.1 在满足本协议规定的条款和条件的前提下，许可方在此授权被许可方在本协议有效期内使用及开发该技术以便生产、制造以及/或者组装及加工该产品之非独占性的、不可转让的、只限于被许可方本身的权利和许可。

Subject to the terms and conditions set out in this Agreement，the Licensor hereby grants to the Licensee a non-exclusive and non-assignable and personal right and license to use and exploit the Technology to produce，manufacture and/or assemble and process the Products during the Term hereof. ①

2.2 该许可权仅授予被许可方本身，除非获得许可方的事先书面批准，该授权并不包括被许可方进行与之相关的任何种类的再授权、特许、权利或优先权，或将该技术用于任何第三方为被许可方生产的任何产品。该许可权是不可分割的，并且不得全部或部分转让，无论是通过合同、法律的实施或是以任何方式转让，但事先获得许可方书面批准的不在此限。

The license is personal to the Licensee and，except with the Licensor's prior written approval，the grant does not include any right for the Licensee to grant any sub-license，concession，right or privilege of any kind relating thereto，or to use the Technology in connection with any products manufactured by any third party for the Licensee. Such license is indivisible and may not be transferred or assigned in whole or in part，by contract，operation of law or in any manner whatsoever，except with the Licensor's prior written approval.

第 3 条　培训

Training

3.1 在本协议有效期内，根据被许可方不时提出的合理要求，许可方应向被许可方派遣技术人员（以下简称"**该等技术人员**"），向被许可方的雇员提供现场技术培训与援助。附件 B 列明了该培训的范围以及许可方的相关责任。

During the Term of this Agreement，the Licensor shall，from time to time as reasonably②requested by the Licensee，dispatch its technicians

---

①　这是极为常用的技术许可授权。根据本条的约定，许可方除了授权被许可方使用该技术之外，还可将该技术授权其他第三方使用；而被许可方仅限于其本身使用该技术，不得转让或转授权其他第三方使用该技术。在技术许可协议中，许可方极少给予被许可方独占性的授权，以避免过度限制许可方本身的权利。

②　这里对被许可方的要求加以"reasonably（合理）"的限定，避免被许可方动辄提出要求，使许可方应接不暇。至于何为"合理"，一般会进行通常意义上的解释，没有具体的规定。

(hereinafter referred to as the "Technicians") to the Licensee to provide on-site technical training and assistance to the Licensee's employees. Schedule B sets forth the scope of the Training and the Licensor's responsibility in this regard.

3.2 被许可方应负担附件 B 中列明的与该培训有关的下述费用：海外旅行费用、中国境内发生的食宿费和交通费以及劳务费。向该等技术人员支付的与该培训相关的费用在本协议第 6.5 条和第 6.6 条中规定。

The Licensee shall be responsible for the following costs related to the Training as set forth in Schedule B: overseas travel expenses, expenses for accommodation, meals and transportation incurred in the PRC and labor costs. The costs relating to the Training payable to the Technicians shall be set out in Articles 6.5 and 6.6 of this Agreement.

3.3 被许可方应协助许可方，以便使受训人员按照该培训计划完成该培训。被许可方应尽其最大努力协助许可方派遣的该等技术人员，以完成与该培训有关的事宜。

The Licensee shall assist the Licensor so that the trainees will complete the Training in accordance with the training plan. The Licensee shall use its best endeavors to assist the Technicians dispatched from the Licensor to complete matters related to the Training.

第 4 条 许可费及其他相关费用
Royalties and Other Related Charges

4.1 在本协议有效期内，被许可方应向许可方支付：

(1) 一笔特殊许可费，其最高限额为【 】美元或双方此后可能以书面形式同意的金额，在被许可方的累计亏损被填补之后支付。[①] 特殊许可费的支付方式如下：

(a) 在被许可方经营期限内的每个年度，被许可方税后净利润的 30％，直到约定的全部金额支付完毕为止；

(b) 根据被许可方年度审计会计报表计算款项；

(c) 在被许可方的年度审计会计报表出具之后 30 天内付款；

以及

(2) 持续发生的许可费，在本协议有效期内的最初 3 年期间按加工装配成本的 3％计算，在每年的 6 月和 12 月各计算一次，并于每个日历半年结束后的 45 天内付款。许可方应根据由被许可方报告并经许可方核查的加工装配成本计算的许可费开具发票，核查方式如下文所述或依照双方不时商定的合理方式。在本协议有效期内，该许可费应每隔 3 年由双方共同协商进行调整或修正。

为避免疑义，在特殊许可费的全部金额支付完毕之前，如果本协议因

[①] 本协议中特殊许可费的计算和支付方式，与一般技术许可协议中支付入门许可费和提成费的方式不同，这是因为本协议双方之间的特殊关系（合营公司与其股东的关系），许可方作为股东之一为了支持被许可方合营公司的业务发展，待合营公司赢利后才开始支付特殊许可费。

任何原因提前解除或期满终止，则被许可方无需支付特殊许可费最高限额与本协议提前解除或期满终止时特殊许可费已付金额之间的差额。

During the continuance of this Agreement，the Licensee shall pay to the Licensor：

(1) a special royalty of up to a maximum amount of US $【 】，or such sum as the Parties may hereafter agree in writing，which shall be payable，only after accumulated losses of the Licensee have been made up，such payment to be made in the following manner，namely：

(a) 30% of the net profit after taxes of the Licensee for each year of the term of the Licensee until the whole of the agreed sum has been paid；

(b) payment to be made based on the annual audited financial statements of the Licensee；and

(c) payments to be made within thirty (30) days of the issuance of the relevant annual audited financial statements of the Licensee；

and

(2) ongoing royalties calculated at 3% of the Processing and Assembly Costs，payment thereof to be calculated half-yearly in June and December each year，during the first three (3) years of the Term. The on-going royalties shall be payable in arrears within 45 days after the end of each calendar half year. The The Licensor shall issue invoices for royalties due based on the Processing and Assembly Costs as reported by the Licensee and verified by the Licensor in the manner described below or as the Parties shall reasonably agree from time to time. The royalties shall be subject to adjustment or amendment by mutual agreement of the Parties every three years during the Term.

For the avoidance of doubt[①]，in the event of early termination of this Agreement for any reason，or expiration before the full amount of the special royalty has been paid，the Licensee shall not be obliged to pay the difference between the maximum of the special royalty and the actual amount of the special royalty paid as of the time of the early termination or expiration of this Agreement.

4.2 上述许可费在按照中国法律规定支付税金后，由被许可方以美元汇入许可方指定的银行账户或以许可方通知的其他方式支付。

The royalties above shall be remitted in United States Dollars by the Licensee to the bank account designated by the Licensor or be paid by

---

① For the avoidance of doubt，意即"为免生疑问""为避免疑义""为免存疑"，是英文合同或其他法律文件中非常有用的短语，后面紧跟的内容是为了避免当事方之间可能发生的误解而特别予以界定和说明的内容。这是因为合同或其他法律文件应极力避免的问题之一是对同一内容可能产生不同理解或误解，影响当事人权利义务的实施履行。

other ways notified by the Licensor after payment of taxes in accordance with PRC law.

4.3　本协议第 4.1 条约定的许可费以及本协议约定的其他全部相关费用，作为该技术的使用许可和相关技术援助及服务的对价，即使在本协议提前解除的情况下也无需退还。

The royalties described in Article 4.1 and all other fees in relation thereto as described in this Agreement as the consideration for the Technology license and related technical assistance and services shall not be returned in the event of early termination of this Agreement.

4.4　在确定上述第 4.1 条（2）项下应付的许可费时，应首先以人民币计算出加工装配成本，然后把计算出的加工装配成本按许可费实际付款当日中国银行公布的买入价和卖出价的中间价折算成等值的美元。

In determining the royalties payable under Article 4.1 (2) above, the Processing and Assembly Costs shall be calculated in RMB and then converted into the equivalent in US Dollars at the median of the buying and selling rates of the Bank of China on the actual payment date.

4.5　本协议项下的许可费和其他相关费用在中国境内汇款产生的银行费用由被许可方承担，在境外产生的银行汇款费用由许可方承担。

The bank charges for remittance of the royalties and other fees hereunder in the PRC shall be borne by the Licensee. The bank charges incurred abroad for such remittances shall be borne by the Licensor.

4.6　如果被许可方支付给许可方的许可费根据中国法律规定须缴付任何代扣所得税，该税金应从许可费中扣除。被许可方应向许可方提供证明向有关税务当局缴税的正式纳税收据的副本。

If the royalties paid by the Licensee to the Licensor are subject to any withholding tax[①]required by PRC law, such tax shall be applied to and deducted from the royalty payment. The Licensee shall provide the Licensor with a duplicate copy of the official tax receipt evidencing the payment of such tax to the appropriate tax authority.

4.7　为确认上述所定许可费金额计算的准确性，被许可方在每月底之后 30 日内应向许可方提交加工装配成本的月度报告，并附上经双方同意的全部成本之资料。

In order to ensure the accuracy of the calculation of the amount of the royalties provided above, the Licensee shall provide reports to the Licensor within thirty (30) days after the end of each month in regards to the monthly Processing and Assembly Costs with information on all costs as agreed by both Parties.

4.8　被许可方应保存并在本协议有效期内每一会计年度结束后 3 个月内提

---

① withholding tax，"预扣所得税""预提所得税"或"预提税"，指付款人按照所适用的法律规定代扣代缴收款人应付的税款。在本协议中，指许可方（外国公司）就收取的技术许可费在中国应缴纳的外国企业所得税，先由被许可方（合营公司）代扣代缴，然后才能汇出到许可方的国外银行账户。

供给许可方在本协议有效期内每一年度全部适当的账目及记录，包括关于加工装配成本的全部必备数据。在许可方给予合理通知后，在被许可方的正常工作时间内，被许可方应允许许可方或其代表审计相关记录及账目，以核实被许可方报告的真实性和准确性，与此有关的费用和开支应由许可方独自负担。

The Licensee shall also keep and provide to the Licensor upon request, within three （3） months following the end of each fiscal year during the Term hereof, the entire and appropriate book keeping entries and records for each year of the Term with the complete and necessary data concerning the Processing and Assembly Costs. Upon the reasonable notice from the Licensor and within the normal operation hours of the Licensee, the Licensee shall allow the Licensor or its representatives to audit the relevant records and accounts to verify the truthfulness and accuracy of the Licensee's reports, all such costs and expenses in relation thereto shall be borne by the Licensor solely.

4.9　在本协议中，**"半年"** 指公历 1 月 1 日至 6 月 30 日或 7 月 1 日至 12 月 31 日。

In this Agreement, **"half year"** means the period from January 1st to June 30th, or July 1st to December 31st.

4.10　如果按照第 4.8 条作出的审计报告显示了差异，被许可方有权聘请双方选定的独立审计师对实际的加工装配成本进行核查。双方应接受该独立审计师的调查结果为终局性的。如果实际的加工装配成本大于被许可方已支付的许可费数额，则被许可方应立即支付已到期的许可费增加额和该增加额从逾期付款日到实际付款日为止日数按年利率【　】%计算的逾期付款利息。如果实际的加工装配成本低于被许可方已支付的许可费数额，许可方应退还多支付的许可费以及该多余部分金额从多余付款日到退款日为止日数按年利率【　】%计算的利息。双方应平均负担由此而发生的相关费用。

If there are discrepancies noted from the audit carried out in accordance with Article 4.8, the Licensee shall have the right to engage an independent auditor chosen by agreement among the Parties to verify the actual Processing and Assembly Costs. The Parties shall accept the findings of the independent auditor as final. If the actual Processing and Assembly Costs is greater than the amount for which the Licensee has paid royalties, the Licensee shall pay the additional royalties due forthwith together with interest on the amount overdue calculated for each overdue day until payment at the rate of 【　】% per annum. If the actual Processing and Assembly Costs is less than the amount for which the Licensee has paid royalties, the Licensor shall refund the excess royalties received together with interest on the excess amount calculated for each overpaid day until receipt at the rate of 【　】% per annum. Both Parties shall share equally the related expenses arising therefrom. ①

4.11 如果被许可方未按本协议规定的期限向许可方支付许可费，许可方有权要求被许可方就逾期日数支付按年利率【 】%计算的逾期付款利息。

If the Licensee fails to pay the royalties to the Licensor within the time limits specified in this Agreement，the Licensor shall be entitled to charge the Licensee interest on the amount overdue calculated for each overdue day at the rate of 【 】% per annum.

第 5 条　声明、保证及其他条件
Representations, Warranties and other Conditions

5.1 许可方在此声明与保证：

（1）许可方具有充分的合法权利将该技术授权被许可方使用。该技术以及与此相关的全部知识产权与任何第三方的权利无关。被许可方使用该技术将不侵犯任何第三方的知识产权或任何其他方的任何权利。

（2）如果按照许可方根据本协议条款不时告知被许可方的标准和规格使用该技术，则本协议所授权使用的该技术，就该加工厂的经营以及该产品的制造、生产及/或加工而言是完整和有效的。

（3）倘若由于超出许可方的充分、完全和排他性控制的情况，致使该技术失灵或未达到要求的标准或规格时，则本第 5 条所规定的保证将不适用；这些情况包括但不限于：（i）合资合同所定义的任何不可抗力事件；（ii）如果许可方已事先给予被许可方有关的详细指示，但被许可方没有遵守该指示，被许可方在其工厂没有保持使用该技术的适当条件；（iii）如果许可方已就正确使用该技术事先给予被许可方详细的指示，但被许可方没有遵守该指示，被许可方对该技术使用不当；（iv）未经许可方事先同意，对任何技术文件的未经授权翻译；（v）在本协议实施过程中所进行的任何该培训、技术支持或其他活动期间，没有遵守许可方给予被许可方的正确指示。

（4）如果许可方违反上述任何保证或者有关该技术质量方面的任何其他责任，许可方在收到被许可方就该违约发出的通知后，应立即向被许可方提供对该技术有缺陷的项目、部分或要素的纠正或替换。

（5）在许可方对该技术作出改进的情况下，许可方应在合理时间内通知被许可方，许可被许可方使用该改进，并尽其最大努力向被许可方的雇员提供现场技术培训与援助。

因许可方违反本第 5.1 条的任何声明或保证或与该技术有关的其他责

---

① 本条款中关于双方平均负担独立审计费用的规定，是由于本协议双方之间的特殊关系（合营公司与其股东的关系）。在一般情况下，往往是由过错方或责任方负担独立审计费用。例如：如属于被许可方的错误，独立审计费用由被许可方负担；如被许可方审计结果与独立审计的一致，独立审计费用由许可方负担。

任而导致被许可方产生或遭受的一切损失、损害或费用，许可方应承担赔偿责任。

The Licensor hereby represents and warrants that:

（1） The Licensor has the full legal right to grant the license of the Technology to the Licensee. The Technology and all intellectual property rights in relation thereto are not subject to any third party right（s）whatsoever. The use of the Technology by the Licensee will not infringe any third party intellectual property right（s）or any right（s）of any other party（ies）.

（2） The Technology licensed hereunder is complete and effective for the operation of the Processing Plant and the manufacture, production and/or processing of the Products if utilized in accordance with the Licensor's standards and specifications as from time to time communicated by the Licensor to the Licensee pursuant to the terms of this Agreement. ①

（3） The warranties set forth in this Article 5 shall not apply if the Technology malfunctions or fails to perform up to the required standards or specifications due to circumstances not within the full, complete and exclusive control of the Licensor, including but not limited to, （i） any Event of Force Majeure as defined in the JV Contract; （ii） failure by the Licensee to maintain appropriate conditions in its plant for the use of the Technology provided that the Licensor shall have given prior detailed instructions to the Licensee in relation thereto and the Licensee shall have failed to observe such instructions; （iii） improper use of the Technology by the Licensee provided that the Licensor shall have given prior detailed instructions to the Licensee on the proper use of the Technology and the Licensee shall have failed to observe such instructions; （iv） unauthorized translation of any of the technical documentation without the prior consent of the Licensor; （v） failure to follow the proper instructions given by the Licensor during any Training, technical support or other activity in the course of the implementation of this Agreement. ②

（4） In the event of any breach by the Licensor of any of the above warranties or any other duty in respect of or relating to the quality of the Technology, the Licensor shall, forthwith upon notice by the Licensee of such breach, provide the Licensee with a correction of or replacement for the defective item, part or

---

① 请注意本条款中许可方对该技术完整有效的承诺，是以"如果按照许可方根据本协议条款不时告知被许可方的标准和规格使用该技术"为前提条件的。

② 本条款对第 5 条的保证适用范围进一步作出详细的限定，以保护许可方的利益。

element of the Technology. ①

（5）In the event that any Improvements to the Technology are developed by the Licensor, the Licensor shall within reasonable time notify the Licensee and license such Improvements to the Licensee and use its best endeavors to provide on-site technical training and assistance to the Licensee's employees.

The Licensor shall indemnify the Licensee for all losses, damages or costs arising or resulting from the breach of any of the representations or warranties given by the Licensor in this Article 5. 1 or other duty in respect of or relating to the Technology.

5.2 被许可方在此声明、保证与承诺如下：

（1）被许可方将严格遵照适用于该技术的规格和要求生产与制造该产品。

（2）被许可方将该技术专用于该产品的装配与制造，并严格按照本协议的条款和条件执行。

（3）被许可方确保对该技术的一切使用、应用和开发以及被许可方根据本协议负责的关于本协议实施的所有方面，将只由完全合格的人员进行。

（4）被许可方始终对全部该技术及技术文件严格保密，该技术及技术文件仅披露给那些因其职责需要知悉或接触该技术及技术文件的人员。

（5）因被许可方生产与销售该产品所发生的产品责任而由顾客提出的全部索赔，由被许可方负责；被许可方应赔偿并使许可方免于受到此类索赔的损害，并应就此风险投保适当的保险。

（6）在许可方不时提出合理要求时，在许可方负担被许可方所发生的全部成本和费用的条件下，被许可方将协助许可方确保在中国境内除被许可方之外的任何实体未经许可方事先书面同意不以任何方式使用或实施该技术。被许可方承诺，未经许可方知悉与同意，不复制该技术或将其披露给任何第三方或为自己的利益使用该技术。本条款应结合下述第 11 条关于保密的条款进行解释。

因被许可方违反本第 5.2 条的任何声明或保证或与该产品质量有关的其他责任而导致许可方产生或遭受的一切损失、损害或费用，被许可方应承担赔偿责任。

The Licensee hereby represents, warrants, covenants and undertakes that:

（1）The Licensee will produce and manufacture the Products strictly in accordance with the specifications and requirements of the applicable Technology.

（2）The Licensee will use the Technology solely in connection with the assembly and manufacture of the Products and strictly in

---

① 本条款是对许可方的违约责任范围作出的限定，即"对该技术有缺陷的项目、部分或要素的纠正或替换"。

accordance with the terms and conditions of this Agreement.

（3）The Licensee will ensure that all use，application and exploitation of the Technology and all aspects of the implementation of this Agreement for which the Licensee is responsible hereunder will be conducted only by fully qualified personnel.

（4）The Licensee will at all times maintain the strict confidentiality of all Technology and technical documentation，shall disclose such Technology and technical documentation only to those of its personnel whose duties require knowledge of or access to such Technology and technical documentation.

（5）The Licensee will bear responsibility for any and all claims by customers based on product liability concerning the Products manufactured and sold by the Licensee，and the Licensee shall indemnify and hold the Licensor harmless from all such claims and shall obtain appropriate insurance coverage of such risk.

（6）The Licensee will assist the Licensor，as reasonably requested by the Licensor from time to time and subject to the condition that the Licensor shall bear all costs and expenses incurred by the Licensee in relation thereto，in ensuring that no entity in the PRC other than the Licensee shall use or practice the Technology in any manner without the prior written consent of the Licensor. In this regard the Licensee covenants not to copy the Technology or disclose it to any third party or make use of it for its own benefit without the knowledge and consent of the Licensor. This Clause is to be read in conjunction with the provisions regarding Confidentiality in Article 11 below.

The Licensee shall indemnify the Licensor for all losses，damages or costs arising or resulting from the breach of any of the representations or warranties given by the Licensee in this Article 5. 2 or other duty in respect of or relating to the quality of the Products.

第 6 条　实施

Implementation[①]

6.1　本协议的实施以及本协议项下该技术的使用和开发，均由许可方不时指派的技术经理负责管理、指导与监督。

The implementation of this Agreement and the use and exploitation of the Technology hereunder shall be under the authority，direction and supervision of the technical manager from time to time appointed by the Licensor.

---

① 本条就许可方对该技术在被许可方的各项实施环节作了详细周密的约定，明确双方的各项权利义务，以避免因事先考虑不周或约定不明确而发生争议。

6.2 为使被许可方能够利用与开发根据本协议许可的该技术，许可方应不时向被许可方派遣合格的技术人员，向被许可方人员提供培训与技术援助。派遣技术人员的人数、时间安排、持续期间、工作时间表、日程以及其他细节，应由双方本着诚信原则协商确定。

To enable the Licensee to utilize and exploit the Technology licensed hereunder, the Licensor shall, from time to time, dispatch certain qualified Technicians to the Licensee for the purpose of providing Training and technical support to the Licensee's personnel. The number of the Technicians to be dispatched and the timing, duration, work schedule, agenda and other details shall be negotiated and agreed upon by the Parties in good faith.

6.3 被许可方应负责协助许可方取得任何及全部所需的签证、工作许可以及/或者其他批准，以使许可方人员能够出入中国并在中国旅行、居住和工作；但这些相关人员应就办理这些手续向被许可方不时提供必要的协助。

The Licensee shall be responsible for assisting the Licensor to obtain any and all visas, work permits and/or other authorizations necessary to permit and enable the Licensor's personnel to enter into, travel, reside and work within and exit from the PRC, provided that such relevant personnel shall render all necessary assistance to the Licensee as from time to time required for processing such visas, work permits and/or other authorizations.

6.4 许可方所提供的培训及技术援助，原则上应用英文进行。被许可方应负责自费安排充足人数的合格翻译。这些翻译不仅需具备英文与中文的双语能力，同时还应具备足够的技术知识，以便准确、高效率地翻译技术资料。

The training and technical support provided by the Licensor shall be conducted principally in the English language. The Licensee shall be responsible for arranging, at its own expense, for the services of a sufficient number of qualified interpreters. Such interpreters shall not only be bilingual in both the English and Chinese languages, but also have sufficient technical understanding to accurately and efficiently interpret technical materials.

6.5 关于许可方派遣人员的劳务费，被许可方负责直接向每一被派遣人员每月支付【 】美元，但被派遣人员每月工资或补贴中超过【 】美元的部分由许可方支付。此外，被许可方还应负责支付下述各项：

生活费：向被派遣人员提供在该加工厂的饮食住宿以及从该加工厂至宿舍的交通；

交通费：每年三次向被派遣人员提供往返于中国和【 】的飞机票，但仅限于经济舱；

其他费用：双方一致同意的与被派遣人员有关的其他实际发生的支出，视实际业务范围而定。

In regard to the labor costs of the personnel assigned by the Licensor, the Licensee shall be responsible to pay directly to each of the assigned personnel US＄【 】 each month, and the Licensor shall pay any amount of salary or allowance exceeding the amount of US＄【 】 each month to each assigned personnel. In addition, the Licensee shall be responsible for the following:

Living Costs: Provide accommodation costs, meals in the Processing Plant and transportation to and from the Processing Plant to the dormitory for the assigned personnel;

Travel Expenses: Costs of economy class air fares between 【 】 and the PRC for the assigned personnel no more than three (3) a year;

Other Fees: Other actual costs or out-of-pocket expenses relating to the assigned personnel as both Parties shall mutually agree and depending on the scope of the actual engagement.

6.6 作为提供技术援助与服务的对价，被许可方应向许可方支付技术服务费（以下简称"**技术服务费**"），按每位被派遣技术人员每天【 】美元计算，从该技术人员为此目的离开【 】国当天开始，直到其离开中国之日为止。

In consideration of the technical assistance and services to be rendered, the Licensee shall pay to the Licensor a Technical Assistance Fee (hereinafter referred to as "**Technical Assistance Fee**") calculated at US＄【 】 for each day for each assigned technician, calculated from the date of departure from 【 】 for such purpose until the date of departure from the PRC.

6.7 许可方应就技术服务费和上述其他费用每月向被许可方发出账单。被许可方应在收到账单后 30 天内向许可方付款。

The Licensor shall bill the Licensee for the Technical Assistance Fee and the other costs described above on a monthly basis. The Licensee shall pay to the Licensor within thirty (30) days after receipt of the invoice.

6.8 上述付款的汇率按照实际付款日中国银行公布的买入价和卖出价的中间价计算。

Exchange rate for the above payment shall be based at the median of the buying and selling rate of the Bank of China on the actual payment date.

6.9 以本协议第 4.1 条的规定为条件，除非双方另有约定，上述全部费用的生效与适用从本协议生效时开始，直至本协议有效期届满时为止。如果本协议被续期，上述列明的费用应由双方协商一致进行调整。

Subject to Article 4.1 hereof, all the above charges shall be valid and applicable from the time this Agreement becomes effective until the expiry of the Term，unless otherwise provided by the Parties. In the event of extension of this Agreement，the above listed charges shall be adjusted accordingly by mutual agreement.

第 7 条　第三方假冒和侵权
Counterfeiting and Infringement by Third Party[①]

7.1　被许可方在知悉对该产品的任何假冒行为以及/或者对该技术或许可方的任何其他专有技术权利或其他知识产权或工业产权的任何侵权行为后，应立即书面通知许可方。许可方在此保留专属权利，针对该产品的假冒者或侵权者，或针对该技术或许可方的任何其他专有技术权利或知识产权或工业产权的假冒者或侵权者，提起并进行一项或数项诉讼或采取其他法律行动。为实现这一目的，许可方在向被许可方事先发出合理通知后，可以以被许可方的名义作为原告或共同原告（单独或与许可方共同行动），但许可方应充分补偿被许可方由此发生的一切相关费用和开支。

The Licensee shall immediately inform the Licensor in writing of any counterfeiting of the Products and/or infringement of any of the Technology or any other proprietary technology right or other intellectual or industrial property right of the Licensor of which the Licensee shall become aware. The Licensor hereby reserves the exclusive right to introduce and pursue one or several suits or other actions against counterfeiters or infringers of the Products, or any of the Technology or any other proprietary or intellectual or industrial property rights of the Licensor. To accomplish this objective, the Licensor may upon giving reasonable prior notice to the Licensee use the name of the Licensee as plaintiff or co-plaintiff，either separately or in conjunction with the Licensor，provided that the Licensee shall be fully indemnified by the Licensor for all its costs and expenses in relation thereto.

7.2　除非许可方和被许可方事先另有书面协议，根据本第 7 条或与侵害该技术或其他相关知识产权有关而提起、继续及进行的所有诉讼或其他法律行动，均由许可方负担费用，而对于在该等诉讼中遭受损失或发生费用的补偿或赔偿金额，均应归许可方所有。倘若许可方和被许可方均参与针对第三方的该等诉讼，应各自负担其费用，并有权获得对其各自损害的赔偿。

Unless otherwise provided by prior written agreement between the Licensor and the Licensee, all suits or other actions under this Article 7 or otherwise in relation to any action against any infringement of the Technology or any intellectual property rights in relation thereto shall

---

①　本条款详细规定了针对可能发生的第三方假冒该产品以及对该技术等的侵权行为采取法律行动的情况及其对策，对于双方权利义务的约定比较平衡、对等。

be introduced, maintained and conducted at the expense of the Licensor, and all sums received as indemnities or compensation for damages suffered or expenses incurred in any such suit shall remain the property of the Licensor. If the Licensor and the Licensee both participate in legal actions against third parties, they shall each bear their own costs thereof and be entitled to their respective damages.

7.3　如果许可方选择不起诉或不采取法律行动，被许可方在事先征得许可方书面同意后，可以自己的名义自费采取上述行动。

In the event that the Licensor elects not to introduce or pursue any such suit or action, the Licensee may take such action in its own name and on its own cost, after receiving prior written consent from the Licensor.

第 8 条　专有权

Proprietary Rights[①]

8.1　该技术及相关技术文件以及其中含有的任何及全部著作权、商业秘密、专有技术和其他知识产权或工业产权的所有权及其全部专有权，应始终归属于许可方及其母公司所有。在本协议期满终止或提前解除时，被许可方须立即将全部技术文件交还给许可方。

The title to the Technology and the related technical documentation and to any and all copyrights, trade secrets, know-how and other intellectual or industrial property rights therein and all proprietary rights thereto, shall at all times vest in and remain with the Licensor and its parent company. All technical documentation shall be returned by the Licensee to the Licensor immediately upon the expiration or earlier termination of this Agreement.

8.2　除了本协议规定的有限使用权之外，被许可方不得获取该技术或技术文件中的任何权利或权益。倘若被许可方采取行动对许可方在该技术或技术文件中的任何专有权进行质疑、损害或以任何方式威胁，许可方有权解除本协议。

The Licensee shall not acquire any right or interest in the Technology or the technical documentation except the limited use rights pursuant to the terms of this Agreement. Any action by the Licensee that challenges jeopardizes or in any way threatens any of the Licensor's proprietary rights in the Technology or technical documentation shall entitle the Licensor to terminate this Agreement.

8.3　尽管双方之间存在上述第 8.2 条的约定，如果被许可方依中国法律规定或以任何其他方式获得任何一项该技术中任何种类的任何权利、所有权或权益，作为对本协议项下授予使用权的部分对价，被许可方在

---

①　许可方提供的该技术既包括经注册登记保护的知识产权，也有通过保密手段保护的专有技术等。本条款确认了许可方对该技术的专有权，并从多方面规定了对该技术及其相关技术文件的保护方式。

此同意：许可方是上述权利、所有权或权益的受益所有权人，作为对本协议项下授予权利的部分对价，被许可方在此不可撤销地和无条件地将此种权利、所有权或权益转让给许可方。被许可方在此明确同意：经许可方要求，被许可方应签署必要或适当的任何文件，以便完成、登记或完善上述转让。许可方应负担本第 8.3 条或下述第 8.4 条项下与该转让或其他权利有关的全部律师费、登记费及其他费用。

In the event that notwithstanding the agreement between the Parties set forth in Clause 8.2 above, the Licensee acquires any right, title or interest of any kind in any item of the Technology by operation of PRC law or by any means whatsoever, the Licensee, in partial consideration of the license granted hereunder, hereby agrees that the Licensor shall be the beneficial owner thereof, and the Licensee, in partial consideration of the rights granted hereunder, hereby irrevocably and unconditionally assigns such right title or interest to the Licensor. The Licensee hereby expressly agrees that upon request from the Licensor, the Licensee shall sign or execute any documents which may be necessary or appropriate to accomplish, register or perfect such assignment. The Licensor shall be responsible for all legal and registration and other costs in relation to such assignment or other right in this Article 8.3 or Article 8.4 below.

8.4 经许可方要求，被许可方应签署或获得签署任何必要或适当的文书、文件或协议以及/或者确保中国政府的任何必要或适当的批准或登记，以便在中国完善或保护许可方在该技术和/或技术文件中的任何专有权。

At the Licensor's request, the Licensee shall execute or obtain the execution of any instrument, document or agreement and/or secure any PRC governmental approval or registration that may be necessary or appropriate to perfect or protect in the PRC any of the Licensor's proprietary rights in the Technology and/or the technical documentation.

第 9 条　修改或改进
Modifications or Improvements①

9.1 任何该改进的所有权以及申请、注册、持有、拥有、使用和开发与该技术的任何该改进有关的任何专利权、著作权或其他任何种类的知识产权或工业产权的任何权利，均归属于许可方所有。

Title to any Improvement and any rights to apply for, register, hold, own, utilize and exploit any patent, copyright or other intellectual or industrial property right of any kind whatsoever relating any such

---

① 在本条款中，在确认对该技术的任何改进所产生的权利均归属于许可方的同时，对于许可方或被许可方所进行的技术改进，作出了双方的使用权利对等的约定。

Improvements to the Technology shall vest in and belong to the Licensor.

9.2　如果被许可方对任何一项该技术作了任何其他改进，被许可方应在本协议的有效期内授权许可方免费使用该改进的技术。

In the event that the Licensee develops any other improvement of any kind to any item of the Technology, the Licensee shall grant the Licensor the right to use all such improved technology freely during the term of this Agreement.

9.3　许可方对本协议附件 A 所列任何一项该技术所作的任何改进，均应授权被许可方免费使用，被许可方在本协议有效期内无需为此负担额外费用和条件。

The Licensor shall grant the Licensee the right to use freely any Improvements developed by the Licensor to any item of the Technology which is listed in Schedule A attached hereto, without imposing additional costs and conditions on the Licensee during the Term of this Agreement.

第 10 条　赔偿

Indemnities[①]

10.1　倘若发生针对被许可方的诉讼，声称任何该技术侵犯了在本协议签署之日依据中国法律存在的某项专利或专有技术权利，则许可方将自费为被许可方进行抗辩，并将支付被许可方在侵权诉讼中最终被判必须缴付的赔偿费和诉讼费；但许可方这样做的前提条件为：（i）被许可方在获悉可能或已被声称索赔后，立即以书面方式通知许可方；（ii）许可方对于索赔的抗辩以及其任何解决或和解的谈判有独家控制权；以及（iii）被许可方并未进行许可方认为是违反许可方利益的任何行动。

If an action is brought against the Licensee claiming that any of the Technology infringes upon a patent or proprietary technology right existing under PRC law as of the date of this Agreement, the Licensor will defend the Licensee at the Licensor's expense and will pay the damages and costs finally awarded against the Licensee in the infringement action, but only if: (i) the Licensee notifies the Licensor in writing promptly upon learning that the claim may be or has been asserted; (ii) the Licensor has sole control over the defense of the claim and any negotiation for its settlement or compromise; and (iii) the Licensee has not taken any action that, in the Licensor's judgment, is contrary to the Licensor's interests.

10.2　被许可方应独自负责并赔偿许可方由于被许可方未按照本协议条款使用该技术而发生的或与之有关而发生的任何及所有索赔、损害、费用

---

① 本条款的赔偿规定对于双方来说是平衡的、相当合理的。

及收费。

The Licensee shall be solely responsible for and shall indemnify the Licensor against any and all claims, damages, expenses and fees arising out of or in connection with any use by the Licensee of the Technology which is not in accordance with the terms of this Agreement.

第 11 条 保密和非竞争
Confidentiality and Noncompetition

11.1 许可方在本协议项下向被许可方提供的任何计划、设计、制造工艺或质量标准等，或有关许可方的业务、财务和计划的任何信息，或因履行本协议或与本协议有关而取得的有关该技术的信息，均须作为秘密进行保密；在本协议有效期内或在本协议终止后，未经许可方事先书面授权，被许可方不得向任何个人、商号、公司或其他实体披露，但按照本协议规定或为本协议目的而披露的则不在此限。

Any plan, design, manufacturing process or quality standard etc. provided by the Licensor to the Licensee under this Agreement, or any information in connection with the business, finance and planning of the Licensor, or information in connection with the Technology obtained through the performance of this Agreement or related with this Agreement, shall be considered confidential and shall not be disclosed to any individual, firm, company or other entity during the term of this Agreement and thereafter without the prior written authorization of the Licensor, save in accordance with this Agreement or for the purposes of this Agreement.

11.2 被许可方应将该技术及技术文件仅提供给那些因其职责有必要熟悉这些技术及技术文件的人员。

The Licensee shall make such Technology and technical documentation available only to those of its personnel whose duties necessitate familiarity with such Technology and technical documentation.

11.3 被许可方确认并同意，如果违反本协议中的保密规定，将对许可方造成无法弥补的严重损害；对于许可方提供的该技术或技术文件的任何项目、部分或要素，任何未经许可方事先书面同意的披露而给许可方造成的任何损害、损失或伤害，均应由被许可方负责。被许可方应立即以书面方式将此种披露通知许可方，并自费采取一切必要措施，回收该技术或技术文件并防止未经授权的使用或传播，包括采取一切可以采取的法律上及/或行政上的措施。

The Licensee acknowledges and agrees that a breach of the confidentiality provisions set forth in this Agreement will result in serious and irreparable harm to the Licensor and that the Licensee shall be responsible for any damage, loss or injury to the Licensor, caused by any disclosure without the prior written consent by the

Licensor of any item，part or element of the Technology or technical documentation provided by the Licensor. The Licensee shall immediately notify the Licensor in writing of any such disclosure and take，at the Licensee's expense，all steps which are necessary to recover such Technology or technical documentation and to prevent its unauthorized use or dissemination，including the taking of all legal and/or administrative measures available.

11.4　除非许可方另以书面方式明确同意，本协议一旦解除，根据本协议授予被许可方的所有权利即随之停止；被许可方应立即将其占有、控制或包含有任何保密信息的全部文件交还给许可方，包括但不限于下列各项：

（1）许可方提供的文件原件和数据的全部复印件；

（2）被许可方根据许可方提供的数据而编撰的文件原件和数据的全部复印件。

Upon termination of this Agreement，all rights granted to the Licensee hereunder shall cease，unless otherwise expressly agreed to in writing by the Licensor，and the Licensee shall immediately deliver to the Licensor all the documents within the Licensee's possession or control that contain any confidential information including but not limited to the following：

（1）Original documents including all photocopies of data supplied by the Licensor.

（2）Original documents including all photocopies of data compiled by the Licensee based on the data supplied by the Licensor.

11.5　在本协议有效期内以及在本协议期满终止或提前解除后，本条的保密规定仍然有效。

The confidentiality provisions set forth in this Article shall remain in effect during the term of this Agreement and after the termination or expiration of this Agreement. ①

11.6　被许可方进一步承诺并同意，对于因其自身或其任何关联公司违反本条款而作出的赔偿可能是不充足的补救措施，许可方在要求对其可能遭受的损害进行赔偿之外，有权要求禁止令救济。

The Licensee further acknowledge and agree that in any breach of this Article by it or its affiliates or any one of them，damages may be an inadequate remedy，and the Licensor shall have the right to claim injunctive②relief in addition to any other claims for damages which

---

①　保密期限可以超过协议的有效期，这种约定方式是很常见的。

②　Injunctive 是 injunction 的形容词形式，后者可译为 "禁令" "禁止令" 或 "禁制令" "强制令"，是衡平法上的一种救济方法，是英美法中法院或行政机构颁发的一种命令，禁止某项行为或不作为，以消除对某项权利的侵害或某种非法状态的持续，给予受害人救济。

they may have. ①

11.7 任何一方均应尽其最大努力诚意支持合营公司的业务。为了使用该技术或其任何改进能够生产该产品，双方同意在实际可能的情况下，向合营企业介绍客户或业务，或者将双方或通过其各自关联公司接到的订单转介给合营公司。

Each of the Parties hereto shall use their best endeavors in good faith to support the business of the JV Company. In this regard，the Parties agree that wherever practicable to do so，they shall introduce to the JV Company's customers or business or orders received by them or through their respective affiliates for the production of the Products which can be produced using the Technology or any Improvements thereof. ②

11.8 本协议各方同意，如果其本身或其任何关联公司或有关企业决定设立或另外从事与合营公司相同或类似的其他生产设施，该方应事前通知另一方并共同协商，以确保合营公司的业务不致因此受到严重的不利影响。该方或通过其关联公司设立或另外从事这些其他生产设施时，该方有义务向另一方解释，在本协议有效期内合营公司业务将不会因此受到严重的不利影响之理由。

Each of the Parties hereto agrees that if it or any of its affiliates or related enterprises decides to establish or otherwise engage in other manufacturing facilities identical or similar to those of the JV Company，it shall inform the other Party beforehand and consult together to ensure that the business of the JV Company is not and will not be materially adversely affected thereby. The Party which，or through its affiliate（s），establishes or otherwise engages in such other manufacturing facilities shall be obligated to explain to the other Party why the business of the JV Company will not be materially adversely affected thereby during the term of this Agreement.

11.9 本第11条的任何规定不得被解释为：（i）向本协议任何一方或其关联公司施加第11.8条规定的义务，或者（ii）阻止任何一方或其关联公司进行或继续进行在本协议签订时正在从事的业务，即使这些业务可能被认为与合营公司的业务存在竞争关系。

Nothing in this Article 11 shall be construed so as（i）to impose the obligations provided under Article 11. 8 on any Party（ies）or their affiliates，or（ii）to prevent any Party（ies）or their affiliates from carrying on or continuing to carry on，any business in which they are currently engaged as of the date hereof，even though such business may be considered to be competitive with the business of the JV Company.

---

① 例如，可请求法院判令侵权人停止对该技术相关权利（专利权、著作权、商业秘密等）的侵权行为等。

② 第11.7～11.9条属于非竞争条款，请参照本书第6章第1节（合资合同）的相关规定。

第 12 条　有效期与提前解约

Term and Termination[①]

12.1 本协议的有效期为 10 年，自被许可方的营业执照颁发之日起开始起算，根据双方的一致协议可以续期。

The Term of this Agreement shall be for a period of ten（10）years from the date of issuance of the business license of the Licensee and renewable upon mutual agreement by the Parties.

12.2 倘若任何一方严重违反其在本协议项下的任何义务，而且在收到守约方指出其违约的书面通知后 30 天内仍未纠正该违约行为，则守约方在该 30 天通知期满后可以解除本协议。

If any Party materially breaches any of its obligations under this Agreement and such breach is not remedied within thirty（30）days after receipt of written notice of the breach from the non-breaching Party, the non-breaching Party may terminate this Agreement upon expiry of such thirty（30）-day notice to the other Party.

12.3 如果任何一方失去偿债能力或破产，或进入清算程序（无论是主动清算或被迫清算），或任何一方的主要资产被任何第三方占有、没收、征用或占用，或被许可方成为无能力或无法充分履行本协议项下义务的，本协议则自动终止。

This Agreement shall automatically cease，in the event that any Party becomes insolvent or bankrupt，or goes into liquidation（no matter whether voluntarily or compelled），or any Party's substantial assets have been possessed，confiscated，expropriated or occupied by any third party，or the Licensee becomes incapable or unable to fully perform its obligations under this Agreement.

12.4 发生下述任何情形之一的，许可方在通知被许可方后可以立即解除本协议：

（1）被许可方多次或连续性地未能及时支付本协议项下的许可费和其他费用，许可方已向被许可方事前发出与此有关的书面警告；

（2）被许可方违反本协议项下的保密规定；

（3）被许可方将该技术用于履行本协议以外的其他目的；

（4）被许可方未经许可方事先书面同意，转让或意图将该技术转让给第三方；

（5）被许可方进行与许可方拥有该技术的所有权、权益和权利不相符的任何行为，且该行为严重地损害许可方的业务、利益或声誉。

The Licensor may terminate this Agreement forthwith upon notice to the Licensee in any of the following events：

（1）repeated or continual failure by the Licensee to make timely

---

① 考虑到双方之间的关系（合营企业与其股东之一的关系），本条款规定的权利义务是相当对等、平等的。而在一般情况下的技术许可协议解约条款中，往往许可方拥有更多的权力和权利。

payments of the royalties and other charges under this Agreement and prior written warning in relation thereto has been given by the Licensor to the Licensee；

（2）breach by the Licensee of confidentiality provisions of this Agreement；

（3）use of the Technology by the Licensee for purposes other than performance of this Agreement；

（4）transfer or purported transfer of the Technology by the Licensee to a third party without the Licensor's prior written consent；

（5）any actions by the Licensee which are inconsistent with the Licensor's ownership interest and rights to the Technology，and which cause material damage to the Licensor's business，interests or reputation.

12.5　在本协议解除或期满时，依据本协议授予被许可方的全部权利和许可应立即停止，被许可方应立即停止使用任何该技术，且从此以后不再使用该技术，但经许可方以书面方式明确同意的除外。

Upon the termination or expiration of this Agreement，all rights and licenses granted to the Licensee hereunder shall cease forthwith and the Licensee shall immediately discontinue any and all use of the Technology and thereafter refrain from any future use thereof，unless such future use is expressly permitted in writing by the Licensor.

第 13 条　不可抗力
Force Majeure

13.1　倘若发生不可抗力事件，以致一方或双方的合同义务由于该事件而无法履行，该等义务应于该不可抗力事件导致的延误期间内暂缓履行，但受该不可抗力影响的一方或双方须尽一切合理的努力并在合理的范围内尽快消除或减轻该不可抗力事件的影响。

If an event of Force Majeure occurs，to the extent that[①]the contractual obligations of the Party or Parties cannot be performed as a result of such event，such obligations shall be suspended during the period of the delay caused by the event of Force Majeure，provided that the Party or Parties affected by such Force Majeure shall use all reasonable efforts to eliminate or reduce the effects of the same with all reasonable scope.

13.2　如果任何一方由于不可抗力事件而无法履行其在本协议项下的任何义务，受影响的一方应立即以传真或电邮通知另一方该不可抗力事件的发生以及随后的终止。

---

① "to the extent that…"，意为"达到……的程度""在……范围内"，是英文合同或其他法律文件中常用的短语，that 后面的内容是限定或排除的程度或范围的具体内容（一般为权利或义务），在理解其原有含义的基础上，在具体翻译时可根据上下文使用符合中文表达习惯的翻译方法，以便使语句更加通顺。

If any Party is prevented from performing any of its obligations under this Agreement due to an event of Force Majeure, the affected Party shall immediately notify the other Party of the occurrence and subsequent termination of the event of Force Majeure by facsimile or e-mail.

13.3 如果任何不可抗力事件造成的延误持续超过 6 个月，双方应通过友好协商解决进一步履行本协议的问题。

In the event that the delay caused by any event of Force Majeure continues for more than six（6）months, the Parties shall settle the problem of further performance of this Agreement through friendly negotiation.

第 14 条　适用法律
Governing Law

本协议适用中国法律，并按照中国法律解释。如果中国法律对争议中的特定问题未作规定，双方同意遵循与此相关的国际惯例。

This Agreement shall be governed by and construed in accordance with the laws of the PRC. In the event that PRC law is silent on any particular point in dispute, the Parties agree to follow relevant international practice with respect thereto. ①

第 15 条　争议解决
Settlement of Disputes

因本协议发生的任何争议或与本协议所处理的事项相关的任何争议，双方同意通过友好协商解决。如协商不成，争议事项应提交香港国际仲裁中心（下称"该仲裁中心"），按照该仲裁中心的仲裁规则在香港进行仲裁，裁决是终局性的，双方在此不可撤销地接受该仲裁中心的管辖权。

In the event of any dispute arising out of this Agreement, or in relation to the matters dealt with herein, the Parties hereto agree to settle such dispute through amicable negotiation, failing which, the matter in dispute shall be finally decided by arbitration in Hong Kong in accordance with the rules of the Hong Kong International Arbitration Centre（hereinafter called "**HKIAC**"）and the Parties hereby irrevocably submit themselves to the jurisdiction of HKIAC.

第 16 条　语言
Languages

本协议用中文和英文制作，两种文本均具有法律效力。如果两种文本有不一致之处，以中文文本为准。

---

① 鉴于中国法律对有些问题还存在一些灰色地带（grey area），如中国法律中无相关规定可依据，双方根据此条款可以适用相关的国际惯例。

This Agreement has been prepared in the Chinese and English languages，all of which have legal effect. In the event of any discrepancies between the two versions，the Chinese version shall prevail.

第 17 条　通知
Notices

17.1　按本协议所要求或允许的所有通知、请求、要求和其他通讯应采用书面形式；如果通过面交、挂号邮寄、速递、传真或电邮方式发出（在传真或电邮发送的情况下，应在发出后的两个营业日内通过面交、快递或已付邮资挂号信，发出该通知的确认副本），发往以下地址（直至书面通知改变地址时为止），应视为正式发出或发送：

许可方：
　　　　地址：
　　　　传真：
　　　　收件人：

被许可方：
　　　　地址：
　　　　传真：
　　　　收件人：

All notices，requests，demands and other communications required or permitted under this Agreement shall be in writing and shall be deemed to have been duly given or made if delivered by hand，registered mail or sent by courier or facsimile transmission or e-mail provided that in the case of the facsimile transmission or e-mail，a confirmation copy of the notice shall be delivered by hand or sent by courier or registered prepaid mail within two（2）Business Days of the transmission①，to the followings（until notice of a change thereof is given in writing）：

To：Licensor：
　　　　Address：
　　　　Facsimile no. ：
　　　　Attention：

To：Licensee：
　　　　Address：
　　　　Facsimile no. ：
　　　　Attention：

17.2　根据上述第 17.1 条发出或发送的所有通讯，如通过面交、邮寄或速递发送，则在交付时生效；如通过传真或电邮发送，则在传送时生效；倘若交付或传送的时间（按目的地时间计算）为营业日的下午六

---

①　为了保证将通知内容切实送达给对方，在以传真或电邮方式发送通知的情况下，在发出后的一定期间内再通过面交、快递或邮寄方式发送该通知的确认副本给对方，是一些英文合同的通知条款中常用的约定方式。

时以后或在星期六、星期日或公众假日，则被视为于下一个营业日生效。

All communications given or made in accordance with Article 17.1 above shall be effective, if delivered by hand, mailed or sent by courier, at the time of delivery, and if communicated by facsimile or e-mail, at the time of transmission, provided that if such delivery or transmission is made at a time which, in the destination, is later than 6 p. m. on a Business Day, or is on a Saturday, Sunday or public holiday, it shall be deemed effective on the next succeeding Business Day.

第 18 条　弃权
Waiver

一方没有行使或延迟行使按本协议或与本协议相关的其他合同或协议规定的任何权利、权力或优先权，不应作为放弃该等权利、权力或优先权；任何单独或部分地行使任何权利、权力或优先权，不应妨碍将来另外行使该等权利、权力或优先权。

Failure or delay on the part of any Party to exercise any right, power or privilege under this Agreement, or under any other contract or agreement relating hereto, shall not operate as a waiver thereof, nor shall any single or partial exercise of any right, power or privilege preclude any other future exercise thereof.

第 19 条　转让和修改
Assignment and Amendments

19.1　在本协议项下发生的权利专属于双方，未经另一方的书面同意，任何一方不得转让或转移这些权利。

　　　The rights arising under this Agreement are personal to the Parties and shall not be assignable or transferable by any of them except with the written consent of the other Party.

19.2　未经双方授权代表签订进一步的书面协议，不得修改本协议。

　　　This Agreement may not be amended other than by a further agreement in writing and signed by authorized representatives of the Parties.

第 20 条　继承人
Successors

为了双方及其各自继承人或许可受让人的利益，本协议有效并对双方及其各自继承人和许可受让人具有约束力。本协议中一方之名称被视为包括其任何继承人或受让人之名称。

This Agreement shall enure for the benefit of and be binding upon the Parties and their respective successors or permitted assigns, and the name of a Party herein shall be deemed to include the names of any such successor or assign.

第 21 条　可分割性
Severability

本协议任何条款的无效，不影响本协议任何其他条款的有效性。

The invalidity of any provision of this Agreement shall not affect the validity of any other provisions herein.

第 22 条　标题
Headings

本协议内的标题仅为方便使用而设，不得用于本协议的解释、分析或以其他方式影响本协议条款的含义。

The headings within this Agreement are used for convenience only and shall not be used to interpret，construe or otherwise affect the meaning of the provisions of this Agreement.

第 23 条　全部协议
Entire Agreement

本协议及其全部附件构成双方之间有关本协议标的之全部协议，并取代此前双方之间的全部讨论、协商和协议。

This Agreement and all the Schedules hereof constitute the entire Agreement between the Parties with respect to the subject matter hereof and supersede all prior discussions，negotiation and agreements between the Parties.

第 24 条　生效和登记
Effectiveness and Registration

24.1　本协议及其附件由双方的法定代表人或授权代表签字并加盖各自公司印章后生效。

This Agreement and the Schedules hereof will come into force after signed by both Parties' legal representatives or by their authorized representatives and sealed with each other's corporate stamp.

24.2　在被许可方与许可方正式签订本协议后，如有必要，双方应尽快将本协议副本以及其他有关文件提交给中国主管机关进行登记备案。

After the formal execution of this Agreement by the Licensor and the Licensee，when necessary, the Parties shall submit a duplicate copy of this Agreement together with other relevant documents to the Chinese competent authorities for registration as soon as possible.

本协议各方已由其正式授权代表于本协议开头所述日期签订，以资证明。

IN WITNESS WHEEOF，each of the Parties hereto has caused this Agreement to be executed by its duly authorized representative on the date first set forth above.

许可方：**ABC** 有限公司
Licensor：ABC CO.，LIMITED

签署（Sign）：_____
姓名（Name）：
职衔（Title）：
公司章（Company Chop）

被许可方：**XYZ** 有限公司
Licensee：XYZ CO.，LTD.

签署（Sign）：_____
姓名（Name）：
职衔（Title）：
公司章（Company Chop）

附件 A
SCHEDULE A

技术说明
DESCRIPTION OF TECHNOLOGY①

1. 用于生产该产品的技术工艺和专有技术，包括【 】等特定产品的精密金属模具的设计、铸造、涂层及装配；
   Technical skill and know-how on the production of the Products including the design of the precise metal molding, casting, coating, and assembly covering for the particular product such as 【 】 and so on;
2. 有关使用【 】生产线的大批量生产该产品所需的技术工艺和专有技术，为生产过程的稳定性提供最合适的条件以及完善的原料管理方法，其结果是保证品质，有助于控制在较低的不合格率；
   Technical skill and know-how on the mass-production of the Products using 【 】 production line. This involves setting up the best conditions and a complete management method for the materials and conducive to stabilizing the production process. The resulting quality assurance will help to achieve a lower defect rate;
3. 与建立夹具（提高生产效率的关键所在）相关的技术工艺和专有技术，这要求开发夹持和遮蔽夹具所需设计的特殊方法和流程；
   Technical skill and know-how concerning the set up of the JIG which is the key point for improving the production efficiency. This requires developing special methods and procedures for the design for holding and masking of the JIG;

---

① 关于许可方在本协议项下向被许可方提供的该技术，在本附件 A 中作了具体描述，以便双方据此实施、检查。

4. 建立有效的管理方法，开发所需工艺以达到适当的一致色调及光泽；建立保障质量的评估方法。

Establishment of effective management methods for developing the skills needed for achieving the proper and consistent color tones and gloss. Setting up methods for the evaluation of quality assurance.

附件 B
SCHEDULE B

培训内容
DETAILS OF TRAINING①

培训被许可方的本地员工将按照下述方式进行：

The training of the local staff of the Licensee will be carried out by the following means：

1. 在投产之前，许可方的某些技术人员将常驻该加工厂，按照许可方对生产线的特殊设计和配置来监督生产线设备和机械的安装及/或重新排列；

Certain Technicians from the Licensor will be stationed at the Processing Plant before commencement of production to supervise the installation and/or realignment of production line equipment and machinery in accordance with the Licensor's specified production line design and configuration；

2. 许可方将从【某外国】派遣更多的技术人员，向被许可方的当地生产人员提供本协议所规定的特殊技术培训；

Additional technicians from Licensor will be sent from 【某外国】 to provide specific training sessions to the local production staff of the Licensee in the Technology as defined herein；

3. 许可方技术人员将监督最初的试产和投产，实施质量保障方法和流程；

Licensor's Technicians will supervise initial test and production runs and implement quality assurance methods and procedures；

4. 根据被许可方不时提出的要求，许可方技术人员协助进行设备维修和保养、采购生产材料、检查和测试完成品，直到被许可方的当地员工能够独立进行操作为止；

Licensor's Technicians will be available to assist with equipment maintenance and repair, procurement of production materials and inspection and testing of finished Products as required by the Licensee from time to time until Licensee's local staff can perform these functions independently；

5. 在被许可方不时提出要求时，为了向被许可方提供培训与技术援助，许可方将努力建立明确的程序、日程和目标，并向被许可方提交相关书面

---

① 附件 B 对许可方培训被许可方人员的内容以及相关方法等作了详细说明，便于具体实施。

报告。

The Licensor shall endeavor to set definite procedures，schedules and targets for the training and technical assistance to be provided and to report thereon in writing to the Licensee from time to time as requested.

第6章

合资合同和章程的精选与解读

第 1 节　合资合同精选与解读

【 】年【 】月【 】日签署

Dated【日】day of【月　年】

【X 有限公司】

【X Co. , Ltd. 】

与

AND

【Y 有限公司】

【Y Co. , Ltd. 】

与

AND

【Z 有限公司】

【Z Co. , Ltd. 】

───────────────

XYZ 有限公司

合资合同书

【XYZ Co. , Ltd. 】

JOINT VENTURE CONTRACT

───────────────

目 录
CONTENTS

【XYZ 有限公司】
合资合同书

【XYZ CO. ，LTD. 】
JOINT VENTURE CONTRACT①

第一章　总　则
Chapter 1　General Provisions

1.【X 有限公司】、【Y 有限公司】与【Z 有限公司】，依据《中华人民共和国中外合资经营企业法》和中国其他相关法律法规（以下合称"**合资经营法律法规**"），本着平等互利的原则，经过友好协商，一致同意依据本合同的条款和条件在中华人民共和国（以下简称"**中国**"）【　】市共同投资设立中外合资经营企业。本合资合同于【　】年【　】月【　】日在中国【　】市签订。

【X Co. ，Ltd. 】，【Y Co. ，Ltd. 】and　【Z Co. ，Ltd. 】，in accordance with the Law of the People's Republic of China on Sino-Foreign Equity Joint Venture Enterprises and other relevant Chinese laws and regulations （jointly called "**the Joint Venture Laws and Regulations**"），based on the principle of equality and mutual benefits and after friendly negotiations，agree to jointly invest in and set up a sino-foreign equity joint venture enterprise in【某市】，the People's Republic of China （"**PRC**"②），under the terms and conditions of this Contract. This Contract is executed on the【日】day of【月】【年】in【某市】，the PRC.

第二章　合营公司各方
Chapter 2　Parties to Joint Venture Company③

2.1　本合同的各方为：

The Parties to this Contract are as follows：

甲方：【X 有限公司】

---

① 关于中外合资经营企业合同的中英文本，最早和最常见的示范文本，是在《中华人民共和国中外合资经营企业法》及其实施条例公布后的初期，由当时合资企业设立的政府审批部门"中华人民共和国对外经济贸易部"条约法律局起草的合资合同参考格式。从该格式的内容来看，是以合同的形式体现中外合资相关法律法规的基本内容，对于中外双方的权利义务作了基本平衡的规定，这在当时缺乏类似合同文本的情况下，对于合资双方起到了一定参考作用。但是，在法律实践中，这样的格式合同文本显然并不能充分体现各方当事人对其权利义务作详细约定的需要。笔者在从事涉外法律工作中接触及制作的中外合资合同文本，绝大多数是由律师参考该示范样本的章节架构（为了易于得到审批机关的批准）、另行制作的侧重保护委托方权益内容的合资合同文本。合资合同的文本内容有简繁之分，取决于各方之间的关系、投资金额的多少、引进技术的高低、各方对合营企业的控制和管理等因素。这里向读者介绍的合资合同文本属于较详细之类，是外国合资方委托律师制作，并经各方多次协商修改后的签约文本。读者在制作合资合同时，可以将此作为参考进行取舍；从繁到简，较之从简到繁，相对更加容易。

② 在英文合同中，对于词语全称之后的简称，可以用"hereinafter referred to as..."或者"hereinafter called..."，也可以在括号内以引号""（""）将其标明，中文均可译为（以下简称"……"）。为了在合同中易于找到第一次定义的简称，可将引号内的简称词语以黑色加粗。

③ 在本合同中，X 公司是中方（中国生产厂家），Y 公司是外方（外国生产厂家），Z 公司也是外方（外国贸易公司）。

登记地址：

公司注册地：

法定代表人：

职务：

国籍：

Party A：【X Co., Ltd. 】

Registered address：

Place of incorporation：

Legal representative：

Position：

Nationality：

乙方：【Y 有限公司】

登记地址：

公司注册地：

法定代表人：

职务：

国籍：

Party B：【Y Co., Ltd. 】

Registered address：

Place of incorporation：

Legal representative：

Position：

Nationality：

丙方：【Z 有限公司】

登记地址：

公司注册地：

法定代表人：

职务：

国籍：

Party C：【Z Co., Ltd. 】

Registered address：

Place of incorporation：

Legal representative：

Position：

Nationality：

（以下合称"**各方**"，单独称"**一方**"）

(Collectively the **"Parties"** and individually the **"Party"**)

2.2 本合同每一方在此向其他方声明与保证，在本合同签署之日，下列陈述是真实和准确的：

（a）本身是根据其注册地法律正式成立并有效存续的公司；

（b）本身拥有签订本合同和履行本合同项下义务的全部权力和授权；

（c）本合同的签订、交付和本合同项下义务的履行或本合同所拟议任何交易的完成均不会违犯、抵触或违反下列各项文件的条款、条件或规定：

（i）本身的章程、组织细则或其他章程性文件；

（ii）本身作为一方或受约束的政府当局的任何命令；

（iii）对其有影响的任何法律规定或其应遵守的任何法规、规则或政策的变更；

（iv）其作为一方或其可能受约束的任何合同、抵押、契约、许可、文书、信托文件或者其他合同或文件；以及

（d）不存在任何法律、行政或仲裁程序，或者任何性质的未决诉讼，或者就其所知被威胁诉讼、怀疑或质疑本合同或本合同所预期的任何交易的有效性。

Each of the Parties hereby①represents and warrants to the other Parties that the following representations are true and correct as at the date hereof②：

（a）It is a company duly established and validly existing under the laws of its registered place；

（b）It possesses full power and authority to enter into this Contract and to perform its obligations hereunder；

（c）Neither the execution and delivery of this Contract nor the performance of its obligations hereunder，nor the consummation of any transactions contemplated hereby will violate，conflict with，or result in a breach of the terms，conditions or provisions of：

（i）its charter，by-laws，articles of association or other constitutional documents；

（ii）any order of any governmental authority to which it is a party or by which it is bound；

（iii）any requirements of law affecting it，or any regulations，rules or policies of any change（s）to which it is subject；or

（iv）any contract，mortgage，indenture，permit，instrument，trust document，or other contract or document to which it is a party or by which it may be bound；and

---

① "hereby"经常用于合同中，在当事人表示同意、声明、确认等内容时使用，意为"兹，特此；由此，以此方式"等，以示当事人以正式、郑重的方式，表达hereby后面的内容。

② 在本条中，各方对于其中各项陈述内容（包括其作为合资合同当事方的主体、资格、合规性等）的声明和保证，对于确保各方具备相应的主体资格和缔约能力至关重要。如果任何当事方对此作出虚假陈述，则会构成违约，须承担相应的违约责任。

（d）There is no legal，administrative or arbitration proceeding，suit or action of any nature pending or，to its knowledge，threatened against it which questions or challenges the validity of this Contract，or any of the transactions contemplated hereby.

第三章　成立合营公司
Chapter 3　Establishment of Joint Venture Company

3.1　甲方、乙方和丙方根据中外合资经营法律法规，同意在中国【　】市成立一家中外合资经营有限责任公司（以下简称"**合营公司**"）。合营各方在合营公司具备必要的条件时拟申请合营公司为先进技术企业。

In accordance with the Joint Venture Laws and Regulations，the Parties have agreed to set up a sino-foreign equity joint venture enterprise with limited liability（"**JV Company**"）in【　】，the PRC. The Parties intend to apply for the JV Company to be granted the status of a technologically advanced enterprise upon fulfillment of the necessary conditions.

3.2　合营公司的中文名称为：【**XYZ 有限公司**】

合营公司的英文名称为：【**XYZ** Co.，Ltd.】

合营公司的法定地址为：

The name of the JV Company in Chinese shall be：【**XYZ 有限公司**】

The name of the JV Company in English shall be：【**XYZ Co.，Ltd.**】

The legal address of the JV Company shall be：

3.3　合营公司在中国注册，具有中国法人资格。合营公司受中国法律的管辖和保护。

The JV Company shall be registered in the PRC and shall be a legal person under PRC law. The JV Company shall be subject to the jurisdiction and protection of PRC law.

3.4　合营公司的组织形式为有限责任公司。合营公司作为一家有限责任公司，仅以其资产为限对其任何性质的全部债务和其他义务承担责任。合营公司各方仅以其各自对合营公司认缴的出资额为限对合营公司的债务承担责任，未经各方以书面形式明确承担责任并经其法定代表人同意并签字，各方均不对合营公司任何性质的债务或其他义务承担责任。合营公司的债权人（包括税务当局和其他政府当局）仅有权依法对合营公司的资产进行追索求偿。以这些限制为前提，各方以其在合营公司注册资本中所占的比例分享合营公司的利润，并承担合营公司的风险和亏损。

The JV Company shall be formed as a company with limited liability. As a limited liability company，the JV Company shall have liability to the extent of its assets for all of its debts and other obligations of any nature whatsoever. The Parties of the JV Company shall bear responsibility with respect to the obligations of the JV Company only to the extent of their respective capital contributions to the JV Company and shall not be liable for any debt or other obligation of any nature whatsoever of the JV Company，unless expressly assumed in writing and agreed to and signed by the legal representatives of the Parties so charged. The creditors of the JV Company (including tax authorities and other government authorities) shall have recourse only to the assets of the JV Company for payment according to law. Subject to these limitations，the Parties shall share the profits and bear the risks and losses of the JV Company in proportion to their respective interests in the registered capital.

3.5 合营公司的财务、管理及经营均应独立。合营公司有权拒绝任何第三方的任何不正当干预，除非这种干预符合中国相关法律法规或本合同或合营公司章程的规定；合营公司有权管理自己的资产并自行承担亏损。

The JV Company shall have independent accounts and be managed and operated independently. The JV Company shall have the right to resist any improper interference from any third party，unless such interference is made in accordance with the provisions of the relevant PRC laws and regulations or the terms of this Contract or the Articles of Association of the JV Company，and shall have the right to administer and manage its own assets and bear its own losses.

3.6 合营公司应努力争取获得税收、海关及其他方面可获得的全部优惠待遇，包括但不限于在中国【 】省【 】市外商投资企业可获得的全部优惠待遇。

The JV Company shall use its endeavors to obtain all available preferential treatment in taxes，customs and other areas for enterprises including but not limited to all preferential treatment available to foreign investment enterprises located at【 】,【 】Province，the PRC.

3.7 任何一方准备的与合营公司成立有关的所有文件，在提交给中国政府有关部门审批或备案之前，均应事先经各方审阅和确认。

All documents prepared by any Party in connection with the establish-ment of the JV Company shall be subject to the prior review and approval of all of the Parties before they are submitted to the relevant PRC government departments for approval or record. ①

---

① 自上个世纪 70 年代末以来的三十多年期间，按照有关设立外商投资企业（即中外合资经营企业、中外合作经营企业、外商独资企业，统称"三资企业"）的中国法律法规（包括《中外合资经营企业法》《中外合作经营企业法》《外资企业法》及其相关实施条例和细则），一直实行逐案审批制度，规定"三资企业"的设立、变更、股权转让和其他相关事项均须取得中国政府商务部门的审批方可生效。2016 年 10 月 1 日起施行的全国人大常委会《关于修改〈中华人民共和国外资企业法〉等四部法律的决定》，取消了以往对于"三资企业"的逐案审批制度，对于不涉及国家规定实施准入特别管理措施（负面清单）的"三资企业"的设立、变更、股权转让和其他相关事项，无需审批，通过向相关政府部门事前及/或事后备案，即可完成设立及变更程序。本条款的约定是为了保障各方合营者能够事先审阅确认向政府主管部门提交的设立合营企业相关文件。

第四章　生产经营目的、范围和规模

Chapter 4　Purpose, Scope and Scale of Operation and Production

4.1 合营公司的生产经营目的是加强经济合作和技术交流，采用适当的先进技术和科学的经营管理方法，满足国内和国际市场的需求，为合营公司获得良好的经济效益，从而为合营各方带来满意的经济回报。

The purpose of operation and production of the JV Company shall be to strengthen the economic cooperation and technology exchange, using appropriate advanced technology and scientific operation and management methods, catering for both the domestic and international markets, so as to achieve beneficial economic results for the JV Company and to enable the Parties to obtain satisfactory economic benefits.

4.2 合营公司的经营范围：研发【　】技术，使用【　】技术加工、制造、生产、销售【　】产品的【　】配件和组件（以下简称"**产品**"）。

The business scope of the JV Company is to perform research and development of【　】technologies, and use of【　】technologies to process, manufacture, produce and sale of【　】parts and components for【　】products（"**Products**"）.

4.3 合营公司的生产规模：年度产值约为【　】万美元。

The scale of production of the JV Company will have an annual production value of approximately US＄【　】.

4.4 合营公司生产的产品在中国国内外市场销售，具体指标可按照国内外市场对合营公司产品的需求和其他情况，根据合营公司董事会决议作出决定并进行适当变更。

The JV Company shall sell its Products in the PRC domestic market and export to the overseas market, provided, however, that specific targets may be decided and revised based on the market demand for the Products manufactured by the JV Company, within or outside of the PRC and other conditions, as appropriate, in accordance with resolutions of the Board of Directors of the JV Company.

第五章　投资总额和注册资本

Chapter 5　Total Investment and Registered Capital

5.1 合营公司的投资总额为【　】美元。

The total investment of the JV Company shall be US＄【　】.

5.2 合营公司的注册资本为【　】美元。合营各方应按如下方式向合营公司出资：

The registered capital of the JV Company shall be United States Dollars【　】（US＄【　】）. The Parties shall make the following contributions to the registered capital of the JV Company：

出资方	在注册资本中所占出资比例	出资金额	出资方式（实物或现金）
甲方	％	【 】美元	机器设备
乙方	％	【 】美元	现金
丙方	％	【 】美元	现金

Party	Percentage contribution in registered capital	Amount of contribution	In kind/cash
Party A	％	US $ 【 】	Machinery & equipment
Party B	％	US $ 【 】	cash
Party C	％	US $ 【 】	cash

5.3 各方的出资分两期缴付。第一期出资应在合营公司的营业执照颁发之日起【 】天内缴付；第二期出资应在合营公司的营业执照颁发之日起【 】天内缴付。

甲方：第一期出资　　价值【 】美元的机器设备

第二期出资　　价值【 】美元的机器设备

乙方：第一期出资　　【 】美元现金

第二期出资　　【 】美元现金

丙方：第一期出资　　【 】美元现金

第二期出资　　【 】美元现金

The Parties shall make their contributions in 2 installments. The first installment shall be paid within 【 】 days from the date of issuance of the business license of the JV Company；and the second installment shall be paid within 【 】 days from the date of issuance of the business license of the JV Company.

Party A：First installment：　US $ 【 】 in machinery and equipment；

Second installment：US $ 【 】 in machinery and equipment.

Party B：First installment：　US $ 【 】 in cash；

Second installment：US $ 【 】 in cash.

Party C：First installment：　US $ 【 】 in cash；

Second installment：US $ 【 】 in cash.

5.4 甲方应根据本合同和中国相关法律法规所规定的期限进行机器设备出资，包括【 】生产线和【 】供应系统（详见本合同**附件1**）；以这种方式出资的机器设备价值应由合营各方协商选定的具有适当资格的独立评估机构按照各方商定的期限和其他程序以及相关法规进行评估。在该等机器设备被运输交付到合营公司场地，并办理完毕中国海关的免税进口手续以及/或者中国法律可能要求的其他程序后，甲方的出资方视为完成。

Party A shall contribute the machinery and equipment including 【 】 production lines and 【 】 supply system （the details as set out in **Schedule 1** hereof） in accordance with the time limit as prescribed under this Contract and the relevant PRC laws and regulations，and the value of such machinery and equipment to be contributed as capital in this manner shall be assessed by a duly qualified independent valuer chosen by agreement among the Parties who shall carry out the valuation in accordance with the time limits and other procedures to be agreed between the Parties and in accordance with relevant regulations. Upon the completion of the transport of such machinery and equipment to the site and delivery to the JV Company as well as completion of the duty/tax free import procedures with the PRC customs authorities and/or any other procedures if required by PRC law，the contribution shall be deemed to have been made by Party A. ①

5.5　乙方和丙方将现金按上述期限汇入合营公司在中国境内的指定账户后，出资方视为完成。

Upon the remittance by Party B and Party C of the cash into the bank account of the JV Company in a bank within the PRC designated by the JV Company in accordance with the schedule set out above, the contributions by Party B and Party C shall be deemed to have been made.

5.6　合营各方完成其出资后，合营公司应委任一名中国注册会计师验资。在进行验资时，会计师应采用由中国有资格的独立评估机构确认的甲方出资机器设备之价值。验资结束后，会计师应出具验资报告。合营公司在收到该验资报告后应向各方颁发由董事长和副董事长签署的出资证书，以确认各方的出资额，证明各方在合营公司中的权益。

After the Parties have made their contributions，the JV Company shall appoint an accountant registered in the PRC to examine the capital contributions. In conducting such examination，the accountant shall use the value of the machinery and equipment contributed by Party A as confirmed by a duly qualified independent valuer in the PRC. After the examination has been completed the accountant shall issue a verification report. The JV Company，upon receipt of the said verification reports，shall issue to each Party an investment certificate signed by the Chairman and Vice Chairman of the Board of Directors of the JV Company，confirming the amount contributed by each Party and evidencing each Party's interest in the JV Company.

5.7　合营各方不得以借款、租赁的机器设备和用合营公司名义担保的其他资产或属于第三方的资产作为其出资。合营各方不得以合营公司的财产和权益或者合营他方的财产或权益为自己的出资作担保。

---

① 因甲方是以实物（免税进口的机器设备）出资，出资时的实际价值需由独立的评估机构进行评估，还需要在海关办理免税进口等手续，才视为甲方完成其对合营公司的出资。本条款详细约定了机器设备的评估和出资手续，具有较强的可操作性，有助于避免各方之间可能发生的争议。

The Parties shall not use the borrowings, leased machinery, equipment and other properties secured under the JV Company's name, or properties belonging to third parties, as the investment contributions. The Parties shall not use the properties and interests of the JV Company or the properties and interests of the other Parties as security for their investment.

5.8 在合营各方均已完成其出资后,在董事会确定其具体用途之前,任何一方或合营公司的任何人员均不得从投资账户中提取任何资金。

After the Parties have made their respective contributions and before the Board of Directors specifies in detail their usage, neither the Parties nor any personnel of the JV Company may withdraw any funds from the investment account. ①

5.9 经合营公司董事会一致同意并向有关政府部门办理法定手续后,合营公司可以增加或减少其注册资本。若董事会批准增加注册资本,合营各方有权依其对合营公司注册资本的出资比例认缴所增加的注册资本。

The Board of the JV Company may increase or decrease the registered capital of the JV Company upon a unanimous vote and completion of legal formalities with the relevant government departments. In the event the Board approves such an increase, all the Parties shall have the right to subscribe to the additional registered capital in proportion to their respective contribution to the registered capital of the JV Company.

5.10 没有合营他方的事前书面同意,各方均不得对其认缴的出资额设定任何抵押、质押或其他担保权益。

None of the Parties may create any mortgage, encumbrance or other security interest rights over the contributions subscribed without the prior written consent of the other Parties.

第六章 借 贷
Chapter 6 Loan

6.1 作为一般原则,合营公司应当从中国国内外金融机构筹借其注册资本与投资总额的差额部分,无需各方提供财务支持。

As a general rule, the JV Company shall borrow the difference between the registered capital and the total investment of the JV Company from domestic PRC or international financial institutions without any financial assistance from the Parties hereto.

6.2 如果合营公司董事会确定合营公司需要额外资金,但无法由合营公司本身提供足够担保,乙方可为此提供担保。为避免发生疑义,除非经甲方或丙方(视情况而定)同意,甲方或丙方不应被要求向合营公司

---

① 本条款约定由董事会决定注册资本的用途,可以避免任何一方或合营公司的任何人员滥用出资金额。

提供进一步的资金和/或任何性质的财务援助、出资或其他援助。但是，如果乙方提供自有资金以满足合营公司所需的额外资金，各方同意该等资金作为乙方向合营公司的贷款，有关当事人应签订借款合同，规定支付本金及合理的利息，为此目的在形式和实质上满足乙方的要求。如果乙方对向合营公司提供贷款的金融机构提供保证或其他方式的担保，乙方有权为此获得合理的担保费，该费用由合营公司支付。该等贷款或担保费（视情况而定）应由合营公司董事会一致同意通过。

If the Board of Directors of the JV Company resolves that JV Company needs additional funds，but cannot provide enough security by itself，such security may be provided by Party B. For the avoidance of doubt，unless otherwise agreed by Party A or Party C，as the case may be，Party A or Party C shall not be required to provide further funds and/or financial assistance of any nature，equity or otherwise，to the JV Company. Provided，however，that，if Party B provides its own funds towards the additional funds required，then the Parties agree that such funds will constitute a loan from Party B to the JV Company，and the parties shall enter into a loan contract providing for payment of principal and reasonable interest in form and substance satisfactory to Party B for that purpose. If Party B provides a guarantee or other security to financial institutions which provide the funds to the JV Company，then Party B shall be entitled to a reasonable guarantee fee in respect thereof，such fee to be payable by the JV Company. Such loan or guarantee fee，as the case may be，shall be subject to the unanimous approval of the Board of Directors of the JV Company. ①

第七章　各方责任
Chapter 7　Responsibility of Parties

7.1　为实现合营公司的生产经营目的，各方应按照本合同相互合作，并与合营公司合作。各方应分别负责完成下列事项；若由此发生任何费用，除非另经各方同意，该等费用应由合营公司负担。

The Parties shall cooperate with each other and with the JV Company in order to achieve the purposes of operation and production of the JV Company in accordance with this Contract. The Parties shall respectively be responsible for the completion of the following matters. However，if any expenses shall arise therefrom，such expenses shall be borne by the JV Company unless otherwise agreed between the Parties.

---

① 合营公司在生产经营活动中经常需要流动资金，采购原材料、购买所需的机器设备、支付租赁房屋的租金及员工薪酬等。中国法律允许合营公司就其注册资本和投资总额之间的差额向境内外金融机构借款；在实践中，合营公司需要为此向金融机构提供担保。本条款对于乙方向合营公司提供股东贷款或者为合营公司的融资向金融机构提供担保作了详细的约定，有助于保证合营企业的正常经营以及保护乙方的合法权益。

7.2　甲方应负责办理的事项如下：

（a）完成本合同第五章规定的甲方全部出资；

（b）办理成立合营公司的一切事项，确保尽快取得所有政府部门的批准（如有必要）、备案、登记、许可或本合同预期的合营公司成立和经营所需的其他确认，包括就合营公司根据合资经营的法律法规有权享受的全部优惠待遇提出申请；

（c）向合营公司出租建筑物作为其办公场所和加工厂；为此目的，在本合同签订日，各方作为合营公司的出资方代表合营公司与甲方签署各方同意内容的租赁协议。在合营公司设立后，合营公司董事会应尽快召开会议，通过决议确认合营公司在该租赁协议项下的权利、义务和责任；

（d）协助合营公司获得足够的基本市政设施的供应与安装，包括但不限于水、电、煤气、蒸汽、压缩空气和废水处理，这些市政供应需连续而不停顿，其数量应当足以满足合营公司全面营运的需要，另外还应包括其他当地设施，如运输服务，包括但不限于车辆许可证和通讯服务（包括但不限于电话、互联网和传真服务）；

（e）以商定价格转让或确保转让给合营公司某些机器设备（【　】生产线和【　】供应系统，详见本合同附件2）。该等机器设备的价款将作为合营公司向甲方的负债，由合营公司以如下方式支付：

（i）从合营公司成立之日起【　】个月内付款不少于【　】%；

（ii）从合营公司成立之日起【　】个月内付款不少于【　】%。
如果发生迟延支付上述款项的情况，合营公司须按年利【　】%向甲方支付从应付款日的次日至完全付清之日止的逾期付款利息；

（f）协助办理合营公司以书面方式要求的其他事宜。

The responsibilities of Party A are to:

（a）make all capital contributions required of Party A under Chapter 5 herein;

（b）handle all matters for the establishment of the JV Company in order to ensure, if possible or practicable, that such formalities are completed for any and all relevant governmental approvals, records, registrations, licenses or other assurances of any kind which may be necessary for the establishment of the JV Company as contemplated by this Contract, including applications for all preferential treatment to which the JV Company is entitled under the Joint Venture Laws and Regulations;

（c）rent out to the JV Company the buildings for its offices and processing plant. For this purpose, a lease agreement will be entered into between Party A and the JV Company, to be signed on the date hereof by, the Parties for and on behalf of the JV Company as its investors and Party A. As soon as practicable after the establishment of the JV Company, the Board of Directors of the JV Company shall convene a meeting to pass a resolution confirming its rights, obligations and liabilities under such lease agreement①;

(d) assist the JV Company in obtaining an adequate supply and installation of basic utilities, including but not limited to, water, electricity, gas, steam, compressed air and waste water treatment on a continuous uninterrupted basis and in quantities sufficient to meet the full operational requirements of the JV Company as well as other local facilities such as transportation services including but not limited to vehicle licenses and communication services including but not limited to telephone, internet and facsimile services;

(e) transfer or procure to be transferred to the JV Company certain machinery and equipment (【 】 production lines and 【 】 supply system as set out in Schedule 2 hereof) at an agreed consideration. Such amount shall be regarded as a debt owing by the JV Company to Party A and shall be repayable by the JV Company in the following manner②:

(i) not less than 【 】% payable within 【 】 month from the date of the establishment of the JV Company;

(ii) not less than 【 】% payable within 【 】 months from the date of the establishment of the JV Company.

In the event of late payment of the above amounts, interest on the overdue sum shall be payable by the JV Company to Party A at the rate of 【 】% per annum for the period commencing on the day immediately following the expiry of the relevant repayment period and ending on the date of full repayment;

(f) assist in completing other matters requested by the JV Company in writing.

7.3 乙方应负责办理的事项如下:

(a) 完成本合同第五章规定的乙方全部出资;

(b) 负责全面监督管理产品的生产以及合营公司及其加工厂的运营;

(c) 负责为 【 】 技术的运用提供技术支持,采购原材料,监督管理产品的生产和加工;

(d) 根据技术许可和援助协议的规定,许可合营公司使用 【 】 技术,向合营公司提供为生产和加工产品以及经营加工厂所需的专有技

① 因在签订本合同时合营公司尚未成立,不能以合营公司的名义与甲方(房屋所有权人)签订租赁合同。但为了办理合营公司的设立手续,需要向审批部门提交合营公司注册地址的证明。在实践中,是由合营公司的投资方(股东)代合营公司与房屋所有权人签订租约;待合营公司成立后,再以合营公司名义与房屋所有权人另行签订同样内容的租约。

② 本条款规定的甲方机器设备,是合营公司成立后从甲方购买的固定资产,区别于按照本合同第五章(投资总额和注册资本)的规定作为甲方向合营公司注册资本出资的机器设备。

术、经验、数据和其他所有技术信息或商业信息，并向合营公司提供其不时要求的相关技术援助和支持；

（e）负责促进合营公司的业务发展、市场销售，并全力提供与合营公司生产加工和销售产品有关的商业机会；

（f）协助办理合营公司以书面方式要求的其他事宜。

The responsibilities of Party B are to:

(a) make all capital contributions required of Party B under Chapter 5 herein;

(b) be responsible for the overall supervision and management of the production of the Products and the operations of the JV Company and the processing plant;

(c) be responsible for the provision of technological and technical support for the application of 【 】 technology, the procurement of materials and overseeing the processing and production of the Products;

(d) license to the JV Company, under the Technical License and Assistance Agreement, 【 】 technology and provide the JV Company with such know-how, experience, data and all other technical or commercial information in relation thereto for the processing and production of the Products and the operation of the processing plant, and provide the JV Company with all such technical support and assistance in relation thereto as may be required thereby from time to time①;

(e) be responsible for promoting the business development, marketing and sales of the JV Company and use its best endeavors to refer business opportunities relating to the processing, production and sales of the Products to the JV Company; and

(f) assist in completing other matters requested by the JV Company in writing.

7.4 丙方应负责办理的事项如下：

（a）完成本合同第五章规定的丙方全部出资；

（b）协助乙方全面监督管理合营公司及其加工厂的产品生产和经营；

（c）协助乙方促进合营公司的业务发展、市场销售，并全力提供与合营公司生产加工和销售产品有关的商业机会；

（d）协助办理合营公司以书面方式要求的其他事宜。

The responsibilities of Party C are to:

(a) make all capital contributions required of Party C under Chapter 5 herein;

(b) assist Party B in the overall supervision and management of the

---

① 合营公司的乙方拥有合营公司生产产品的主要技术，乙方将与合营公司另行签订技术许可和援助协议，该协议具体内容详见本合同第八章（技术援助）以及本书第5章第2节（技术许可与援助协议）。

production of the Products and the operations of the JV Company and the processing plant;

(c) assist Party B in promoting the business development, marketing and sales of the JV Company and use its best endeavors to refer business opportunities relating to the processing and production and sales of the Products to the JV Company; and

(d) assist in completing other matters requested by the JV Company in writing.

第八章　技术援助
Chapter 8　Technology Assistance

8.1　合营公司成立后，乙方应许可合营公司使用【　】技术，向合营公司提供为生产和加工产品以及经营加工厂所需的专有技术、经验、数据和其他全部技术信息或商业信息，并向合营公司提供其不时要求的相关技术支持和援助。

Upon the establishment of the JV Company, Party B shall license to the JV Company the 【　】 technology and provide the JV Company with such know-how, experience, data and all other technical or commercial information in relation thereto for the processing and production of the Products and the operation of the processing plant of the JV Company, and shall provide the JV Company with all such technical support and assistance in relation thereto as may be required thereby from time to time.

8.2　为实现这一目的，合营公司应与乙方签订各方同意内容的技术许可与援助协议（下称"**技术许可与援助协议**"）。在合营公司设立后，合营公司董事会应尽快召开会议以通过决议，确认合营公司在该技术许可与援助协议项下的权利、义务和责任。

For this purpose, a technical license and assistance agreement ("**Technical License and Assistance Agreement**") shall be entered into between Party B and the JV Company. As soon as practicable after the establishment of the JV Company, the Board of Directors of the JV Company shall convene a meeting to pass a resolution confirming its rights, obligations and liabilities under the Technical License and Assistance Agreement.

第九章　董事会和监事
Chapter 9　Board of Directors and Supervisor

9.1　合营公司营业执照颁发之日即为合营公司董事会成立之日。董事会是合营公司的最高权力机构，负责决定合营公司的所有重大事宜。

The Board of Directors of the JV Company shall be formed on the same day the business license of the JV Company is issued. The Board of Directors shall be the highest authority of the JV Company responsible for deciding all significant matters of the JV Company.

9.2 董事会由三名董事组成，甲、乙、丙三方各委派一名董事。董事长由甲方委派，副董事长由乙方委派。合营公司设监事一名，由丙方委派。合营公司的所有董事和监事的任期均为 3 年，若由原委派方继续委派，可以连任。

The Board of Directors shall consist of three（3）Directors，of which one Director shall be appointed by Party A，Party B and Party C respectively. The Chairman shall be appointed by Party A and the Vice Chairman by Party B. The JV Company shall have a Supervisor who shall be appointed by Party C. All Directors and Supervisor of the JV Company shall have a term of office of three（3）years and may serve successive terms if they continue to be appointed by the respective Parties.

9.3 各方有权随时撤换其委派的董事。若某位董事在其任期中被撤换，接替董事的任期应为离任董事的剩余任期。

Any Director may be removed by the Party who appointed him. If a Director is removed during the term of his office，the term of the in-coming Director shall be for the remaining term of the out-going Director.

9.4 董事长是合营公司的法定代表人。若董事长不能行使其职权，可授权副董事长或其他董事代为行使。

The Chairman shall be the legal representative of the JV Company. Should the Chairman be unable to perform his duties and responsibilities，he shall empower the Vice Chairman or other Director to act on his behalf.

9.5 董事、董事长和副董事长不得因其担任的董事、董事长或副董事长职务而从合营公司领取报酬。若某位董事、董事长或副董事长兼任总经理、副总经理或其他高级管理职务，他仅以担任这些高级管理职务的身份获取报酬，不因其同时担任董事、董事长或副董事长而获取额外的报酬。

The Directors，Chairman and Vice Chairman shall not be compensated by the JV Company in their capacity as Directors，Chairman or Vice Chairman. Where a Director，Chairman or Vice Chairman concurrently holds such offices as general manager，deputy general manager or other senior management offices，then he will receive compensation only in his capacity as the holder of such senior management office，and shall receive no additional compensation for also acting in the capacity of a Director，Chairman or Vice Chairman. ①

9.6 董事会每年至少召开 4 次会议，由董事长召集并主持。如果董事长不能履行其职责，由副董事长召集并主持董事会会议。经任何一名董事

---

① 担任合营公司的董事、董事长或副董事长是否领取报酬，完全取决于合营各方的约定，基本上应采取对等原则，不可一合资方派遣的董事领取报酬，另一方派遣的董事不领取报酬。

提议，董事会应召开临时会议。董事会会议记录应由合营公司保管。

The Board shall convene at least 4 meetings every year which are to be called and presided over by the Chairman of the Board. Should the Chairman be absent，the Vice Chairman shall call and preside over the Board meetings. An interim meeting of the Board may be held based on a request made by any one Director. The records of the meetings shall be maintained with the JV Company.

9.7　董事会会议的法定人数至少需要两名董事，包括甲方委派的一名董事、乙方或丙方委派的一名董事。若某一董事不能出席董事会会议，他可出具授权书委托他人出席会议并代为投票。

The meetings of the Board require a quorum of at least two Directors，with one Director appointed by Party A and one by Party B or Party C being present at such meetings. Should a Director be unable to attend the Board meeting，he may appoint a proxy in written form to attend and vote in the meeting.

9.8　董事可以亲自或委托他人出席董事会会议，也可用电话会议或所有与会者均能相互接听和交谈的其他沟通方式出席会议。董事会也可以所有董事签名的书面方式作出决议。

The Directors may participate in a meeting of the Board in person or by proxy or by conference telephone or other communication method whereby all persons participating in such meeting can hear and speak to each other. Decisions of the Board of Directors may also be made by written resolution signed by all the Directors. ①

9.9　除本合同第 9.10 条规定的事项之外，合营公司的董事会决议应由出席会议的董事过半数同意方可通过。

Subject to Clause 9.10 below，decisions of the Board of the JV Company shall be reached by a majority of votes of the Directors who are present at the relevant Board meeting.

9.10　下列事项应由全体董事一致同意方可通过：

（a）合营公司章程的修改或变更；

（b）合营公司名称的变更；

（c）合营公司注册资本的增加、减少或转让；

（d）合营公司提前终止、清算或解散；

（e）合营公司与其他经济组织合并；

（f）开始从事任何新业务、向任何第三方或新业务投资或撤销任何业务；

（g）对合营公司的价值（包括资本性交易）在【　】美元以上资产或财产的购买或处置（包括进行任何资本性质的交易）；

（h）向任何第三方提供信用额度，但在正常经营过程中给予合营公司

---

①　由于中外方董事平时分处不同国家，本条款规定了召开及参加董事会会议的不同方式（亲身参加会议、委托代理人参加会议、电话会议、书面签署文件方式等），董事可以灵活召开董事会会议，及时作出相关决议。

客户不超过【　】美元授信额度的除外；

(i) 在正常业务经营的过程之外或预先批准的预算之外，从银行、其他金融机构、第三方或根据本合同第 6.2 条规定从乙方借款；或合营公司任何对外贷款或为他人提供担保；

(j) 批准合营公司的年度经营计划（包括预算）、财务报表或利润分配；

(k) 合营公司与其任何股东之间的合同或协议，包括对该等合同或协议的修改和续期；

(l) 决定合营公司董事的报酬；

(m) 聘任和解聘合营公司的审计师；

(n) 对涉及合营公司的任何重大法律诉讼行为（包括和解）作出重要决定（预计负债或索赔超过【　】美元）；

(o) 雇用或解雇合营公司的任何主要管理人员或重要雇员；

(p) 批准或修改销售和授信政策、人力资源计划、管理层薪酬制度（包括合营公司主要管理层的任命和合营公司董事（如果领取报酬）或总经理的报酬）。

The following matters must be decided by a unanimous resolution of the Board of Directors[1]：

(a) Amendment to or alteration of the Articles of Association of the JV Company；

(b) Change in the JV Company's name；

(c) Increase, decrease or transfer of the registered capital of the JV Company；

(d) Early termination, liquidation, winding up or dissolution of the JV Company；

(e) Merger of the JV Company with another entity；

(f) Commencement of any new business, or investment in or with any third party or new business or withdrawal from any business；

(g) Acquisition or disposition of assets or property of the JV Company (including the entering into of any transaction of a capital nature) having a value (including capital commitment) equal to US$ 【　】or more；

(h) Extending credit to any party, except those given in the ordinary course of business to customers of the JV Company, in an amount not exceeding US$ 【　】；

(i) Borrowing funds from a bank or other financial institution or from a third party or from Party B as provided under Clause 6.2 of this Contract, except in the ordinary course of business or for amounts already approved in the budget, or making of any loans

---

① 本条款规定应由合营公司董事会一致通过的事项比法定事项多出不少事项，是合营公司三方根据其意愿和实际情况作出的约定，体现了三方对于合营公司重大事项决定权的互相制约和限定。

by the JV Company or giving any guarantees in favor of any party；

(j) Approval of annual business plans（including budgets），financial statements or dividends of the JV Company；

(k) Contracts or agreements by the JV Company with any of its respective shareholders or any amendment thereto or renewal thereof；

(l) Compensation to the Directors of the JV Company①；

(m) Appointment and removal of the auditors of the JV Company；

(n) Any major decisions relating to the conduct（including the settlement）of material legal proceedings, for a potential liability or claim of more than an amount of US＄【　】，to which the JV Company is a party；

(o) Employment or dismissal of any main officers or important employees of the JV Company；and

(p) The approval of or amendment to the sales and credit policies, human resource plan, management compensation programs, including the appointment of the key management of the JV Company and remuneration（if any）of Directors or the general manager of the JV Company.

第十章　经营管理机构
Chapter 10　Operation and Management Office

10.1　合营公司设立董事会领导下的经营管理机构，负责合营公司的日常经营管理。

The JV Company shall establish an operation and management office under the Board of Directors responsible for the daily operation and management of the JV Company.

10.2　经营管理机构最初由一名总经理、一名副总经理、一名销售经理、一名生产采购经理以及一名行政财务经理组成，他们均在总经理领导下工作。总经理、副总经理、销售经理和生产采购经理由乙方提名，行政财务经理由甲方提名，均由董事会委任。总经理和副总经理的任期为 3 年，经连续委任可以连任。若总经理或副总经理在其任期内被撤换，接替者的任期应为离任者的剩余任期。

The operation and management organization shall initially consist of one General Manager, one Assistant General Manager, one Sales Manager, one Production and Procurement Manager, and one Administration and Finance Manager, each working under the leadership of the General Manager. The General Manager, Assistant

---

① 按照本合同第 9.5 条的规定，如果合营公司董事不兼任管理职务，不应领取报酬，如果领取报酬，则是对前述第 9.5 条的例外，因此需要董事会一致通过决定。

General Manager, the Sales Manager and the Production and Procurement Manager shall be recommended by Party B, the Administration and Finance Manager by Party A, and all of them shall be appointed by the Board of Directors. The term of office of the General Manager and Assistant General Manager shall be three（3）years and each of them may be reappointed to serve consecutive terms. If the General Manager or Assistant General Manager shall be replaced during their term of office, the term of the in-coming person shall be for the remaining term of the out-going person.

10.3　总经理是合营公司日常经营管理的最高负责人，在日常经营管理的范围内，对外代表合营公司，对内负责作出最终决定。总经理应依照中国相关法律法规行使其职权，其主要职权如下：

(a) 准备各种讨论材料并提交董事会考虑，执行董事会决议；

(b) 监督行政财务经理报告的所有日常财务和会计事务；

(c) 决定除高级管理人员之外的雇员的雇用、解雇和惩罚的一切事项；

(d) 签署和履行与第三方之间的关于日常事务的一切合同；

(e) 决定和执行日常经营管理的各项规章制度；

(f) 董事会不时指定的其他职责。

副总经理协助总经理处理上述所有事项。

The General Manager shall be the highest officer-in-charge of the day-to-day operation and management of the JV Company, and shall, within the scope of the day-to-day operation and management, represent the JV Company externally and be responsible for making final decisions internally. The General Manager shall perform his duties in accordance with the relevant laws and regulations of the PRC, and such duties are set out as follows：

(a) prepare and submit to the Board for consideration various types of discussion materials and execute the resolutions of the Board；

(b) oversee all day-to-day financial and accounting matters as reported by the Administration and Finance Manager；

(c) decide on all matters relating to the employment, dismissal and punishment of employees other than senior management personnel；

(d) conclude and implement all contracts with third parties for day-to-day matters；

(e) adopt and implement various rules and regulations for the day-to-day operation and management；and

(f) other responsibilities as assigned by the Board from time to time.

The Assistant General Manager shall assist the General Manager in all the matters set forth above.

10.4　若总经理、副总经理或其他高级管理人员有渎职或严重失职行为，董事会可通过决议对其进行惩罚或撤换。

If the General Manager，Assistant General Manager or other senior management staff commit graft or serious dereliction of duties，they shall be punished or dismissed by resolution of the Board of Directors.

第十一章　机器、设备和材料的采购
Chapter 11　Purchase of Machinery，Equipment and Materials

11.1 甲方应向合营公司转让上述第 7.2 条（e）款规定的机器设备。

Party A shall transfer to the JV Company certain machinery and equipment as described above in Clause 7.2（e）.

11.2 合营公司在购入其所需的材料、燃料、零部件、交通工具和办公设备时，应考虑具有竞争力的质量、价格、实用性和其他商业因素以及基本采购条款和条件。

In its purchase of required materials，fuel，parts，means of transportation and office equipment，the JV Company shall take into consideration competitive quality，price，availability and other commercial factors，as well as the general terms and conditions for the purchase.

第十二章　劳动管理
Chapter 12　Labor Management

12.1 与合营公司雇员的雇用、辞退、薪酬、社会保险、生活福利和奖罚有关的政策、规章和制度，应由董事会根据中国相关法律法规经研究后确定。

Policies，rules and regulations on matters relating to the employment，dismissal，wages and salaries，social insurance，living welfare and reward and punishment of the employees of the JV Company shall be studied and determined by the Board of Directors in accordance with the relevant PRC laws and regulations.

12.2 合营公司有权根据董事会的决定自主雇用员工。招聘均应通过考核择优录取。合营公司应与被录取的员工个人签订劳动合同。

The JV Company shall have the right to employ any employees at the discretion of the Board of the JV Company. All employment shall be through examination and by merit. The JV Company shall enter into labor contracts with the selected personnel individually.

12.3 合营公司有权根据员工违反合营公司规章制度的情节轻重，给予警告、罚款、减薪、降级、停职、劝退或辞退的处罚。以上处罚的实施应不违反相关法律法规的规定。

The JV Company shall have the right to，in accordance with the seriousness of any violation or breach of any rules or regulations of the JV Company，give a warning to，impose fines on，reduce the salaries of，demote to a lower rank，suspend from duty，give advice to resign or dismiss such employee. Any or all of such measures may be carried out unless they are restricted by the relevant laws and regulations.

12.4 有关合营公司高级管理人员（如总经理、副总经理和各方派遣的其他境外人员）的工资和报酬事项，由董事会依据下列原则制定规章制度：

（a）高级管理人员和各方派遣的境外人员的工资，应考虑合营公司的盈利状况，本着平等互利、同工同酬的原则，在统一及合理的基础上确定；

（b）高级管理人员和境外人员的薪金，应当用人民币支付；但是，在前述人员回国时，合营公司应当将该人员持有的累积人民币金额兑换成外币，兑换价格应为兑换日的中国银行买入价和卖出价的中间值。

With respect to matters relating to the salaries and remuneration of the senior management personnel of the JV Company such as the General Manager, the Assistant General Manager and other expatriate personnel dispatched by the Parties, the Board of Directors shall formulate rules and regulations in accordance with the principles set out below[①]:

（a）The salaries of senior management personnel and expatriate personnel dispatched by the Parties shall be determined on an integrated and reasonable basis after taking into consideration the profitability of the JV Company and on the principle of equality and mutual benefits as well as equal pay for equal work;

（b）The salaries to the senior management and expatriate personnel shall be paid in RMB. However, when the person shall return to his home country, the JV Company shall convert any accumulated amounts held by such person in RMB into foreign currency at the median of the buying and selling rates of the Bank of China on the exchange date.

12.5 合营公司应当建造或租赁宿舍以及居住、福利及卫生设施，按照董事会制订的规章制度向高级管理人员和雇员提供前述宿舍和设施。

The JV Company shall construct or lease accommodation quarters as well as living, welfare and hygiene facilities and provide the same to senior management personnel and employees in accordance with rules and regulations determined by the Board of Directors.

第十三章 工 会
Chapter 13   Trade Union

13. 合营公司的员工有权组成工会组织，并按《中华人民共和国工会法》及

---

① 合营公司的高级管理人员以及合营各方向合营公司派遣的境外人员，其工资薪酬的确定关系着多方利益。本条款对此作出具体的原则性约定，有助于公平合理地确定相关人员的薪酬，平衡各方的利益。

其他相关法律法规开展工会活动。

Employees of the JV Company shall have the right to set up a trade union and conduct union activities in accordance with the Trade Union Law of the People's Republic of China and other relevant laws and regulations.

第十四章　税收、财务和审计
Chapter 14　Taxation, Finance and Audit

14.1　合营公司应当按照中国的相关法律法规缴纳税款。合营公司在其经营期限内，应尽可能申请并维持其作为先进技术企业所能获得的最优惠税收待遇。

The JV Company shall pay all taxes in accordance with the pertinent laws and regulations of the PRC. The JV Company shall, if possible or practicable, apply for and maintain the most favorable preferential tax treatment available to technologically advanced joint ventures during the term of the JV Company.

14.2　合营公司的员工应按照《中华人民共和国个人所得税法》及其他相关法律法规缴纳所得税。

The employees of the JV Company shall pay income tax in accordance with the Individual Income Tax Law of the People's Republic of China and other relevant laws and regulations.

14.3　根据相关法律法规，合营公司应当从其税后利润中提取储备基金、员工奖励和福利基金以及企业发展基金。提取的数额由董事会根据合营公司的经营状况每年作出决定。

In accordance with the relevant laws and regulations, the JV Company shall make allocations for the reserve fund, reward and welfare fund for the staff and workers and enterprise development fund from the JV Company's after-tax profits. The amount of such allocations shall be determined by the Board of Directors each year in accordance with business conditions of the JV Company.

14.4　合营公司应按照中国法律法规制订财务会计制度。

The JV Company shall formulate financial and accounting rules in accordance with the pertinent laws and regulations of the PRC.

14.5　合营公司的会计年度从每年的 1 月 1 日起，至 12 月 31 日止。但合营公司的第一个会计年度应从合营公司营业执照签发之日起至同年 12 月 31 日止。

The fiscal year of the JV Company shall be the period beginning on January 1 and ending on December 31 each year. However, the first fiscal year of the JV Company shall begin on the date of the issuance of the business license of the JV Company and end on December 31 of the same calendar year.

14.6　合营公司应当采用国际通用的权责发生制和借贷记账法，遵守程序完备、内容完整和及时的原则。

The JV Company shall adopt the internationally accepted accrual system and double entry bookkeeping method, conduct on the principles of completeness of procedures and contents without delay.

14. 7 合营公司的会计凭证、账簿、收据和统计报告原则上应当用中文书写，但如果任何一方要求，上述材料可同时用英文书写。

The accounting vouchers, books, receipts and statistical statements and reports of the JV Company shall in principle be written in Chinese; however, if required by any Party, such materials shall also be written in English.

14. 8 合营公司的账目用人民币记录。若将人民币换算为外币，应采用中国银行（或任何其他适当的中国外汇管理机关）于外汇交易结算日公布的汇率。

The accounts of the JV Company shall be denominated in RMB. In converting RMB into foreign currency, the exchange rate quoted by the Bank of China (or any other appropriate PRC authority of foreign exchange control) on the day the foreign exchange transaction is settled shall be adopted.

14. 9 合营公司应当采用中英文制作月度、季度和年度的损益报告、资产负债表和财务报告，提交给各方，并按中国相关法律法规向有关当局提交。

The JV Company shall prepare monthly, quarterly and annual profit and loss accounts, balance sheet and financial statements in both Chinese and English and submit the same to the Parties as well as to the relevant authorities in accordance with the pertinent laws and regulations of the PRC.

14. 10 每月财务报告应当在下个月的 12 日以前向各方提交；年度财务报告的草案应当于下一年度的 3 月底之前完成，经中国注册会计师审计后提交董事会讨论通过，然后向各方提交。

The monthly financial statements shall be delivered to the Parties before the twelfth (12th) day of the following month; a draft of annual financial statements shall be prepared before the end of March of the immediately following year which shall be submitted to the Board of Directors for consideration and approval after having been audited by accountant (s) registered in the PRC, and the statements shall then be delivered to the Parties.

14. 11 董事会应聘请具有良好声誉的中国注册会计师审计、核查合营公司的账目，并向董事会和总经理报告审计结果。如果任何一方认为有必要从外国聘请会计师审计合营公司相关年度的财务报表，其他当事方应当同意。除各方另行达成一致协议外，聘请这些额外会计师的所有费用由有关当事方负担。

Accountants registered in the PRC and with good reputation shall be appointed by the Board of Directors to audit and inspect the accounts of the JV Company，and the result of the audit shall be reported to the Board of Directors and the General Manager. If any Party considers it necessary to appoint accountant（s）from another country to audit the financial accounts of the JV Company of the relevant year，other Parties shall give their consent. All expenses incurred in retaining such additional accountant（s）shall be borne by the relevant Party unless otherwise agreed by the Parties. ①

14.12　合营公司应在中国的适当银行开立并维持人民币和外币账户。

The JV Company shall open and maintain bank accounts in both RMB and foreign currency at an appropriate bank in the PRC.

第十五章　利润分配
Chapter 15　Distribution of Profits

15.1　合营公司的利润及亏损应以下列方式处理：

（a）在依本合同第 14.3 条规定提取三项基金之前，不得分配利润。

（b）在弥补任何累积亏损之前不得分配利润。

（c）利润按各方对注册资本的出资比例分配给各方。

（d）利润在董事会考虑合营公司的中长期发展计划、提取合营公司发展所需的合理数额后，按照董事会确定的方法可每年分配一次。

（e）向甲方分配的利润应采用人民币，向乙方和丙方分配的利润应采用美元或任何其他符合中国法律法规且乙方和丙方可接受的自由兑换货币。

The profits and losses of the JV Company shall be dealt with in the following manner：

（a）Profits shall not be distributed until allocations have been made for the three funds described in Clause 14.3 hereof.

（b）Profits may not be distributed before all accumulated losses are made up.

（c）Profits shall be distributed to the Parties in accordance with the proportion of contribution by each Party in the registered capital.

（d）Profits may be distributed once each year through methods to be determined by the Board of Directors after a reasonable amount needed for the development of the JV Company has been set aside by the Board of Directors，taking into consideration the JV Company's mid-term and long-term development plans.

（e）Profits shall be distributed to Party A in RMB，and to Party B and Party C in USD or any other freely convertible currency under the PRC laws and regulations and acceptable to Party B and Party C.

---

① 如果合营公司的外方股东不认可中国会计师对合营公司账目的审计，可以根据本条款另行聘请外国会计师进行审计。

15.2 董事会应于每一会计年度结束后 3 个月内决定利润分配和投资准备的方案。

The plan of profit distribution or retention for investment shall be decided by the Board of Directors within three（3）months after the end of each fiscal year.

第十六章　合营期限
Chapter 16　Term of Joint Venture

16.1 除非提前终止，合营公司的经营期限从合营公司营业执照颁发之日起 15 年。

Unless otherwise terminated，the term of the JV Company shall be a term of fifteen（15）years commencing on the day the business license of the JV Company is issued.

16.2 任何一方提议并经董事会会议一致通过决议，在合营公司期满前 6 个月，合营公司可向相关政府部门办理延长经营期限的手续。

At the proposal of either Party and by unanimous resolution adopted in the meeting of the Board of Directors，the formalities for the extension of the term may be completed with the relevant government departments six（6）months before the expiry of the term of the JV Company.

第十七章　转让注册资本出资额
Chapter 17　Transfer of Contribution to Registered Capital①

17.1 除按本章规定或经合营公司其他方当事人事先书面同意之外，合营公司任何一方均不得进行下列各项行为：

（a）转让对注册资本的任何出资额；

（b）授予、宣称、创设或处置任何出资额中的任何权利或权益；

（c）在任何出资额上设立或允许存在任何质权、留置权、担保或其他权利负担。

Except as permitted by this Chapter or with the prior written consent of the other Parties of the JV Company，none of the Parties shall：

（a）transfer any contribution to the registered capital；

（b）grant，declare，create or dispose of any right or interest in any contribution；or

（c）create or permit to exist any pledge，lien，charge or other encumbrance② over any contribution. ③

---

① 本章对各方就其在合营公司注册资本出资额的转让事宜约定了多种情况下的具体处理方式和程序，在出现相关问题时，当事方可以据此办理，避免无据可依。

② encumbrance 在法律英语中的意思是财产负担或权利负担，包括担保、租赁、扣押等。"权利负担"包括期权、收购权、优先权、抵押、押记、质押、留置、押汇、抵付权、反诉、信托安排或其他担保、或者股权、限制（包括有关法律规定的任何有关限制）。

③ 任何当事方对于其出资额设定的任何担保权益，涉及其他方当事人对于合营公司的权益，可能影响合营公司的正常运营，必须事先取得其他方当事人的书面同意。

17.2　除按照第 17.1 条同意转让或第 17.8 条允许的集团内部转让之外，任何一方当事人或其关联公司只有在转让其共同持有的全部出资（不包括部分出资）时，方可进行出资额的转让；第 17.3 条至第 17.7 条（包含这两条）也应据此解释。①

Except for transfers for which consent is given under Clause 17.1 or for intra-group transfers permitted under Clause 17.8，neither of the Parties or any of its affiliates may transfer a capital contribution unless it and/or its affiliates transfer all（and not part only）of the contribution collectively held by it/them，and Clauses 17.3 to 17.7（inclusive）shall be construed accordingly. ①

17.3　希望转让其出资额（以下简称"**待售权益**"）的本合同一方当事人（以下简称"**转让方**"），应首先向本合同其他当事人发出书面通知（以下简称"**转让通知**"），作为向本合同其他当事人（以下简称"**存续方**"）发出的关于转让待售权益的要约，该要约应载明任何经提议的第三方受让人的具体情况、购买价格和其他实质性条款。该要约在存续方收到转让通知之日起 90 天的承诺期内有效，在 90 天的承诺期内，存续方应当通知转让方其是否愿意根据该等条款购入全部（非部分）待售权益。

A Party of this Contract who wishes to sell（"**Seller**"）its contribution（"**Sale Interest**"）must first give written notice（"**Transfer Notice**"）to the other Parties of this Contract to offer to sell the Sale Interest to the other Parties of this Contract（"**Continuing Parties**"）together with details of any proposed third party purchaser，the purchase price and other material terms. The offer to sell shall remain open for acceptance for a period of ninety（90）days following the Continuing Parties' receipt of the Transfer Notice，and within such ninety（90）day period the Continuing Parties shall notify the Seller whether the Continuing Parties want to buy the entire amount（but not part only）of the Sale Interest on those terms. ②

17.4　如果仅有一家存续方决定购入待售权益，本合同各方应促使合营公司采取符合相关法律和合营公司章程规定的必要行动以使待售权益的转让生效。如果多家存续方决定购入待售权益，应按照转让通知日期之前一日该等存续方所持有的出资比例来转让待售权益给每一家存续方。待售权益的转让应在 90 天承诺期届满后 30 天内完成。

---

①　在一方当事人向合营当事方以外的第三方转让其全部出资额后，如果转让方在转让前以合营公司名义进行任何商业行为、留下任何未披露的债务，从而使合营公司遭受任何损害或损失，合营公司以及存续的当事方将难以从转让方取得赔偿、获得救济。为避免发生这些问题，本章对一方向合营当事方以外的第三方转让其全部出资额的情况作了具体的限制、规定了详细的程序。而对于一方向合营公司当事方以外的第三方转让其部分出资额的情况，由于该方仍在合营公司注册资本中保留有股份，所发生的风险相对较低。

②　第 17.3 条至第 17.7 条的规定是对于一方向合营公司当事方以外的第三方转让其全部出资额情况的具体程序约定，以保证出资额的转让对于各方来说均公平、合理、适当、有效。

If only one Continuing Party decides to buy the Sale Interest, then the Parties shall, and shall cause the JV Company to, take all requisite actions to effect the transfer of the Sale Interest to the Continuing Party in accordance with relevant laws and the Articles of Association of the JV Company. If more than one Continuing Party decide to buy the Sale Interest, the Sale Interest to be transferred to each Continuing Party shall be in proportion to that Continuing Party's contribution to the registered capital as recorded immediately prior to the date of the Transfer Notice. Completion of the sale and purchase of the Sale Interest shall take place within thirty (30) days after the expiry of such ninety (90) days period.

17.5 如果存续方决定不购买待售权益或者在该 90 天之内没有通知其意愿，则转让方有权向第三方转让待售权益，但是转让方向第三方提供的条件不得优于向存续方提供的条件；存续方应确保其委派的董事会成员按照转让方的要求（无需额外对价）签署并交付给该第三方使待售权益转让生效所需的文件。如果向第三方转让的条件优于在转让通知中载明的条件，或向第三方转让待售权益没有在 90 天承诺期届满后 60 天内完成（除非此种延迟是由于存续方的原因所造成），在此种情况下，应重新适用本合同第 17.3 条、第 17.4 条和第 17.5 条规定的程序。

If no Party decides to buy the Sale Interest, or if they fail to notify their intention within such ninety (90)-day period, then the Seller is entitled to sell the same to a third party, but on terms no more favorable than those offered to the Continuing Parties, and the Continuing Parties shall, and shall cause their appointees to the Board of Directors, upon the Seller's request and without further consideration, to execute and deliver such documents and instruments as may be required to effect the transfer of the Sale Interest to the third party. Once terms for sale to a third party are more favorable than those set forth in the Transfer Notice or if the sale to the third party is not completed within sixty (60) days of the expiry of the ninety (90)-day period (unless such delay was caused by the Continuing Parties or any one of them), and in such case the procedures as set forth in Clauses 17.3 and 17.4 and this Clause 17.5 above shall be applicable again.

17.6 出资额的受让方应签署适当的遵守契约书或由存续方同意的确认备忘录，以接受本合同的约束。只要受让方尚未承担本合同项下的义务，就不得解除转让方在本合同项下的任何义务，除非存续方已经同意解除转让方的该等义务。出资额转让须经中国相关政府部门的批准或备案。

Any sale or transfer of the equity interest shall be subject to the condition that the transferee shall become bound by this Contract by executing a suitable deed of adherence or memorandum of acknowledgement approved by the Continuing Parties. Nothing in this Contract shall relieve the transferor of any obligation under this Contract in so far as such obligation has not been assumed by the transferee and unless the Continuing Parties have agreed to release the transferor from such obligation. Such transfer must also be approved or recorded by the relevant PRC government authorities.

17.7　向存续方或第三方转让待售权益，应当符合下列规定：

（a）待售权益在被转让时应不存在任何留置权、担保、权利负担及第三方权利；待售权益应具有全部固有权利，包括在转让完成日后宣布、支付或产生的任何获分配红利的权利或其他分配的权利；

（b）自转让完成之日起，存续方及第三方应承担转让方及其任何关联公司与合营公司业务有关的任何保证、赔偿保证、安慰函以及／或者对于第三方的反赔偿保证中的任何义务。

The sale of the Sale Interest to the Continuing Parties or a third party shall be on the following terms：

（a）The Sale Interest will be sold free from all liens, charges and encumbrances and third party rights and together with all rights of any nature attaching to them including all rights to any dividends or other distributions declared, paid or made after the date of the completion of transfer；

（b）The Continuing Parties and the third party shall assume, with effect from the completion date, any obligations of the Seller and any of its affiliates under any guarantees, indemnities, letters of comfort and/or counter-indemnities to third parties in relation to the business of the JV Company.

17.8　如果转让方将其持有的出资额转让给其全资拥有的子公司，则此种转让不适用第 17.3 条的规定，但应当：（i）提前向其他当事方发送书面通知；（ii）继续办理合营公司的业务和履行其合同；（iii）如果其他当事方有要求，则转让方应当保证其全资拥有的子公司履行其在本合同项下的义务。本合同其他当事方应协助转让方完成该出资额的转让。

Any sale or transfer of equity interest by any Seller to its wholly-owned subsidiary shall not be subject to Clause 17. 3 provided always that (i) prior written notice is given to the other Parties； (ii) the business of the JV Company and the performance of its contracts shall not be interrupted, and (iii) if required by the other Parties, the Transferor shall guarantee its wholly-owned subsidiary's performance of its obligations hereunder. The other Parties of this Contract shall assist the Seller in effecting such sale or transfer.①

---

① 由于合营公司当事方可以实际控制其全资子公司，将其出资额转让给全资子公司，与转让给其他第三方的情况完全不同，因此第 17.8～17.9 条对与此相关的情况作了具体约定。

17.9 如果任何一方的关联公司终止作为其关联公司，则该当事方承诺确保该关联公司将其当时所持有的全部出资额转让给该当事方自身或其另一家关联公司。

Each Party undertakes to ensure that its affiliate which holds any contribution shall transfer all of the contribution which that affiliate then holds to that Party or to another affiliate if the first affiliate ceases to be an affiliate.

17.10 如果任何一方（以下简称"**违约方**"）：

（a）严重违反本合同项下的义务或者严重违反技术许可与援助协议或本合同所预定的任何合同项下的义务，在接到本合同其他当事方（以下简称"**守约方**"）对该违约行为的投诉通知后 30 日内，可以纠正该违约行为却没有采取任何必要措施以纠正该违约行为；或者

（b）开始自愿清算程序（除非是为了重组或合并目的），或者法院或相关政府当局发出强制清算命令，或者就其财产中的实质性部分已委任接管人或类似人员，或者与其债权人达成和解或还债协议，或者无力偿债；

在守约方向合营公司和违约方发出通知书（以下简称"**解约通知**"）后，违约方应被视为：

（i）已向守约方或其指定的第三方发出转让其在合营公司所持有的全部而非部分股东权益的要约，该股东权益应由一家独立的会计师事务所（以下简称"**专家**"）所确定的解约通知之日股东权益的账面净值来确定（专家应由守约方指定，专家应以专业人士的身份而非仲裁人的身份行事，专家的决定是终局性的，对所有当事方均具有约束力；专家的费用应由各方平摊）；以及

（ii）不可撤销地委派合营公司作为办理上述转让的代理人。

If any of the Parties（"**Defaulting Party**"）[①]:

(a) shall commit any material breach of its obligations under this Contract，or shall commit any material breach of the Technical License and Assistance Agreement or any contracts contemplated hereby and，if remediable，shall fail to take all necessary action to remedy such breach within thirty（30）days upon the service of notice by the other Parties of this Contract complaining of such breach（"**Non-defaulting Party**（ies）"）to the Defaulting Party；or

(b) shall go into voluntary liquidation otherwise than for the purpose of reconstruction or amalgamation or an order of the court or relevant government authority is made for its compulsory liquidation，or shall have a receiver or similar

---

[①] 在发生一方严重违约时，守约方根据第 17.10～17.13 条的规定，有权单方面解除本合同、强制违约方转让出资额，并追究违约方的赔偿责任。

officer appointed in respect of any substantial part of its assets or shall compound or make any composition or arrangement with its creditors or shall become insolvent;

then upon notice（**"Termination Notice"**）to such effect by the Non-defaulting Parties to the JV Company and the Defaulting Party，the Defaulting Party shall be deemed：

（i）to have offered to sell to the Non-defaulting Parties or third parties to be nominated by the Non-defaulting Parties all but not part of，its equity interest in the JV Company at the net book value of the equity interest determined as of the date of the Termination Notice by an independent firm of accountants（**"Expert"**）to be appointed by the Non-defaulting Parties（the Expert shall act as an expert and not as an arbitrator and its decision shall be final and binding on the Parties；the Expert's fees and expenses shall be shared equally among the Parties）；and

（ii）to have irrevocably appointed the JV Company as its agent for the abovementioned sale.

17.11　守约方可在合营公司收到解约通知后 90 天内通知合营公司接受或者指定第三方以接受要约购买违约方在合营公司中所拥有的全部（非部分）股东权益。违约方所持有的股东权益应按照合营公司章程的规定向守约方或守约方指定的第三方转让。如果存在多家受让方，则按照其各自的出资比例进行转让。在此种情况下，违约方有义务采取所有必要的行动使转让生效，这些行动包括确保其委派的董事会成员同意转让行为。

The Non-defaulting Parties may within ninety（90）days following the JV Company's receipt of the Termination Notice accept or nominate a third party to accept the offer to purchase the Defaulting Party's entire equity interest in the JV Company（but not part thereof）by notifying the JV Company，and then the Defaulting Party's equity interest in the JV Company shall be transferred to the Non-defaulting Parties or the third party（ies）nominated by the Non-defaulting Parties in accordance with the Articles of Association of the JV Company，and if more than one，in proportion to their respective capital contributions. In such case the Defaulting Party shall have the obligation to take all the actions to effect the transfer to the Non-defaulting Parties or the third party（ies）nominated by the Non-defaulting Parties of the Defaulting Party's equity interest in the JV Company，including causing its appointees to the Board to approve such transfer.

17.12　如果守约方决定不购买或者指定第三方购买违约方在合营公司中的股东权益，应立即通知合营公司。

If the Non-defaulting Parties decide not to buy or to nominate a third party to buy the Defaulting Party's equity interest in the JV Company，they shall promptly notify the JV Company.

17.13　违约方对守约方所承担的违约损害赔偿责任，不因上述预定的强制转让股东权益而受到影响或者被免除。

The Defaulting Party's liability to the Non-defaulting Parties for damages caused by the Defaulting Party's breach of this Contract shall not be affected by or waived as the result of the compulsory transfer contemplated above.

第十八章　合营公司的解散和终止
Chapter 18　Dissolution and Termination of JV Company

18.1　如果任何一方按照本合同的规定转让其在合营公司所持有的全部股东权益，其在本合同项下所负的全部义务应予免除；但是在转让日之前发生的累积义务和债务则不予免除。

If any of the Parties sells or transfers all of its equity interest in the JV Company in accordance with the provisions of this Contract，it shall be released from all of its obligations hereunder other than accrued obligations and liabilities arising before the date of the transfer. ①

18.2　在本合同期限内发生下列情况之一的，任何一方可以选择向其他有关当事方（以下简称"**有关当事方**"）发出意图解散和清算合营公司的书面通知：

（a）任何有关当事方严重违反本合同，或其关联公司严重违反其在技术许可与援助协议或本合同所预定的其他合同项下的义务，倘若该违约行为是可以被纠正的，但有关当事方在收到对方发出的书面投诉通知后 30 日内仍未纠正该违约行为；

（b）任何有关当事方没有足额缴纳其所认缴的合营公司出资额；

（c）合营公司停止经营或者资不抵债；

（d）任何有关当事方开始自愿清算程序（除非是为了重组或合并目的），或者法院或相关政府当局发出强制解散命令，或者就其财产中的实质性部分已委任接管人或类似人员，或者与其债权人达成和解或还债协议，或者无力偿债；

（e）超过有关当事方不时同意的合营公司账面净资产数额或部分被政府当局临时或永久征用，以致影响合营公司的业务经营；

（f）如果任何当事方或其控股公司的政府主管当局要求对本合同的任何条款进行修改，或对本合同的履行附加条件或限制，以致对合营公司或任何当事方产生重大不利影响；或者

（g）如果不可抗力（详见下述定义）的情形或影响持续 6 个月以上，各方仍未能找到公平的解决办法。

---

① 本条款对于转让方和受让方在股权转让前后责任义务分割的时间分界点作了明确约定。

在收到有关当事方意图解散合营公司的通知后，其他有关当事方应采取所有必要的公司行动，以促成合营公司按照其章程和中国相关法律法规进行解散和清算，包括但不限于确保各有关当事方委派的董事会成员投票同意解散及清算合营公司。

During the term of this Contract，any Party may elect to cause the JV Company to be dissolved and liquidated by delivery to the other relevant Party（ies）（**"Relevant Party（ies）"**）of a written notice of intention to dissolve the JV Company under any of the following circumstances①：

（a）If any Relevant Party commits any material breach of its obligations under this Contract or any affiliate of such Relevant Party commits any material breach of the Technical License and Assistance Agreement or any contracts contemplated hereby，and such breach，if remediable，is not remedied by such Relevant Party within thirty（30）days upon receipt of complaining notice of such breach from the other Party（ies）；

（b）If any Relevant Party fails to fulfill its capital contribution obligations in respect of the JV Company；

（c）If the JV Company ceases to carry on business or becomes unable to pay its debts as they become due；

（d）If any Relevant Party shall go into voluntary liquidation otherwise than for the purpose of reconstruction or amalgamation or an order of the court or relevant government authority is made for its compulsory liquidation，or shall have a receiver or similar officer appointed in respect of any substantial part of its assets or shall compound or make any composition or arrangement with its creditors or shall become insolvent；

（e）If any part of the assets of the JV Company with a net book value exceeding such amount or proportion of its net book value as the Relevant Parties may agree from time to time is temporarily or permanently expropriated by any government authority，thereby adversely affecting the business of the JV Company；

（f）If any government authority having authority over a Party（ies）or its/their holding company requires any provision of this Contract to be revised or imposes conditions or restrictions upon the implementation of this Contract in such a way as to cause significant adverse consequences to the JV Company or any Party；or

---

① 本条款是在发生违约或其他意外情况时，赋予合营公司当事方选择权，解散及清算合营公司。

(g) If the conditions or consequences of Force Majeure（as defined hereinafter）prevail for a period in excess of six（6）months and the Parties have been unable to find an equitable solution.

Upon receipt by the other Relevant Party（ies）of one Relevant Party's notice of intention to dissolve the JV Company，the Relevant Parties shall take all the requisite corporate actions to effect the dissolution and liquidation of the JV Company as per the provisions of its Articles of Association and the relevant laws and regulations of the PRC，including without limitation causing each Relevant Party's appointees to the Board to vote to dissolve and liquidate the JV Company.

18.3 除非各方另有约定，本合同的终止以及任何有关当事方终止持有合营公司股权，并不影响各方在该等终止前所发生的任何权利或义务，对于本合同中明示或默示规定在该等终止后生效或继续有效的条款也不产生任何影响。任何一方因违反本合同而对其他当事方所承担的损害赔偿责任，并不因本合同的终止而受到影响或免责。

The termination of this Contract however caused and the ceasing by any Relevant Party to hold any equity interest in the JV Company shall be without prejudice to any obligations or rights of any of the Parties hereto which have accrued prior to such termination，and shall not affect any provision of this Contract which is expressly or by implication provided to come into effect on or to continue in effect after such termination，unless otherwise agreed by the Parties. In particular，any Party's liability to the other Parties for damages caused by the first Party's breach of this Contract shall not be affected by or waived as the result of the termination of this Contract.

18.4 无论由于何种原因导致本合同终止，第 22 条和第 23 条以及在该等终止前所累积的任何权利和义务仍然存续。

In the event of termination of this Contract for any reason whatsoever，Clauses 22 and 23 and any rights and liabilities accrued prior to such termination shall survive.

第十九章　保　险
Chapter 19　Insurance

19.1 合营公司原则上应向经批准在中国开展业务的保险公司投保。

The JV Company shall procure insurance in principle from insurance companies approved to carry on business in the PRC.

19.2 保险的种类、价值和期限由董事会根据提供保险的保险公司的规章制度加以确定。

The types，value and terms of insurance shall be determined by the Board of Directors in accordance with the rules and regulations of the insurance companies from which the insurance is taken.

第二十章　合资合同的修订
Chapter 20　Amendment and Alteration of Joint Venture Contract

20. 对本合同的任何修正或变更，应由各方讨论，由各方授权代表或法定代表人签署书面文件方可生效；如有必要，需经相关政府部门批准或备案。

Any amendments or alteration to this Contract shall be discussed by the Parties hereto and shall become effective only when a written instrument concerned is signed by the authorized or legal representative of the Parties，and the approval or record with the relevant government departments may be necessary.

第二十一章　违约责任
Chapter 21　Liability for Breach

21. 倘若本合同任何一方严重违反或违背本合同或合营公司章程的任何条款和条件，守约方可以书面要求违约方纠正其违约行为。如果违约方在收到守约方的纠正违约要求后 30 天内仍未纠正违约行为，守约方有权要求违约方赔偿因此造成的任何经济损失。

When any of the Parties to this Contract materially breaches or violates any of the terms and conditions of this Contract or the Articles of Association of the JV Company，the non-defaulting Party or Parties may request in writing the defaulting Party to remedy such breach. If the defaulting Party fails to remedy such breach within thirty（30）days from the day the non-defaulting Party makes the request for remedy，the non-defaulting Party shall have the right to claim compensation against the defaulting Party for any economic losses caused therefrom.

第二十二章　保　密
Chapter 22　Confidentiality①

22.1 各方应当（并确保其关联公司及其关联公司的职员、雇员、代理人、专业人士和其他顾问）对其所拥有或持有的商业秘密严格保密；这些商业秘密包括：（ⅰ）在本合同、技术许可与援助协议以及本合同所预定的其他合同的协商或履行过程中所获得或披露的保密信息，或者（ⅱ）与合营公司有关的保密信息，或者（ⅲ）任何一方在提供技术援助时所披露的保密信息（以下统称"**商业秘密**"）。商业秘密仅为合营公司经营目的而使用，不得为任何第三方的利益或接受方当事人的自身目的而使用。该等限制在本合同终止后以及合营公司解散后永久有效；一方转让其在合营公司的全部股东权益后仍受该等限制。但对于下列信息或知识，该等限制停止适用：

（a）在被其他方当事人披露前，已被接受方合法而正当地占有；

（b）在披露前或披露后，并非因接受方的过错，商业秘密进入公众信

---

① 由于合资外方股东向合营公司提供高新技术，以使合营公司生产高科技产品，外方股东对商业秘密保护的要求标准较高。本条款对保密事项作了详细的约定，以便确保合营公司、各方股东及其关联公司等保守商业秘密，防止泄密。

息领域；

（c）从外部来源可无限制地合法取得；

（d）接受方能够证明该信息是由其独立开发而来的；

（e）由各方联合声明而公开。

倘若对接受方有管辖权的司法或行政当局明确命令接受方披露其持有的商业秘密，接受方在给予披露方对该命令或其披露范围提出反对或质疑的合理机会后，方可在该当局命令的范围内披露该等商业秘密。但在任何情况下，本条所规定的义务（包括但不限于不得披露和不得使用）在商业秘密尚未进入公众领域时依然有效。

Each Party shall maintain （and shall ensure that its affiliates and its affiliates' officers, employees, agents and professional and other advisers maintain） the strictest secrecy and confidentiality of any information owned or possessed by such Party （i） that is disclosed or obtained at any time in connection with the negotiation or performance of this Contract, the Technical License and Assistance Agreement and any of the contracts contemplated hereby, or （ii） in respect of the JV Company, or （iii） disclosed by any of the Parties in the course of providing technology and technical support （collectively **"Confidential Information"**）. Such Confidential Information shall be used for no purpose other than for the business of the JV Company, and shall not be used for the benefit of any third party or for the receiving Party's own purpose. This restriction shall apply for an indefinite period after termination of this Contract and the dissolution of the JV Company, or in the event a Party transfers all of its equity interest in the JV Company, after such transfer. This restriction shall cease to apply to the information or knowledge which：

（a）is lawfully and properly in the possession of the receiving Party prior to disclosure thereof by the other Party （ies）；

（b）is, or through no fault of the receiving Party becomes, part of the public knowledge or literature before or after disclosure；

（c）lawfully becomes available without limitation from an outside source；

（d）the receiving Party can prove that the information was developed by it independently; or

（e）is publicly announced jointly by the Parties.

In the event that Confidential Information is expressly ordered to be disclosed by a judicial or administrative authority having jurisdiction over the receiving Party, the receiving Party shall only disclose such Confidential Information to the extent ordered by such authority after having given the disclosing Party （ies） a reasonable opportunity to challenge or dispute such order or the scope thereof. In any event, the obligations imposed by this Clause, including but not limited to nondisclosure and non-use, however, shall endure so long as the Confidential Information does not become part of the public domain.

22.2　接受方不得（并确保其关联公司及其关联公司的职员、雇员、代理人、专业人士或其他顾问不得）向任何第三方披露、出售或转让商业秘密。各方仅在为本合同目的向其关联公司或其关联公司的职员、雇员、代理人、专业人士或其他顾问作合理披露时，方可披露商业秘密。披露方应当向商业秘密的接受方作出如下指示：

（a）该等信息是商业秘密；

（b）必须对此保密；

（c）不得向任何第三方披露该等信息（除非根据本合同条款已经向该第三方披露此类信息），不得为合营公司利益以外的任何其他目的使用该等信息。

如果商业秘密的接受方违反了本条款规定，披露方必须对此承担责任。

The receiving Party shall not (and shall ensure that its affiliates and its affiliates' officers, employees, agents and professional and other advisers shall not) disclose, sell or transfer to any third party any such Confidential Information. Each Party shall not disclose any Confidential Information to its affiliate or to its affiliates' officers, employees, agents or professional or other advisers unless such disclosure is reasonably incidental to the purpose of this Contract. The disclosing Party (ies) shall instruct whomever it provides the Confidential Information:

（a）that such information is confidential;

（b）to keep it confidential; and

（c）not to disclose it to any third party (other than those persons to whom it has already been disclosed in accordance with the terms of this Contract) or to use it for any purpose other than for the benefit of the JV Company.

The disclosing Party (ies) is/are responsible for any breach of this Clause by the person to whom the Confidential Information is disclosed.

22.3　如果本合同终止，任何一方可以通知其他方，要求其归还该方的商业秘密。其他方（并确保其关联公司以及关联公司的职员、雇员、代理人、专业人士和其他顾问）必须实施下列行为：

（a）按照提供商业秘密并要求归还的一方要求，向其归还包含商业秘密的全部文件；

（b）销毁该等文件的任何复印件或者复制、包含或参考商业秘密制作的其他文件。

（在上述各种情况下，为了向有关政府、税务或其他主管当局提交或者备案，其他方仅可以在其法务部保存一份复印件），其他方在接到通知后应尽快归还或销毁商业秘密。

If this Contract terminates，any Party may by notice require the other Parties to return the first Party's Confidential Information. If so，the other Parties shall（and shall ensure that its/their affiliates and its/their affiliates' officers，employees，agents and professional and other advisers shall）：

（a）return all documents containing the Confidential Information which have been provided by the Party demanding the return of Confidential Information；and

（b）destroy any copies of such documents or other record reproducing，containing or made from or with reference to the Confidential Information.

（Save，in each case，for one copy in the files of its legal department for record purposes only or for any submission to or filings with governmental，tax or regulatory authorities），the other Parties shall return or destroy the Confidential Information as soon as practicable after receiving notice.

第二十三章　互相协商与合作
Chapter 23　Mutual Consultation and Cooperation

23.1　本合同各方应尽最大努力诚意支持合营公司的业务。为了能够使用由一方向合营公司许可的技术或其改进的技术生产合营公司的产品，各方同意在可能的情况下，向合营公司介绍客户、业务或将其关联企业接到的订单转介给合营公司。

Each of the Parties hereto shall use their best endeavors in good faith to support the business of the JV Company. In this regard，they agree that wherever practicable to do so，they shall introduce to the JV Company customers or business or orders received by them through their affiliated enterprises for the production of any products which can be produced using the technology which has been licensed to the JV Company by a Party or any improvements thereof. ①

23.2　本合同各方同意，如果其本身或其任何关联企业或有关企业决定设立或另外从事与合营公司相同或类似的其他生产设施，该方应事前通知其他当事方并共同协商，以确保合营公司的业务不致因此受到严重的不利影响。该方或通过其关联企业或有关企业设立或另外从事这些其他生产设施时，该方有义务向其他当事方作出解释，在本合同期限内合营公司的业务将不会因此受到严重的不利影响。

Each of the Parties hereto agrees that if it or any of its affiliated or related enterprises decides to establish or otherwise engage in other

---

①　合营各方所生产的产品与合营公司的产品类似，二者之间存在竞争关系；但是合营公司的业务能否成功关系到各方的共同利益，特别是在合营公司设立的初期，需要各方的实际支持和帮助。本条款就各方向合营公司介绍客户、业务、订单等的约定，不是强制性的，而是由各方尽力而为，需要各方诚意合作。

manufacturing facilities identical or similar to those of the JV Company，it shall inform the other Parties beforehand and consult together to ensure that the business of the JV Company is not and will not be materially adversely affected thereby. The Party which，or through its affiliated or related enterprises，establishes or otherwise engages in such other manufacturing facilities shall be responsible to explain to the other Parties that the business of the JV Company will not be materially adversely affected thereby during the term of this Contract. ①

23.3 各方在此确认，第 23 章不应被解释为阻止各方继续从事任何一方当事人或其关联或相关企业目前从事的任何业务，该等业务经营并不构成违反第 23 章的规定。

The Parties hereby confirm that this Chapter 23 shall not be construed so as to prevent the Parties from continuing any of the businesses operated currently by any Party or its affiliated or related enterprises，and such business operations shall not constitute a breach of the provision of this Chapter 23. ②

第二十四章　不可抗力
Chapter 24　Force Majeure

24.1 倘若由于受影响的当事方所不能合理控制的原因（以下简称"不可抗力"），导致受影响当事方无法履行本合同项下的义务，则不构成违约，受影响当事方不应承担因此产生的任何责任。不可抗力包括但不限于暴风雨、洪水、地震、叛乱、暴动、火灾、爆炸、旱灾、政府行为或规定。但是：

（a）本条任何规定不得被解释为免除或解除可归咎于一方自身、其代理人及雇员的过失，从而给其他当事人造成人身伤害或财产损失所应负的法律责任；

（b）受影响当事方应当立即通过传真或其他通讯方式通知其他当事方不可抗力的原因、性质和预期的持续时间。

No failure or omission by any Party hereto in the performance of any obligation of this Contract shall be deemed a breach of or default under this Contract or create any liability if such failure or omission shall arise from any cause or causes beyond the reasonable control of the Party whose performance hereunder is affected（"**Force Majeure**"），including，but not limited to，storm，flood，earth-quake，rebellion，riot，fire，explosion，drought，or government

---

① 在合营公司设立后，如果各方或通过其关联公司等设立或从事其他生产设施、从而与合营公司形成竞争，则势必影响合营公司的正常发展。但是，各方本身的业务原本是与合营公司的业务相类似的，难以完全禁止各方进行这方面的商业行为，本条款仅就这方面规定各方的协商和解释义务，在一定程度上对此作出竞争限制。

② 本条款是对各方目前经营业务现状的承认，设立合营公司并不影响各方现有的业务经营。

act or regulation, provided however:

(a) nothing herein shall be construed to relieve or discharge a Party for any loss, damage, or injury to person or property of the other Party (ies) hereto caused by or attributable to the negligence of such Party, its agents and employees;

(b) the Party so affected shall immediately notify the other Party (ies) of such cause by facsimile or other communications, specifying the nature and anticipated duration thereof.

24.2 第 24 章所规定的受影响当事方应尽最大努力排除无法履行义务的原因。如果不可抗力事件持续 6 个月以上，各方应协商决定是否终止本合同。

A Party so affected under this Clause 24 shall use its best efforts to remove the cause of its inability to perform. If the duration of any event of Force Majeure exceeds six (6) months, then the Parties shall decide through consultation whether to terminate this Contract.

第二十五章　法律适用
Chapter 25　Applicable Law

25. 本合同的成立、签订、生效、解释和执行均适用中华人民共和国法律。

The formation, execution, validity, interpretation and implementation of this Contract shall be governed by the laws of the PRC. [①]

第二十六章　争议解决
Chapter 26　Settlement of Disputes

26.1 各方同意通过友好协商解决彼此之间发生的有关本合同的争议。因此，在任何一方将争议提交仲裁前，各方应采取以下步骤：

(a) 受损害的一方应书面通知被申诉方有关争议的性质、范围和依据。在通知发出后 15 日内，各方应各自派遣一名高级代表在各方所能接受的时间和地点召开会议，各方的高级代表应亲自出席会议，并就受损害一方通知中描述的争议进行诚意协商，讨论解决方案。各方的代表律师不得参加该等会议。

(b) 如果在采取上述（a）项步骤后仍未解决争议，各方的董事长或者授权代表应在 30 日内亲自参加会议，就争议的解决方案进行友好协商。如果律师与一方当事人共同参加会议，该方当事人应当事先合理地通知其他方当事人。

(c) 如果在采取上述（b）项步骤后仍未解决争议，此时一方可以提起仲裁。

按照第 26.1 条所进行的全部协商均应保密。任何一方不得将协商中其他方所作的承认、建议和提供的信息作为在仲裁或司法程序中的证据。

---

① 根据中国法律的强制性规定，中外合资经营企业合同必须适用中国法律。

The Parties agree to resolve through good faith negotiations any dispute between them in relation to this Contract. Accordingly，prior to any Party initiating any arbitration proceedings, the Parties shall undertake the following steps①：

（a）The aggrieved Party shall notify the respondent Parties in writing regarding the nature，scope and basis of the dispute. Within fifteen（15）days of such notice，a senior representative of each Party will meet at a mutually acceptable time and place，in person，to negotiate in good faith a resolution to the dispute or controversy described in the aggrieved Party's notice. No attorneys representing a Party may be present at this meeting.

（b）If there is no resolution after（a）above，the chairman of each of the Parties or an authorized representative of each of such Parties will meet，in person，within thirty（30）days to negotiate in good faith the resolution of the dispute. If an attorney will accompany a person at the meeting，he shall give reasonable prior notice to the other.

（c）If there is no resolution after（b）above，then，and only then，may a Party commence arbitration.

All negotiations pursuant to this Clause 26.1 shall be kept confidential. No Party shall rely on or introduce as evidence in arbitration or judicial proceedings，any admission，proposal or information provided by the other Party（ies）in the course of the negotiations.

26.2　如果各方未能通过友好协商方式解决争议，则应通过仲裁方式最终解决争议。由本合同引起或与本合同有关的任何争议（包括本合同的存续、生效或终止事项），均应提交香港国际仲裁中心，按照联合国国际贸易法委员会的现行仲裁规则进行终局仲裁，该仲裁规则通过在本条款中的引用而构成本条款的一部分。仲裁庭应由三位仲裁员组成，各方各自指定一名仲裁员。全部仲裁程序以英语进行。仲裁裁决是终局性的，对各方均有约束力。除非仲裁庭就仲裁费用另行作出裁决，各方应自行负担其在仲裁过程中发生的费用或开支。

If the Parties are unable to reach an amicable resolution，then such dispute shall be finally settled by arbitration. Any dispute arising out of or in connection with this Contract，including any question regarding its existence，validity or termination，shall be referred to and finally resolved by arbitration at Hong Kong International Arbitration Centre in accordance with the UNCITRAL Arbitration Rules for the time being in force which rules are deemed to be

---

① 本条款对于仲裁之前的协商过程作了详细约定，其目的是尽可能通过各方的友好协商解决争议，体现了各方努力自行解决争议、维护友好合作关系的精神。

incorporated by reference to this Clause. The arbitration court shall be composed of three （3） arbitrators. Each Party shall select one arbitrator. All proceedings shall be in English language. The arbitration award shall be final and binding upon the Parties. Each Party shall bear its own cost or expense incurred in the course of arbitration，unless otherwise awarded by the arbitration court. ①

第二十七章　通　知
Chapter 27　Notice

27.1　任何一方在其股东或所有权人的构成或股权发生重大变更之日起 14 日内，应以书面方式通知其他当事方。

Each of the Parties shall notify the other Party （ies） in writing of any material change in the composition and shareholding of its shareholders or owners within fourteen （14） days of such change.

27.2　在不影响第 27.3 条约定的前提下，在未得到其他当事方的事前书面同意之前（该同意不得被无理拒绝或拖延），任何一方或其关联公司均不得就本合同的签署或标的发表正式公告或新闻发布会。②

Without prejudice to Clause 27.3，no formal public announcement or press release in connection with the signature or subject matter of this Contract shall be made or issued by or on behalf of any Party or any of their affiliates without the prior written approval of the other Parties （such approval not to be unreasonably withheld or delayed）.

27.3　如果一方根据法律、任何证券交易所或政府当局的要求有义务进行或发布任何公告，该方应事前给予其他当事方合理机会，对将要进行或发布的公告作出评论。

If a Party has an obligation to make or issue any announcement required by law or by any stock exchange or by any governmental authority, the relevant Party shall give the other Parties every reasonable opportunity to comment on any announcement or release before it is made or issued.

27.4　本合同项下发送的任何通知、索赔、要求、法院程序、文件或其他通知（本章中合称"通知"）均应以英语书写、以书面形式制作；通知应当向相关当事方送达，通过当面递交、快递或发送到其传真号码（若有），注明收件人，并且/或者抄送给第 27.7 条载明的其他人员。

Any notice, claim, demand, court process, document or other communication to be given under this Contract （collectively **"Com-**

---

①　本条款是对境外仲裁的详细约定，对仲裁机构、仲裁规则、仲裁员人数及指定方法、仲裁语言、裁决效力、仲裁费用的负担等均作了具体约定。据此作出的仲裁裁决，可以依据纽约公约在中国内地和其他缔约国得到承认和执行。

②　因合营当事方中有上市公司或在业界有影响的大公司，对于设立合营公司、成为合营公司股东的事宜，需要按照适用的法律向公众披露。第 27.2 条和第 27.3 条的规定有助于确保该等公司的合规性、防止合资一方单方面提前向外界公布、或不适当地公布合营事宜。

munication" in this Chapter) shall be in writing in the English language and must be served or given personally or sent by courier or to the facsimile numbers (if any) of the relevant Party and marked for the attention and/or copied to such other person as specified in Clause 27. 7. ①

27.5 按照本合同送达或抄送通知的收件人的地址或传真号码如有变更，在书面变更通知上特别注明为本合同的目的，并按本章规定送达到全部其他当事方 5 日后，该变更通知方为生效。

A change of address or facsimile number of the person to whom a Communication is to be addressed or copied pursuant to this Contract shall not be effective until five（5）days after a written notice of change has been served in accordance with the provisions of this Chapter on all other Parties to this Contract with specific reference in such notice that such change is for the purposes of this Contract.

27.6 除本合同中另有规定外，所有通知按照下列方式送达，收件人在下列规定的时间内被视为已收到通知：

发送方式	视为收到通知的时间
本地邮件	24 小时
本地快递或当面递交	3 小时
传真	发送当时
航空快递或特快专递	3 日
航空邮件	5 日

Except as otherwise provided herein，all Communications shall be served by the following means and the addressee of a Communication shall be deemed to have received the same within the time stated as follows：

Means of despatch	Time of deemed receipt
Local mail	24 hours
Local courier/personal delivery	3 hours
Facsimile	on despatch
Air courier/Speedpost	3 days
Airmail	5 days

27.7 各方用于送达通知的初始地址、传真号码以及通知的收件人如下：

如果向甲方发送通知：

地址：

传真：

收件人：

如果向乙方发送通知：

---

① 合营合同项下的很多通知（如对于违约、索赔、解约、终止、股权转让、解散和清算合营公司等）关系到当事人的重大权利义务，会产生重要的法律后果，特别是由于外国合资方的收件人和收件地址通常处于国外，通知的有效送达具有重要的意义。因此，第 27.4～27.9 条的详细规定是必要的。

　　　　　　　　地址：

　　　　　　　　传真：

　　　　　　　　收件人：

　　　　　　如果向丙方发送通知：

　　　　　　　　地址：

　　　　　　　　传真：

　　　　　　　　收件人：

The initial addresses and facsimile numbers of the Parties for the service of Communications，and the person for whose attention of such Communications is to be marked shall be as follows：

If to Party A：

Address：

Facsimile no.：

Attention：

If to Party B：

Address：

Facsimile no.：

Attention：

If to Party C：

Address：

Facsimile no.：

Attention：

27.8 按照本章规定送达的通知应被视为已经有效送达；如要证明一项通知已被有效送达及/或被接收，仅需证明该项通知已留置在收件人的地址或者信封上收件人的地址书写正确、已付邮资并发送到收件人的地址，或者已通过传真方式发送给收件人。如果使用传真方式传送，在传送通知的传真机上打印出发送成功报告，即被视为已有效送达。

A Communication served in accordance with this Chapter shall be deemed sufficiently served and in proving service and/or receipt of a Communication it shall be sufficient to prove that such Communication was left at the addressee's address or that the envelope containing such Communication was properly addressed and posted or despatched to the addressee's address or that the Communication was properly transmitted by facsimile to the addressee. In the case of facsimile transmission，such transmission shall be deemed properly transmitted on receipt of a report of satisfactory trans-mission printed out by the sending machine.

27.9 本章中的任何规定均不排除法律所允许的通知送达方式或者证明通知已送达的方式。

Nothing in this Chapter shall preclude the service of Communications or the proof of such service by any mode permitted by law.

第二十八章　其他条款

Chapter 28　Miscellaneous[①]

28.1　即使本合同中的任何条款可能被证明是违法的或不可执行的，本合同的其余部分应继续充分有效。

Notwithstanding that any provision of this Contract may prove to be illegal or unenforceable, the remaining provisions of this Contract shall continue in full force and effect.

28.2　对于本合同任何条款的拟议变更和废止须采用书面形式，经各方签署后方能生效，并在必要时报相关政府部门批准或备案。

No purported variation or waiver of any provision of this Contract shall be effective unless made in writing, signed by all Parties and, if necessary, approved or recorded by the relevant government departments.

28.3　对于本合同任何违约行为的弃权，不应视为对于该条款或本合同其他条款的其后违约行为之弃权。任何当事方没有行使以及延迟行使本协议项下的任何权利、权力或优先权，不构成放弃该项权利、权力或优先权；任何单独或部分行使任何权利、权力或优先权，并不妨碍任何其他或进一步行使，或者行使任何其他权利、权力或优先权。本合同所规定的权利和救济是累积性的，也不排除法律规定的其他任何权利或救济。

Any waiver of any breach of this Contract shall not be deemed to apply to any succeeding breach of the provision or of any other provision of this Contract. No failure to exercise and no delay in exercising on the part of any of the Parties hereto any right, power or privilege hereunder shall operate as a waiver thereof nor shall any single or partial exercise of any right, power or privilege preclude any other or further exercise thereof or the exercise of any other right, power or privilege. The rights and remedies provided in this Contract are cumulative and not exclusive of any rights or remedies otherwise provided by law.

28.4　本合同的任何规定均未在各方之间形成合伙关系或者建立委托人和代理人的关系或者任何其他类似性质的关系。

Nothing in this Contract shall constitute a partnership or establish a relationship of principal and agent or any other relationship of a similar nature between or among any of the Parties.

28.5　本合同中包含的任何保证、条款、规定和拟议的合同，对于各方及其各自的继承人以及经许可的受让人均具有约束力，且为其利益而订立。除非本合同中另有规定，本合同或任何一方在本合同项下的权利（或由该权利赋予或产生的任何权利或权益）或义务，未经其他当事

---

① 本章第 28.1 条、第 28.3 条、第 28.4 条、第 28.5 条均属于商务合同中的通用法律条款，请参考本书第 2 章第 3 节（合同主文）的说明。

方的事先书面同意，不得全部或部分转让。

Each and all of the covenants, terms, provisions and contemplated contracts contained in this Contract shall be binding upon and inure to the benefit of the Parties hereto and to their respective successors and permitted assigns. Save as otherwise permitted under this Contract, this Contract, or any of a Party's rights or obligations hereunder, may not be assigned (or any right or interest granted or created over it) in whole or in part by any Party without the prior written consent of the other Parties.

28.6 各方自行负担其在协商、准备和执行本合同及其预期交易的过程中所发生的律师费、会计费用及其他费用和开支。但与合营公司设立有关的全部费用和开支（包括为准备合营公司章程所发生的律师费及其开支、登记费、按照任何主管当局的规定应缴纳的费用），均应由合营公司负担。

Each of the Parties shall pay its own legal, accountancy and other costs, charges and expenses incurred in connection with negotiating, preparing and implementing this Contract and the transactions contemplated hereby. All costs and expenses (including legal fees and the expenses to be incurred in relation to the preparation of the Articles of Association of the JV Company, registration fees, and the compliance of rules and regulations of any competent regulatory authority) to be incurred in connection with the setting up of the JV Company shall be borne by the JV Company. ①

28.7 本合同以中文和英文书写，两种文本具有同等法律效力。倘若两种文本有不一致之处，以中文文本为准。

This Contract shall be written in Chinese and English. Two versions are of equal legal effect. In the event of any discrepancies between the two versions, the Chinese version shall prevail. ②

28.8 本合同及其附件在必要时需获得中国相关政府部门的批准或备案。本条规定同样适用于本合同及其附件的修改。

This Contract and its schedules may, when necessary, require the approval or record from the relevant government departments of the PRC.. The same applies to amendments to this Contract and its

---

① 合资各方是彼此独立的法人，其在合营公司中的权益既有共同之处，而更多方面是互不相同，有时甚至是冲突的。在通常情况下，各方会分别委托律师或会计师等专业人士，向其提供独立的专业意见，起草和修改法律文书，有些时候会与委托方一起参加会谈，代表委托方与对方当事方进行协商、交涉。因此，在合营合同的协商、准备和执行以及预期交易的过程中所发生的律师费、会计费用、差旅费等，是各方为保护其自身权益而发生的，理应由各方自行负担。而合营公司的章程制作、登记手续以及为设立合营公司向政府部门缴纳的费用，是因合营公司的设立而发生的，应由合营公司负担。

② 虽然外国合资方希望中英两种文本的合同具有同等法律效力，但因合营合同在必要时需经过中国政府有关部门的批准或备案，因此中英两种文本的合同应以中文文本为准。如果是不需要经中国政府部门批准或备案的合同，当事方可以选择中外文本具有同等法律效力，甚至可以选择以外文文本为准。

schedules.

本合同各方的授权代表已于本合同开头所述日期签订了本合同，以作为证明。

IN WITNESS WHEREOF the Parties hereto have executed this Contract by their authorized representatives on the date first above written.

甲方：**X** 有限公司（公章）
Party A：X Co.，Ltd. （Company chop）

_____

授权代表签署/Signed by authorized representative

乙方：**Y** 有限公司（公章）
Party B：Y Co.，Ltd. （Company chop）

_____

授权代表签署/Signed by authorized representative

丙方：**Z** 有限公司（公章）
Party C：Z Co.，Ltd. （Company chop）

_____

授权代表签署/Signed by authorized representative

附 件 1
Schedule 1

甲方出资的清单和评估价
Contents and Evaluation of Contribution by Party A[1]

附 件 2
Schedule 2

从甲方购买的机器设备清单及其约定价值
List of Machinery and Equipment to be Purchased
from Party A and Agreed Value Thereof[2]

_____

① 请详见本合同第 5.4 条。
② 请详见本合同第 7.2（e）条。

第2节　合资企业章程精选与解读

XYZ 有限公司

章　程

XYZ Co. , Ltd.

Articles of Association

目　录

CONTENTS

【XYZ 有限公司】

章　程①

【XYZ CO.，LTD.】

ARTICLES OF ASSOCIATION②

第一章　总　则

Chapter 1　General Provisions

第一条　X 有限公司（以下简称"**甲方**"）、Y 有限公司（以下简称"**乙方**"）与 Z 有限公司（以下简称"**丙方**"）根据《中华人民共和国中外合资经营企业法》及其他相关法律法规的规定，遵照平等互惠的原则，通过友好协商，同意在中华人民共和国（以下简称"**中国**"）共同投资设立中外合资经营企业 XYZ 有限公司（以下简称"**合营公司**"）。据此制订合营公司章程。

Article 1　X Co.，Ltd.（"**Party A**"），Y Co. Ltd.（"**Party B**"）and Z Co.，Ltd.（"**Party C**"），in accordance with the Law of the People's Republic of China on Sino-Foreign Equity Joint Ventures and other relevant Chinese laws and regulations，based on the principle of equality and mutual benefits and after friendly negotiations，agree to jointly invest in and set up a sino-foreign equity joint venture enterprise XYZ Co.，Ltd.（"**JV Company**"）in the People's Republic of China（"**PRC**"）. This Articles of Association hereby is formulated.

第二条　合营公司名称：XYZ 有限公司

Article 2　The name of the JV Company in Chinese shall be：XYZ 有限公司

合营公司英文名称：XYZ Co.，Ltd.

The name of the JV Company in English shall be：XYZ Co.，Ltd.

合营公司的法定地址：

The registered address of the JV Company shall be：

---

①　关于中外合资经营企业章程的中英文本，最早和最常见的示范文本，是在《中华人民共和国中外合资经营企业法》及其实施条例公布后的初期，由当时设立合资企业的政府审批部门"中华人民共和国对外经济贸易部"条约法律局起草的合资企业章程参考格式。从该格式文本的内容来看，是以公司章程的形式体现中外合资相关法律法规的基本内容，这在当时缺乏类似章程文本的情况下，对于合资双方起到了一定参考作用。但是，正如合营合同的情况一样，在法律实践中，这类的官方格式文本显然并不能充分体现具体情况下各方当事人对合资企业章程内容的要求。笔者在从事涉外法律工作中接触及制作的中外合资企业章程，绝大多数是由律师仅参考该示范文本的章节架构（为了易于得到审批机关的批准）、另行制作可以满足各方当事人要求的公司章程。本章程与前面的合营合同是为同一中外合资经营企业的委托方而制作的，并经各方多次协商修改后的文本。

②　关于中外合资经营企业合同与章程的关系，可从以下几方面考虑：（1）合营合同是合营各方为设立合营企业而就彼此之间的权利和义务关系达成一致意见而签订的法律文件；（2）合营企业章程是根据合营合同规定的基本原则，经营营各方一致同意，规定合营企业的宗旨、组织原则和经营管理方式等事项的法律文件；（3）合营合同和合营企业章程在内容上有很多重复之处，但是两者的侧重点不同，两者分别约定了不同的内容，可以起到互相补充的作用。因此，建议读者对本章程的内容与前面的合营合同互相对照和参考，对有些相同或类似内容的解读，已经在合营合同中详述，在本章程中不再重复说明。这里仅对章程中特有的内容或有必要详述的内容进行解读。

第三条　甲乙丙三方的名称和法定地址为：

Article 3　The names and registered addresses of the Parties to the JV
　　　　　　Company are as follows：

　　　　甲方：　　　　　【X 有限公司】

　　　　　　登记地址：

　　　　　　公司注册地：

　　　　　　法定代表人：

　　　　　　职务：

　　　　　　国籍：

　　　　Party A：　　　　【X Co.，Ltd.】

　　　　　　Registered address：

　　　　　　Place of incorporation：

　　　　　　Legal representative：

　　　　　　Position：

　　　　　　Nationality：

　　　　乙方：　　　　　【Y 有限公司】

　　　　　　登记地址：

　　　　　　公司注册地：

　　　　　　法定代表人：

　　　　　　职务：

　　　　　　国籍：

　　　　Party B：　　　　【Y Co.，Ltd.】

　　　　　　Registered address：

　　　　　　Place of incorporation：

　　　　　　Legal representative：

　　　　　　Position：

　　　　　　Nationality：

　　　　丙方：　　　　　【Z 有限公司】

　　　　　　登记地址：

　　　　　　公司注册地：

　　　　　　法定代表：

　　　　　　职务：

　　　　　　国籍：

　　　　Party C：　　　　【Z Co.，Ltd.】

　　　　　　Registered address：

　　　　　　Place of incorporation：

　　　　　　Legal representative：

　　　　　　Position：

　　　　　　Nationality：

第四条　合营公司为有限责任公司，仅以其本身的资产为限对其任何性质的
　　　　全部债务或其他义务承担责任。合营公司各方仅以其各自向合营公
　　　　司认缴的出资额为限对合营公司的债务承担责任；未经各方以书面

形式确认承担责任并经其法定代表人同意并签字，各方均不对合营公司任何性质的债务或其他义务承担责任。各方以其在合营公司注册资本中所占的比例分享合营公司的利润，并承担合营公司的风险和亏损。

Article 4　The JV Company is a limited liability company and shall have liability to the extent of its assets for all of its debts or other obligations of any nature whatsoever. The Parties of the JV Company shall bear responsibility with respect to the obligations of the JV Company only to the extent of their respective capital contributions to the JV Company and shall not be liable for any debt or other obligation of any nature whatsoever of the JV Company，unless expressly assumed in writing and agreed to and signed by the legal representatives of the Parties so charged. Subject to these limitations，the Parties shall share the profits and bear the risks and losses of the JV Company in proportion to their respective interests in the registered capital.

第五条　合营公司为中国法人，受中国法律管辖和保护。合营公司的所有活动均应遵守中国的法律、法规的相关规定。合营公司实行独立核算、自主经营，有权对其全部资产进行自主支配和管理经营。

Article 5　The JV Company has the status of a Chinese legal person and is subject to the jurisdiction and protection of the PRC laws. All its activities shall be governed by the PRC laws and regulations. The JV Company shall have independent accounts and all its assets shall be managed and operated independently.

第二章　宗旨和经营范围
Chapter 2　Purpose and Scope of Business

第六条　合营公司的宗旨为：发挥甲乙丙三方各自的优势，采用先进的技术和科学的经营管理方法，生产加工和销售【　】产品的【　】配件和组件，满足国内国际市场的需求，为合营公司获得良好的经济效益，从而为合营各方带来满意的经济回报。

Article 6　The purpose of the JV Company shall be for the advantage of all Parties to manufacture, process and sell 【　】 parts and components for 【　】 products, by using appropriate advanced technology and scientific operation and management methods，catering for both the domestic and international markets，so as to achieve beneficial economic results for the JV Company and to enable the Parties to obtain satisfactory economic benefits.

第七条　合营公司的经营范围：研发【　】技术，使用【　】技术加工、制造、生产及销售【　】产品的【　】配件和组件（以下简称"产品"）。

Article 7　The business scope of the JV Company is to perform research and development of 【　】 technologies，and use of 【　】 technologies to process, manufacture, produce and sale of 【 】 parts and components for 【 】 products ("Products").

第八条 合营公司生产规模：年度产值约为【 】万美元。

Article 8 The scale of production of the JV Company will have an annual production value of approximately US$ 【 】.

第九条 合营公司生产的产品在中国国内外市场销售，具体指标可按照中国国内外市场对合营公司产品的需求和其他情况，根据合营公司董事会决议作出决定并进行适当变更。

Article 9 The JV Company shall sell its Products in the PRC domestic market and export to the overseas market, provided, however, that the specific targets may be decided and revised based on the market demand for the Products manufactured by the JV Company, within or outside of the PRC and other conditions, as appropriate, in accordance with resolutions of the Board of Directors of the JV Company.

第三章 投资总额和注册资本
Chapter 3 Total Investment and Registered Capital

第十条 合营公司的投资总额为【 】美元，注册资本为【 】万美元。

Article 10 The total investment of the JV Company shall be US$ 【 】. The registered capital of the JV Company shall be US$ 【 】.

第十一条 甲乙丙三方的出资如下：

Article 11 The investment contributed by each Party is as follows：

甲　方：以【 】万美元的机器设备作为出资，占注册资本之【 】%。

Party A：Investment subscribed in machinery and equipment is US$ 【 】, which accounts for 【 】% of the registered capital；

乙　方：以【 】万美元的外汇现金作为出资，占注册资本之【 】%。

Party B：Investment subscribed in cash is US$ 【 】, which accounts for 【 】% of the registered capital；

丙　方：以【 】万美元的外汇现金作为出资，占注册资本之【 】%。

Party C：Investment subscribed in cash is US$ 【 】, which accounts for 【 】% of the registered capital.

第十二条 甲乙丙三方应按合资合同规定的期限缴清各自出资额。出资分两期缴付。第一期出资应在合营公司的营业执照颁发之日起【 】天内缴付；第二期出资应在合营公司的营业执照颁发之日起【 】天内缴付。其中乙方和丙方用外币缴付的出资额按照缴款当日中国银行公布的外汇汇率中间价折算成人民币。

甲方：第一期出资　　　　价值【 】万美元的机器设备

乙方：第一期出资　　　　【 】万美元现金

丙方：第一期出资　　　　【 】万美元现金

　　　第二期出资　　　　【 】万美元现金

Article 12 The Parties shall pay in all the investment subscribed according to the time limit stipulated in the Joint Venture Contract. The contributions shall be made in 2 installments. The first installment shall be paid within 【 】 days from the date of issuance of the business license of the JV Company; and the second installment shall be paid within 【 】 days from the date of issuance of the business license of the JV Company. The capital investment subscribed in foreign currency by Party B and Party C shall be converted into RMB based on the median of the buying rate and selling rate quoted by the Bank of China on the payment date.

Party A：First installment：　　　US＄【 】 in machinery and equipment.

Party B：First installment：　　　US＄【 】 in cash.

Party C：First installment：　　　US＄【 】 in cash.

Second installment：US＄【 】 in cash.

第十三条　甲乙丙三方缴付出资额后，由合营公司聘请在中国注册的会计师验资。在进行验资时，会计师应采用由在中国具有独立评估资格的机构所确认的甲方出资机器设备之价值。验资结束后，会计师应出具验资报告。出具验资报告后，由合营公司正副董事长签署出资证明书并发给各方，以确认各方的出资额，并证明各方在合营公司中的权益。出资证明书主要内容是：合营公司名称、成立日期、合营者名称及出资额、出资日期、发给出资证明书日期等。

Article 13　After the Parties have made their contributions，the JV Company shall appoint an accountant registered in the PRC to examine the capital contributions. In conducting such an examination，the accountant shall use the value of the machinery and equipment contributed by Party A as confirmed by a duly qualified independent valuer in the PRC. After the examination has been completed，the accountant shall issue a verification report. The JV Company，upon receipt of said verification report，shall issue to each Party an investment certificate signed by the Chairman and Vice Chairman of the Board of Directors of JV Company，confirming the amount contributed by each Party and evidencing each Party's interest in the JV Company. The contents of the investment certificate shall include the following items：name of the JV Company；date of establishment of the JV Company；names of the Parties and the investment contributed；date of the contribution of the investment；and the date of issuance of the investment certificate.

第十四条　如合营公司投资总额或生产规模等发生变化，经合营公司董事会一致同意并办理有关法定手续后，合营公司可以增加或减少其注册资本。若董事会批准增加注册资本，合营各方有权依其对合营公司注册资本的出资比例认缴所增加的注册资本。

Article 14 Should the total amount of investment or the scale of production of the JV Company undergo changes, the Board of the JV Company may increase or decrease the registered capital of the JV Company upon a unanimous vote and completion of the relevant legal formalities. . In the event the Board approves such an increase, all the Parties shall have the right to subscribe to the additional registered capital in proportion to their respective contribution to the registered capital of the JV Company.

第十五条 任何一方转让其出资额，不论全部或部分，都须经其他两方同意。在转让时，其他两方可按投资比例享有优先购买权。合营一方向非合营者转让其出资额的条件，不得比向合营他方转让的条件优惠。违反本条款规定的，其转让无效。

Article 15 Should one Party assign all or part of its investment, consent shall be obtained from the other Parties. When one Party assigns its investment, the other Parties have preemptive rights. The terms of assignment to any external parties shall not be more favorable than those offered to the other Parties of the JV Company. Any non-compliance with this Article shall render the assignment invalid.

第十六条 合营公司注册资本的增加、减少、转让，应由董事会一致通过后，报相关政府部门批准或备案。

Article 16 Any increase, decrease or assignment of the registered capital of the JV Company shall be approved by the Board of Directors and submitted to the relevant government departments for approval or record.

第四章　董事会
Chapter 4　Board of Directors

第十七条 合营公司设立董事会，董事会是合营公司的最高权力机构。合营公司营业执照颁发之日即为合营公司董事会成立之日。

Article 17 The JV Company shall establish the board of directors（"Board of Directors"），which is the highest authority of the JV Company. The Board of Directors of the JV Company shall be formed on the same day the business license of the JV Company is issued.

第十八条 董事会决定合营公司的一切重大事宜，其职权主要如下：

（1）决定和批准总经理提出的重要报告（如生产规划、年度营业报告、资金、借款等）；

（2）批准年度财务报表、收支预算、年度利润分配方案；

（3）通过公司的重要规章制度；

（4）决定设立分支机构；

（5）修改公司章程；

（6）讨论决定合营公司停产、终止或与其他经济组织合并；

（7）决定聘用总经理、副总经理等高级职员；

（8）负责合营公司终止和期满时的清算工作；

（9）其他应由董事会决定的重大事宜。

Article 18　The Board of Directors shall decide all major issues concerning the JV Company. Its functions and powers are as follows[①]:

（1）Deciding and approving the important reports submitted by the General Manager（for instance, production plan, annual business report, funds, loans, etc.）;

（2）Approving annual financial reports, budget of receipts and expenditures, distribution plan of annual profits;

（3）Adopting major rules and regulations of the JV Company;

（4）Deciding to set up branches;

（5）Amending the Articles of Association of the JV Company;

（6）Discussing and deciding the cessation of production, the termination of the JV Company or merging with other economic entity;

（7）Deciding the engagement of senior management staff such as the General Manager, Assistant General Manager;

（8）Taking charge of the liquidation matters upon the expiration or termination of the JV Company; and

（9）Other major issues which are normally decided by the Board of Directors.

第十九条　董事会由 3 名董事组成，甲乙丙三方各委派一名董事。合营公司设监事一名，由丙方委派。合营公司的所有董事和监事的任期均为 3 年，若由原委派方继续委派，可以连任。

Article 19　The Board of Directors shall consist of three（3）Directors, of which one Director shall be appointed by Party A, Party B and Party C respectively. The JV Company shall have a Supervisor who shall be appointed by Party C. All Directors and Supervisor of the JV Company shall have a term of office of three（3）years and may serve successive terms if they continue to be appointed by their respective Parties.

第二十条　董事长由甲方委派，副董事长由乙方委派。董事长是合营公司的法定代表人。若董事长不能行使其职权，可授权副董事长或其他

---

① 本条列举了合营公司的重大事项，根据后面第二十九条的规定，除第二十九条规定需由董事会一致决定的事项之外，其他事项需要出席董事会会议人数的过半数同意通过。

董事代为行使。董事、董事长和副董事长不得因其担任的董事、董事长或副董事长职务而从合营公司领取报酬。若某位董事、董事长或副董事长兼任总经理、副总经理或其他高级管理职务，他仅以担任这些高级管理职务的身份获取报酬，不因其同时担任董事而领取额外的报酬。

Article 20 The Chairman of the Board shall be appointed by Party A and the Vice Chairman by Party B. The Chairman shall be the legal representative of the JV Company. Should the Chairman be unable to perform his duties and responsibilities, he shall empower the Vice Chairman or other Director to act on his behalf. The Directors, Chairman and Vice Chairman shall not be compensated by the JV Company in their capacity as Directors, Chairman or Vice Chairman. Where a Director, Chairman or Vice Chairman concurrently holds such offices as General Manager, Assistant General Manager or other senior management offices, then he will receive compensation only in his capacity as the holder of such senior management office, and shall receive no additional compensation for also acting in the capacity of a Director.

第二十一条 甲乙丙三方在委派和更换董事人选时，应书面通知董事会。

Article 21 When appointing and replacing Directors, a written notice shall be submitted to the Board of Directors by each Party.

第二十二条 董事会例会每年召开至少 4 次。经任何一名董事提议，董事会应召开临时会议。

Article 22 The Board of Directors shall convene at least 4 meetings every year. An interim meeting of the Board of Directors may be held based on a proposal made by any one of the Directors.

第二十三条 董事会会议原则上在合营公司所在地举行，经所有董事同意后，也可以在其他地点召开（包括中国以外的地区）。

Article 23 The Board meetings shall be held in principle at the location of the JV Company, and if necessary, at other venues (including outside China).

第二十四条 董事会会议由董事长召集并主持，董事长缺席时由副董事长召集并主持。

Article 24 The Board meetings shall be called and presided by the Chairman of the Board. Should the Chairman be absent, the Vice Chairman shall call and preside the Board meetings.

第二十五条 董事长应在董事会开会前至少 10 天但不早于 30 天内书面通知各董事，写明会议内容、时间和地点。

Article 25 The Chairman shall give each Director a written notice at least 10 days but not more than 30 days before the date of the Board meeting. The notice shall detail the agenda, time and venue of the meeting.

第二十六条　董事可以亲自或书面委托代理人出席董事会会议，也可以用电话会议或所有与会者均能相互接听和交谈的其他沟通方式出席会议。董事会也可以用所有董事签名的书面方式作出决议。如董事届时未出席也未委托代理人出席董事会会议，则作为弃权。

Article 26　The Directors may participate in a meeting of the Board in person or by proxy or by conference telephone or other communication method whereby all persons participating in such meeting can hear and speak to each other. Decisions of the Board of Directors may also be made by written resolution signed by all the Directors. In case a Director does not attend the Board meeting in person or by proxy, he will be regarded as absent.

第二十七条　董事会会议的法定人数至少须两名董事，包括甲方委派的一名董事、乙方或丙方委派的一名董事。出席董事会会议的董事不够法定人数时，其通过的决议无效。

Article 27　Meetings of the Board require a quorum of at least two Directors, with one Director appointed by Party A and one by Party B or Party C being present at such meetings. When the quorum is less than two Directors, the decisions adopted by the Board meeting are invalid.

第二十八条　董事会每次会议，须作详细的书面记录，并由全体出席董事签字，代理人出席时，由代理人签字。记录文字使用中文和英文，该记录由合营公司存档。

Article 28　Detailed written minutes shall be prepared for each Board meeting and signed by all the Directors who attended or by their proxy. The minutes shall be written in Chinese and English, and shall be filed with the JV Company.

第二十九条　除应由全体董事一致通过方可作出决定的事项之外，合营公司其他事项的决定，应由出席董事会会议的董事过半数同意方可通过。下列事项必须由全体董事一致通过方可作出决定：

（1）合营公司章程的修改或变更；

（2）合营公司名称的变更；

（3）合营公司注册资本的增加、减少或转让；

（4）合营公司提前终止、清算或解散；

（5）合营公司与其他经济组织的合并；

（6）开始从事任何新业务、向任何第三方或新业务投资或撤销任何业务；

（7）对合营公司的价值（包括资本性交易）【　】万美元以上资产或财产的购买或处置（包括进行任何资本性质的交易）；

（8）提供任何第三方的信用额度，但在正常的经营过程中给予合营公司客户不超过【　】万美元信用额的除外；

(9) 在正常经营过程之外或预先批准的预算之外从银行、其他金融机构、第三方或从乙方借款；或合营公司任何向外贷款或为他人提供的任何担保；

(10) 批准合营公司的年度经营计划（包括预算）或财务报表，或决定合营公司的利润分配；

(11) 合营公司和其任何股东之间的合同或协议，包括对该合同或协议的修改和续期；

(12) 决定合营公司董事的报酬；

(13) 聘任和解聘合营公司的审计师；

(14) 对任何涉及合营公司的重大法律诉讼行为（包括和解）作出重要决定（预计负债或索赔超过【 】万美元）；

(15) 雇用或解雇合营公司的任何主要管理人员或重要雇员；

(16) 对销售和授信政策、人力资源计划、管理层薪酬制度（包括合营公司主要管理层的任命和合营公司董事（如果领取报酬的话）或总经理的报酬）的批准或修改。

Article 29 Decisions of the Board of the JV Company concerned with general matters shall be reached by a majority of votes of the Directors who are present at the relevant Board meeting. The following matters require unanimous agreement of all the Directors: -

(1) Amendment to or alteration of the Articles of Association of the JV Company;

(2) Change in the JV Company's name;

(3) Increase, decrease or transfer of the registered capital of the JV Company;

(4) Early termination, liquidation, winding up or dissolution of the JV Company;

(5) Merger of the JV Company with another entity;

(6) Commencement of any new business, or investment in or with any third party or new business or withdrawal from any business;

(7) Acquisition or disposition of assets or property of the JV Company (including the entering into of any transaction of a capital nature) having a value (including capital commitment) equal to US$ 【 】 or more;

(8) Extending credit to any party, except those given in the ordinary course of business to customers of the JV Company, in an amount not exceeding US$ 【 】;

(9) Borrowing funds from a bank or other financial institution or from a third party or from Party B, except in the ordinary course of business or for amounts already approved in the budget; or making of any loans by the JV Company or giving of any guarantees in favour of any party for any

amount；

(10) Approval of annual business plans (including budgets) or financial statements of the JV Company or declarations of dividends by the JV Company；

(11) Contracts or agreements by the JV Company with any of its respective shareholders or any amendment thereto or renewal thereof；

(12) Compensation to the Directors of the JV Company；

(13) The appointment and removal of the auditors of the JV Company；

(14) Any major decisions relating to the conduct (including the settlement) of material legal proceedings, for a potential liability or claim of more than an amount of US $【 】, to which the JV Company is a party；

(15) Employment or dismissal of any main officers or important employees of the JV Company；

(16) The approval or amendment of the sales and credit policies, human resource plan, management compensation programs, including the appointment of the key management of the JV Com-pany and remuneration (if any) of Directors or the general manager of the JV Company.

第五章 经营管理机构
Chapter 5　Business Management Organization

第三十条 合营公司设经营管理机构，下设生产、技术、销售、财务和行政等部门。

Article 30 The JV Company shall establish an operational management organization. It consists of production, technology, marketing, finance and administration departments etc.

第三十一条 经营管理机构最初由一名总经理、一名副总经理、一名销售经理、一名生产采购经理以及一名行政财务经理组成。总经理、副总经理、销售经理和生产采购经理由乙方提名，行政财务经理由甲方提名，均由董事会任命。

Article 31 The operation and management organization shall initially consist of one General Manager and one Assistant General Manager, one Sales Manager, one Production and Procurement Manager and one Administration and Finance Manager. The General Manager, Assistant General Manager, the Sales Manager and the Production and Procurement Manager shall be recommended by Party B, the Administration and Finance Manager by Party A, and all of them shall be appointed by the Board of Directors.

第三十二条　总经理是合营公司日常经营管理的最高负责人，在日常经营管理的范围内，对外代表合营公司，对内负责作出最终决定。总经理应依照中国法律和法规行使其职权，其主要职权如下：

（1）准备各种讨论材料并提交董事会考虑，执行董事会决议；

（2）监督财务经理报告的所有日常财务和会计事务；

（3）决定除高级管理人员之外的雇员的雇用、解雇和惩罚的一切事项；

（4）签署和履行与第三方之间关于日常事务的一切合同；

（5）决定和执行日常经营管理的各种规章制度；

（6）董事会不时指定的其他职责。

副总经理应当协助总经理处理上述所有事项，当总经理不在时，代理行使总经理的职责。

Article 32　The General Manager shall be the highest officer-in-charge of the day-to-day operation and management of the JV Company, and shall, within the scope of the day-to-day operation and management, represent the JV Company externally and be responsible for making final decisions internally. The General Manager shall perform his duties in accordance with the laws and regulations of the PRC, and such duties are set out as follows:

（1）Prepare and submit to the Board for consideration various types of discussion materials and execute the resolutions of the Board;

（2）Oversee all day-to-day financial and accounting matters as reported by the Administration and Finance Manager;

（3）Decide on all matters relating to the employment, dismissal and punishment of employees other than senior management personnel;

（4）Conclude and implement all contracts with third parties for day-to-day matters;

（5）Adopt and implement various rules and regulations for the day-to-day operation and management; and

（6）Other responsibilities as assigned by the Board from time to time.

The Assistant General Manager shall assist the General Manager in all the matters set forth above.

第三十三条　总经理、副总经理的任期为 3 年。经董事会批准，可以连任。若总经理或副总经理在其任期中被撤换，接替者的任期应为离任者的剩余任期。

Article 33　The term of office of the General Manager and Assistant General Manager shall be three（3）years and each of them may be reappointed to serve consecutive terms upon the approval of the Board of Directors. If the General Manager and Assistant General

Manager shall be replaced during their term of office，the term of the in-coming person shall be for the remaining term of the out-going person.

第三十四条　董事长或副董事长、董事经董事会聘请，可兼任合营公司总经理、副总经理及其他高级职位。

Article 34　At the discretion of the Board of Directors，the Chairman，Vice-Chairman or Directors of the Board may concurrently be the General Manager，Assistant General Managers or other senior management staff of the JV Company.

第三十五条　总经理、副总经理不得兼任其他经济组织的总经理或副总经理，不得参与其他经济组织对本合营公司的商业竞争活动。

Article 35　The General Manager or Assistant General Manager shall not concurrently hold posts as general manager or assistant general manager of other economic entities，or take part in commercialcompetition activities organized by other economic entities.

第三十六条　生产和采购经理、销售经理和行政财务经理由总经理领导。
生产和采购经理负责领导合营公司的生产、技术支援、品质控制及材料采购方面的工作。
销售经理负责推销合营公司的产品、开拓其市场。
行政财务经理负责领导合营公司的财务会计工作，组织合营公司开展全面经济核算，实施经济责任制。

Article 36　The Production and Procurement Manager，Sales Manager and Administration and Finance Manager shall be under the supervision of the General Manager.
The Production and Procurement Manager shall be responsible to lead the production，technical support，quality control and procurement of materials of the JV Company.
The Sales Manager shall be responsible for the marketing of the products and promoting the business development of the JV Company.
The Administration and Finance Manager shall head the financial and accounting affairs of the JV Company，organize the JV Company to carry out overall business accounting，human resource affairs and implement the economic responsibility system.

第三十七条　总经理、副总经理、生产和采购经理、销售经理、行政财务经理和其他高级职员请求辞职时，应提前向董事会提出书面报告。以上人员如有营私舞弊或严重失职行为的，经董事会决议，可随时解聘。如触犯刑律的，要依法追究刑事责任。

Article 37　The General Manager，Assistant General Manager，Production and Procurement Manager，Sales Manager，Administration and

Finance Manager and other senior management staff who seek for resignation shall be required to submit their written notices to the Board of Directors in advance. In case any one of the above-mentioned persons commits graft or serious dereliction of duty，they may be dismissed at any time upon the decision of the Board. Those who violate the criminal law shall be under criminal sanction.

第六章　财务会计
Chapter 6　Finance and Accounting

第三十八条　合营公司应当按照中国有关的法律法规缴纳税款。合营公司在其经营期限内，应尽可能申请并保持其作为先进技术企业所能享受的最优惠税收待遇。

Article 38　The JV Company shall pay all taxes in accordance with the pertinent laws and regulations of the PRC. The JV Company shall, if possible or practicable, apply for and, if successful, maintain the most favorable preferential tax treatment available to technologically advanced joint ventures during the term of the JV Company.

第三十九条　合营公司的员工应按照《中华人民共和国个人所得税法》及其他相关法律法规缴纳个人所得税。

Article 39　The employees of the JV Company shall pay income tax in accordance with the Individual Income Tax Law of the People's Republic of China and other relevant laws and regulations.

第四十条　合营公司的财务会计事务按照中国相关法律法规的规定办理。

Article 40　The financial accounting of the JV Company shall be managed in accordance with the relevant laws and regulations of the PRC.

第四十一条　合营公司会计年度采用日历年制，自每年1月1日起至12月31日止为一个会计年度。但合营公司的第一个会计年度应从合营公司营业执照签发之日起至同年12月31日止。

Article 41　The fiscal year of the JV Company shall coincide with the calendar year，i. e. from January 1 to December 31 based on the Gregorian calendar. However the first fiscal year of the JV Company shall begin on the date of the issuance of the business license of the JV Company and end on December 31 of the same year.

第四十二条　合营公司的会计凭证、账簿、收据和统计报告原则上应当用中文书写，但如果任何一方要求，上述材料可同时用英文书写。

Article 42　All vouchers, accounting records, receipts, statistic schedules and reports of the JV Company shall in principle be written in Chinese；however，if required by any Party，such materials shall also be written in English.

第四十三条　合营公司采用人民币为记账本位币。人民币同外币的折算，按实际发生之日中国银行公布的汇价计算。

Article 43　The JV Company shall adopt RMB as its book keeping currency. The conversion of RMB into foreign currencies shall be based on the exchange rates quoted by the Bank of China at the transaction date.

第四十四条　合营公司应在中国的适当银行开立人民币和外币账户。

Article 44　The JV Company shall open and maintain bank accounts in both RMB and in foreign currency at an appropriate bank in the PRC.

第四十五条　合营公司采用国际通用的权责发生制和借贷记账法记账，遵守程序完备、内容完整和及时的原则。

Article 45　The JV Company shall adopt the internationally accepted accrual system and double entry book keeping method，conducted on the principles of comprehensive procedures，completeness of contents and timeliness.

第四十六条　合营公司财务会计账册上应记载如下内容：

（1）合营公司所有的现金收入、支出数额；

（2）合营公司所有的产品及物资销售及购入情况；

（3）合营公司注册资本及负债情况；

（4）合营公司注册资本的缴纳时间、增加、减少及转让情况。

Article 46　The following items shall be recorded in the financial accounts of the JV Company：

（1）All the cash receipts and spending of the JV Company；

（2）All products and materials purchases and sales of the JV Company；

（3）The registered capital and liabilities of the JV Company； and

（4）The time of payment，increase，decrease and transfer of the registered capital of the JV Company.

第四十七条　合营公司应当采用中英文制作每月、季度和年度的损益报告、资产负债表和财务报告。每月财务报告应当在下一个月的第十二日以前向各方提交；年度财务报告的草案应当于下一个会计年度头 3 个月内编制完成，经中国注册会计师审计后提交董事会讨论通过，然后向各方提交，并按中国的有关法律法规向有关当局提交。

Article 47　The JV Company shall prepare monthly，quarterly and annual profit and loss accounts，balance sheet and financial statements in both Chinese and English. The monthly financial statements shall be delivered to the Parties before the twelfth （12th） day of the following month；a draft of annual financial statements shall be prepared by the end of March of the immediately following year which shall be submitted to the Board of Directors for consideration and approval after having been audited by accountant（s）registered in the PRC and the statements shall then be delivered to the Parties and submitted to relevant governmental authorities according to pertinent rules and regulations of the PRC.

第四十八条 合营各方有权自费聘请审计师查阅合营公司账簿。查阅时，合营公司应提供方便。如果任何一方认为有必要从外国聘请会计师审计相关年度的财务报告，其他方应予同意。除各方达成一致协议外，聘请这些额外会计师的所有费用由有关当事方承担。

Article 48 The Parties shall have the right to engage auditors to review the accounts of the JV Company at their own expense. The JV Company shall cooperate in such review. If any Party shall consider it necessary to appoint accountant（s）from another country to audit the financial accounts of the relevant year, other Parties shall give their consent. All expenses incurred in retaining such additional accountant（s）shall be borne by the relevant Party unless otherwise agreed by the Parties.

第四十九条 合营公司按照中国相关法律法规的规定，由董事会决定其固定资产的折旧年限。

Article 49 The depreciation period for the fixed assets of the JV Company shall be determined by the Board of Directors in accordance with the relevant laws and regulations of the PRC.

第五十条 合营公司的一切外汇事宜，按照《中华人民共和国外汇管理条例》和有关规定以及合营合同的规定办理。

Article 50 All matters concerning foreign currencies shall be handled in accordance with the Regulations for Exchange Control of the People's Republic of China，and other related regulations as well as the terms and conditions of the JV Contract.

第七章　利润分配
Chapter 7　Profit Sharing

第五十一条 合营公司从缴纳所得税后的利润中提取储备基金、企业发展基金和职工奖励及福利基金。提取的比例由董事会根据合营公司的经营状况每年确定。

Article 51 The JV Company shall allocate reserve funds，enterprise-development funds，staff bonuses and welfare funds from the profits after payments of income taxes. The percentage of allocation shall be decided by the Board of Directors annually based on the business performance of the JV Company.

第五十二条 合营公司依法缴纳所得税和提取各项基金后的利润，按照甲乙丙三方在注册资本中的出资比例进行分配。向甲方分配的利润应采用人民币，向乙方和丙方分配的利润应采用美元或任何其他符合中国法律法规且乙方和丙方可接受的自由兑换货币。

Article 52 After paying income taxes in accordance with law and the allocation of the various funds, the remaining profits of the JV Company shall be distributed according to the capital ratios of each Party in the registered capital. Profits shall be distributed to Party A in RMB, and to Party B and Party C in USD or any other freely convertible currency under the PRC laws and regulations and acceptable to Party B and Party C.

第五十三条 合营公司每年分配利润一次。每个会计年度后 3 个月内公布利润分配方案及各方应分的利润额。利润应当在董事会考虑合营公司的中长期发展计划，提取合营公司发展所需的合理数额后，按照董事会确定的方法每年分配一次。

Article 53 The JV Company shall distribute its profits once a year. The profit distribution plan and the amount of profit to be distributed to each Party shall be announced within the first three months following each fiscal year. Profits shall be distributed once each year through methods to be determined by the Board of Directors after a reasonable amount needed for the development of the JV Company has been set aside by the Board of Directors, taking into consideration the JV Company's middle and long term development plans.

第五十四条 合营公司的累积亏损未弥补前不得分配利润。上一个会计年度未分配的利润，可并入本会计年度利润分配。

Article 54 The JV Company shall not distribute profits unless the accumulated losses of previous financial years have been made up. The un-distributed profits from previous financial years shall be added to the distributable profits of the current financial year.

第八章 职 工
Chapter 8 Staff and Workers

第五十五条 合营公司职工的招收、招聘、辞退、工资、福利、社会保险、劳动纪律等事宜，应由董事会根据有关的中国法律法规作出决定。

Article 55 The matters concerning employment, recruitment, dismissal, salaries, welfare, social insurance, labor discipline etc. shall be decided by the Board of Directors under the relevant laws and regulations of the PRC.

第五十六条 合营公司有权自主雇用员工。招聘均应通过考核择优录取。合营公司应当与每个被选定的员工签订劳动合同。

Article 56 The JV Company shall have the right to employ any employees at the discretion of the Board of the JV Company. All employment shall be through examination and by merit. The JV Company shall enter into employment contracts with the selected personnel individually.

第五十七条 合营公司有权根据员工违反合营公司规章制度的情节轻重，给予警告、罚款、减薪、降级、停职、劝退或辞退的处罚。以上处罚的实施应符合中国相关法律法规的规定。

Article 57 The JV Company shall have the right to，in accordance with the seriousness of any violation or breach of any rules or regulations of the JV Company，give a warning to，impose fines on，reduce the salaries of，demote to a lower rank，suspend from duty，give advice to resign or dismiss such employee. Any or all of such measures may be carried out unless they are restricted by the relevant laws and regulations of the PRC.

第五十八条 职工的工资待遇，参照中国有关法律法规的规定，根据合营公司具体情况，由董事会确定，并在劳动合同中具体规定。合营公司随着生产的发展，职工业务能力和技术水平的提高，适当提高职工的工资。

Article 58 Salary scales of the employees shall be determined by the Board of Directors with reference to the relevant laws and regulations of the PRC and the specific situations of the JV Company，and the details shall be specified in the employment contract. The salaries of the employees shall be increased in accordance with the production development，capabilities and technical levels of the employees.

第五十九条 职工的福利、奖金、劳动保护和社会保险等事宜，合营公司将分别在各项制度中加以规定，确保职工可在正常条件下从事生产和工作。

Article 59 Matters concerning the employees' welfare，bonuses，labor protection and social insurance etc. shall be regulated in the various systems of the JV Company in order to ensure that the employees may engage in work under normal conditions.

第六十条 合营公司董事会就高级管理人员（如总经理、副总经理和各方派遣的其他海外人员）的工资和报酬事项将依据下列原则制定规章制度：

（1）高级管理人员和海外派遣人员的工资应考虑合营公司的盈利状况，本着平等互利、同工同酬的原则，在综合和合理的基础上确定；

（2）高级管理人员和海外派遣人员的薪金应当用人民币支付；但是，在前述人员回国时，合营公司应当将该人员持有的累积人民币金额兑换成外币，兑换价格应为兑换日的中国银行买入价和卖出价的中间值。

Article 60　With respect to matters relating to the salaries and remuneration of the senior management personnel of the JV Company such as the General Manager, the Assistant General Manager and other expatriate personnel dispatched by the Parties, the Board of Directors shall formulate rules and regulations in accordance with the principles set out below:

(1) The salaries of senior management personnel and expatriate personnel shall be determined on an integrated and reasonable basis after taking into consideration the profitability of the JV Company and on the principle of equality and mutual benefits as well as equal pay for equal work.

(2) Salaries to the senior management and expatriate personnel shall be paid in RMB; however, when the person shall return to his home country, the JV Company shall convert any accumulated amounts held by such person in RMB into foreign currency at the median of the buying and selling rates of the Bank of China on the exchange date.

第六十一条　合营公司应当建造或租赁宿舍和居住、福利及卫生设施，并按董事会制订的规章制度向高级管理人员和雇员提供前述宿舍和设施。

Article 61　The JV Company shall construct or lease accommodation quarters as well as living, welfare and hygiene facilities and provide the same to senior management personnel and employees in accordance with rules and regulations determined by the Board of Directors.

第九章　工会组织
Chapter 9　Trade Union

第六十二条　合营公司职工有权按照《中华人民共和国工会法》及其他相关法律法规建立工会组织，开展工会活动。

Article 62　The employees of the JV Company shall have the right to form a trade union organization and carry out activities in accordance with the Trade Union Law of the People's Republic of China and other relevant laws and regulations.

第六十三条　合营公司应按有关法律规定拨交工会经费，并为工会活动提供必要的条件。

Article 63　The JV Company shall allocate trade union's funds in accordance with the relevant laws and regulations and provide necessary assistance for the trade union's activities.

第十章　期限、终止、清算
Chapter 10　Term, Termination and Liquidation

第六十四条　合营期限为 15 年，自营业执照签发之日起计算。

Article 64   The term of the JV Company shall be 15 years，commencing from the date when business license is issued.

第六十五条   甲乙丙三方如一致同意延长合营期限，经董事会会议作出决议，应在合营期满前 6 个月向相关政府部门办理延长经营期限的法定手续。

Article 65   If the three Parties agree unanimously to extend the term of the JV Company，the legal formalities for the extension of term shall be completed with the relevant government departments after the approval of the Board six（6）months before the expiration of the term…

第六十六条   甲乙丙三方如一致认为终止合营符合各方最大利益时，可提前终止合营。合营公司提前终止，需董事会召开全体会议作出一致决定，并报相关政府部门批准或备案。

Article 66   The JV Company may be terminated before the expiration of its term if the three Parties agree unanimously that the termination of the joint venture is for the best interests of all Parties. The termination resolution shall be made by the Board of Directors and the decision shall be reported to the relevant government departments for approval or record.

第六十七条   发生下列情况之一时，甲乙丙任何一方有权依法终止合营：

（1）合营公司期满，合营各方不同意续办时；

（2）合营各方一致同意提前终止合营公司；

（3）一方或其关联公司实质性地违反其在合资合同、技术许可与援助协议或合资合同所预定的其他合同项下的义务，在收到非违约方发出的书面投诉通知后 30 日内未对其违约行为予以纠正，非违约方欲终止合营公司；

（4）一方没有足额缴纳其所认缴的出资额，非违约方欲终止合营公司；

（5）合营公司停止经营或者资不抵债；

（6）如果对任何一方或其控股公司有管辖权的政府机构要求对合资合同的任何条款进行修改，或对合资合同的履行附加条件或限制以至于对合资合同或任何一方产生重大不利影响；

（7）如果因自然灾害、战争等不可抗力（如合营合同中所定义）的条件或影响持续了 6 个月以上，而且合营公司没有能够找到合适的解决办法；

（8）任何一方开始自愿清算程序，除非是为重组或合并的目的；法院或相关政府机构所发布的强制解散命令；就其财产中的实质部分已委任清算人或类似官员；与债权人达成和解或还债协议；或破产；

（9）超过有关当事方不时同意的合营公司的账面净资产数额或比例被政府部门暂时性或永久性征收，因而影响到合营公司的经营；

（10）合资合同所规定的提前终止合营公司的其他情况。

上述情况发生时应由董事会提出解散申请书，报相关政府部门批准或备案。批准或备案后，应立即对合营公司的财产进行清算。

Article 67　Any Party shall have the right to terminate the joint venture in any of the following events：

（1）Expiration of the term and there has been no agreement to extend；

（2）All Parties agree unanimously to early terminate the JV Company；

（3）If any relevant Parties commit any material breach of its/their obligations under the JV Contract or any affiliate of such relevant Parties commits any material breach of the Technology License and Assistant Agreement or any contracts contemplated hereby, and such breach, if remediable, is not remedied within thirty（30）days upon the service of notice by the non-defaulting Party complaining of such breach, and the non-defaulting Party intends to terminate the JV Company；

（4）If a Party fails to fulfill any of its capital contribution obligations in respect of the JV Company and the non-defaulting Party intends to terminate the JV Company；

（5）If the JV Company ceases to carry on business or becomes unable to pay its debts as they become due；

（6）If any government authority having authority over a Party（ies）or its/their holding company（ies）requires any provision of the JV Contract to be revised or imposes conditions or restrictions upon the implementation of the JV Contract in such a way as to cause significant adverse consequences to the JV Company or any Party；

（7）If the conditions or consequences of Force Majeure as defined in the JV Contract such as act of God, war etc. prevail for a period in excess of six（6）months and the Parties have been unable to find an appropriate solution；

（8）If any of the Parties shall go into voluntary liquidation otherwise than for the purpose of reconstruction or amalgamation, or an order of the court or relevant government authority is made for its/their compulsory liquidation or shall have a receiver or similar officer appointed in respect of any substantial part of its/their assets or shall compound or make any composition or arrangement with its/their creditors or shall become insolvent;

(9) If any part of the assets of the JV Company with a net book value exceeding such amount or proportion of its net book value as the relevant Parties may agree from time to time is temporarily or permanently expropriated by any government authority, thereby adversely affecting the business of the JV Company; and

(10) Other situations provided in the JV Contract in relation to early termination of the JV Company.

When any of the above events occurs, the Board of Directors shall put forward a termination application for approval or record with the relevant government departments. After obtaining the approval or record, liquidation process shall commence immediately.

第六十八条 合营期满或提前终止合营时，董事会应提出清算程序、原则和清算组人选，组成清算组，对合营公司财产进行清算。

Article 68 Upon the expiration or early termination of the joint venture, the Board of Directors shall work out procedures and principles for liquidation and nominate the liquidation committee for liquidating the JV Company's assets.

第六十九条 清算组任务是对合营公司的财产、债权、债务进行全面清查，编制资产负债表和财产目录，制订清算方案，提请董事会通过后执行。

Article 69 The task of the liquidation committee is to conduct a thorough check against the assets, liabilities and indebtedness of the JV Company, to prepare the statement of assets and liabilities and list of properties and to formulate a liquidation plan for the approval of the Board of Directors.

第七十条 清算期间，清算组代表合营公司起诉或应诉。

Article 70 During the process of liquidation, the liquidation committee shall represent the JV Company to sue and be sued.

第七十一条 清算费用和清算组成员的酬劳应从合营公司现存财产中优先支付。

Article 71 The liquidation expenses and remuneration of the members of the liquidation committee shall be paid in priority from the existing assets of the JV Company.

第七十二条 清算组对合营公司的债务全部清偿后，其剩余的财产按甲乙丙三方在注册资本中的出资比例进行分配。

Article 72 The remaining assets after the clearance of debts of the JV Company shall be distributed among the Parties according to the proportion of each Party's contribution to the registered capital.

第七十三条 清算结束后，合营公司应向相关政府部门提出报告，并向原登记机关办理注销登记手续，缴回营业执照，同时对外公告。

Article 73　After the completion of the liquidation process，the JV Company shall submit a liquidation report to the relevant government departments, nullify its registration with the original registration authority, return its business license and at the same time, make an announcement to the public.

第七十四条　合营公司结业后，其各种账册由甲方保存。

Article 74　After winding up the JV Company, its various accounting records shall be in the custody of Party A.

第十一章　规章制度
Chapter 11　Rules and Regulations

第七十五条　合营公司董事会应制定以下的规章制度：

（1）经营管理制度，包括所属各个管理部门的职权与工作程序；

（2）职工守则；

（3）劳动工资制度；

（4）职工考勤、升级与奖惩制度；

（5）职工福利制度；

（6）财务制度；

（7）公司解散时的清算程序；

（8）其他必要的规章制度。

Article 75　The following rules and systems shall be formulated by the Board of Directors of the JV Company：-

（1）Management operational system，including the functions and responsibilities of the management departments and their work procedures；

（2）Employment regulations；

（3）Employees' salaries system；

（4）System for employees' attendance, promotion and incentives/punishments；

（5）Employees' welfare system；

（6）Financial system；

（7）Liquidation procedures upon the dissolution of the JV Company；and

（8）Other necessary rules and systems.

第十二章　附　则
Chapter 12　Supplementary Articles

第七十六条　本章程的修改，必须经董事会会议一致通过决议，并报相关政府部门批准或备案。

Article 76　The amendments to the Articles of Association shall be unanimously agreed and decided by the Board of Directors and submitted to the relevant government departments for approval or record.

第七十七条 本章程用中文和英文书写，两种文本具有同等效力。上述两种文本如有不一致之处，以中文本为准。

Article 77 The Articles of Association is written in Chinese and English. Both languages shall be equally valid. In the event of any discrepancies between the two versions，the Chinese version shall prevail.

第七十八条 本章程须经中国相关政府部门批准或备案才能生效；本条规定同样适用于本章程的修改。

Article 78 The Articles of Association shall come into effect upon obtaining the approval or record of the relevant government departments. The same applies in the event of amendments hereto.

第七十九条 本章程于【 】年【 】月【 】日，由甲乙丙三方的授权代表签署。

Article 79 The Articles of Association are executed by each Party's duly authorized representatives on【 】.

甲方：**X** 有限公司（盖章）
授权代表（签名）：_____

Party A：X Co.，Ltd. (Company chop)
Signed by authorized representative：_____

乙方：**Y** 有限公司（盖章）
授权代表（签名）：_____

Party B：Y Co.，Ltd. (Company chop)
Signed by authorized representative：_____

丙方：**Z** 有限公司（盖章）
授权代表（签名）：_____

Party C：Z Co.，Ltd. (Company chop)
Signed by authorized representative：_____